The Planters of Colonial Virginia

The PLANTERS OF
COLONIAL VIRGINIA

By THOMAS J. WERTENBAKER

New York

RUSSELL & RUSSELL

1959

COPYRIGHT 1922 BY PRINCETON UNIVERSITY PRESS
COPYRIGHT 1958, 1959 BY THOMAS J. WERTENBAKER

LIBRARY OF CONGRESS CATALOG CARD NUMBER 59-11228

PRINTED IN THE UNITED STATES OF AMERICA

PREFACE

America since the days of Captain John Smith has been the land of hope for multitudes in Europe. In many an humble home, perhaps in some English village, or an Ulster farm, or in the Rhine valley, one might find a family assembled for the reading of a letter from son, or brother, or friend, who had made the great venture of going to the New World. "Land is abundant here and cheap," the letter would state. "Wages are high, food is plentiful, farmers live better than lords. If one will work only five days a week one can live grandly."

In pamphlets intended to encourage immigration the opportunities for advancement were set forth in glowing colors. In Virginia alone, it was stated, in 1649, there were "of kine, oxen, bulls, calves, twenty thousand, large and good." When the traveller Welby came to America he was surprised to "see no misery, no disgusting army of paupers, not even beggars; while Henry B. Fearson noted that laborers were "more erect in their posture, less careworn in their countenances" than those of Europe.

In Virginia, as in other colonies, it was the cheapness of land and the dearness of labor which gave the newcomer his chance to rise. The rich man might possess many thousands of acres, but they would profit him nothing unless he could find the labor to put them under cultivation. Indentured workers met his needs in part, but they were expensive, hard to acquire, and served for only four years. If he hired freemen he

would have to pay wages which in England would have seemed fantastic.

Thus the so-called servants who had completed their terms and men who had come over as freemen found it easy to earn enough to buy small plantations of their own. That thousands did so is shown by the Rent Roll which is published as an appendix to this book. One has only to glance at it to see that the large plantations are vastly outnumbered by the small farms of the yeomen. It proves that Virginia at the beginning of the eighteenth century was not the land of huge estates, worked by servants and slaves, but of a numerous, prosperous middle class.

Owning plantations of from fifty to five hundred acres, cultivating their fields of tobacco, their patches of Indian corn and wheat, their vegetable gardens and orchards with their own labor or the labor of their sons, the yeomen enjoyed a sense of independence and dignity. It was their votes which determined the character of the Assembly, it was they who resisted most strongly all assaults upon the liberties of the people.

As the small farmer, after the day's work was over, sat before his cottage smoking his long clay pipe, he could reflect that for him the country had fulfilled its promise. The land around him was his own; his tobacco brought in enough for him to purchase clothes, farm implements, and household goods.

But he frowned as he thought of the slave ship which had come into the nearby river, and landed a group of Negroes who were all bought by his wealthy neighbors. If Virginia were flooded with slaves, would it not cheapen production and lower the price of tobacco? Could he and his sons, when they hoed their fields with their own hands, compete with slave labor?

The event fully justified these fears. The yeoman class in Virginia was doomed. In the face of the oncoming tide they had three alternatives—to save enough money to buy a slave or two, to leave the country, or to sink into poverty.

It was the acquiring of a few slaves by the small planter which saved the middle class. Before the end of the colonial period a full fifty per cent. of the slaveholders had from one to five only. Seventy-five per cent. had less than ten. The small farmer, as he led his newly acquired slaves from the auction block to his plantation may have regretted that self-preservation had forced him to depend on their labor rather than his own. But he could see all around him the fate of those who had no slaves, as they became "poor white trash." And he must have looked on with pity as a neighbor gathered up his meager belongings and, deserting his little plantation, set out for the remote frontier.

It was one of the great crimes of history, this undermining of the yeoman class by the importation of slaves. The wrong done to the Negro himself has been universally condemned; the wrong done the white man has attracted less attention. It effectively deprived him of his American birthright—the high return for his labor. It transformed Virginia and the South from a land of hard working, self-respecting, independent yeomen, to a land of slaves and slaveholders.

Princeton, New Jersey   Thomas J. Wertenbaker
August, 1957

iii

CONTENTS

CHAPTER I

ENGLAND IN THE NEW WORLD

At the beginning of the Seventeenth century colonial expansion had become for England an economic necessity. Because of the depletion of her forests, which constituted perhaps the most important of her natural resources, she could no longer look for prosperity from the old industries that for centuries had been her mainstay. In the days when the Norman conquerors first set foot upon English soil the virgin woods, broken occasionally by fields and villages, had stretched in dense formation from the Scottish border to Sussex and Devonshire. But with the passage of five centuries a great change had been wrought. The growing population, the expansion of agriculture, the increasing use of wood for fuel, for shipbuilding, and for the construction of houses, had by the end of the Tudor period so denuded the forests that they no longer sufficed for the most pressing needs of the country. Even at the present day it is universally recognized that a certain proportion of wooded land is essential to the prosperity and productivity of any country. And whenever this is lacking, not only do the building, furniture, paper and other industries suffer, but the rainfall proves insufficient, spring floods are frequent and the fertility of the soil is impaired by washing. These misfortunes are slight, however, compared with the disastrous results of the gradual thinning out of the forests of Elizabethan England. The woods were necessary

7

for three all-important industries, the industries upon which the prosperity and wealth of the nation were largely dependent —shipbuilding, for which were needed timber, masts, pitch, tar, resin; the manufacture of woolens, calling for a large supply of potash; smelting of all kinds, since three hundred years ago wood and not coal was the fuel used in the furnaces. It was with the deepest apprehension, then, that thoughtful Englishmen watched the gradual reduction of the forest areas, for it seemed to betoken for their country a period of declining prosperity and economic decay. "When therefore our mils of Iron and excesse of building have already turned our greatest woods into pasture and champion within these few years," says a writer of this period, "neither the scattered forests of England, nor the diminished groves of Ireland will supply the defect of our navy."[1]

From this intolerable situation England sought relief through foreign commerce. If she could no longer smelt her own iron, if she could not produce ship-stores or burn her own wood ashes, these things might be procured from countries where the forests were still extensive, countries such as those bordering the Baltic—Germany, Poland, Russia, Sweden. And so the vessels of the Muscovy Company in the second half of the Sixteenth century passed through the Cattegat in large numbers to make their appearance at Reval and Libau and Danzig, seeking there the raw materials so vitally necessary to England. "Muscovia and Polina doe yeerly receive many thousands for Pitch, Tarre, Sope Ashes, Rosen, Flax, Cordage, Sturgeon, Masts, Yards, Wainscot, Firres, Glasse, and such like," wrote Captain John Smith, "also Swethland for Iron and Copper."[2]

But this solution of her problem was obviously unsatisfactory to England. The northern voyage was long, dangerous and costly; the King of Denmark, who controlled the entrance to the Baltic, had it within his power at any moment to exclude the English traders; the Muscovy company no longer enjoyed exemption from customs in Prussia, Denmark and Russia.   In case war should break out among the northern nations this trade might for a time be cut off entirely, resulting in strangulation for England's basic industries.   "The merchant knoweth," said the author of *A True Declaration*, "that through the troubles in Poland & Muscovy, (whose eternall warres are like the Antipathy of the Dragon & Elephant) all their traffique for Masts, Deales, Pitch, Tarre, Flax, Hempe, and Cordage, are every day more and more indangered."[3] Moreover, the trade was much impeded by the ice which for several months each year choked some of the northern ports.

The most alarming aspect of this unfortunate situation was the effect of the shortage of shipbuilding material upon the merchant marine.   Situated as it was upon an island, England enjoyed communication with the nations of the world only by means of the ocean pathways.   Whatever goods came to her doors, whatever goods of her own manufacture she sent to foreign markets, could be transported only by sea.   It was a matter of vital import to her, then, to build up and maintain a fleet of merchant vessels second to none.   But this was obviously difficult if not impossible when "the furniture of shipping" such as "Masts, Cordage, Pitch, Tar, Rossen" were not produced in quantity by England itself, and could be had "only by the favor of forraigne potency."[4]   Already, it was stated, the decay of shipping was manifest, while large numbers of able mariners were forced to seek employment in other countries.   "You know how many men for want of imploiment, betake themselves to Tunis, Spaine and Florence," declared one observer, "and to serve in courses not warrantable, which would better beseeme our own walles and borders to bee spread with such branches, that their native countrey and not forreine Princes might reape their fruit, as being both exquisite Navigators, and resolute men for service, as any the world affords."[5]

It must be remembered that the merchant vessel three hundred years ago constituted an important part of the nation's sea defence. The fleet which met the mighty Spanish Armada in the Channel and inflicted upon it so decisive a defeat, was made up in large part of volunteer ships from every English port. And the Britisher knew full well that the merchant marine constituted the "wooden walls" of his country, knew that its decay would leave England almost defenseless. At the moment when one able writer was pointing out that "the Realme of England is an Island impossible to be otherwise fortified than by stronge shippes," another was complaining that there were scarce two vessels of 100 tons belonging to the whole city of Bristol, and few or none along the Severn from Gloucester to Land's End on one side, and to Milford Haven on the other.[6]

For this intolerable situation there could be but one remedy —England must secure colonial possessions to supply her with the products for which her forests were no longer sufficient. Her bold navigators had already crossed the Atlantic, returning with alluring stories of the limitless resources of the New World, of mighty forests spreading in unbroken array for hundreds of miles along the coast and back into the interior as far as the eye could see.[7] Why, it was asked, should Englishmen be forced to make the hazardous journey to the Baltic in order to procure from other nations what they might easily have for themselves by taking possession of some of the limitless unoccupied areas of America? It was folly to remain in economic bondage while the road to independence stretched so invitingly before them.

Long before the Goodspeed, the Discovery and the Sarah

Constant turned their prows into the waters of the James, able English writers were urging upon the nation the absolute necessity for colonial expansion. In 1584 the farseeing Hakluyt pointed out that the recent voyage of Sir Humphrey Gilbert had proved that "pitche, tarr, rosen, sope ashes" could be produced in America in great plenty, "yea, as it is thought, ynoughe to serve the whole realme."[8] Captain Christopher Carleill had the previous year made an effort to persuade the Muscovy Company to divert its energies toward America. Why remain under the power of the King of Denmark, he asked, or other princes who "command our shippes at their pleasure," when all the products of the Baltic regions were to be had from unoccupied territories which so easily could be placed under the English flag?

It has often been taken for granted that the statesmen and merchants of three centuries ago pursued always a mistaken and shortsighted economic policy. John Fiske assures us that even at the close of the Eighteenth century the barbarous superstitions of the Middle Ages concerning trade between nations still flourished with scarcely diminished vitality. Yet it requires but a cursory study of the theories and arguments of the Elizabethan economists to realize that they were men of ability and vision, that they knew what was needed and how to procure it, that they were nearer right than many have supposed. In fact, they acted upon sound economic principles a century and a half before Adam Smith formulated and expounded them.

These men realized keenly that England's safety demanded a larger measure of economic independence and they pointed out what seemed to be the only available means of securing it. Since her forests upon which her prosperity in the past had been so largely based, were nearing the point of exhaustion, she must expand to embrace new lands where the virgin growth of trees stood untouched. If this is barbarous, then the recent efforts of Italy to gain an independent coal supply, of Great Britain to get control of various oil fields, of the United States to build up a dye industry, are all likewise barbarous. In fact the world today in matters of economic policy has by no means gotten away from the conceptions of the men whose able writings cleared the way for the beginning of the British colonial empire.

But it must not be supposed that England in this matter was concerned only for her supply of naval stores, potash and pig iron. There were other products, not so vital it is true, but still important, which she was forced to seek abroad. From the south of Europe came salt, sugar, wine, silk, fruits; from the Far East saltpetre and dyes, together with spices for making palatable the winter's stock of food; from Holland came fish, from France wine and silk. And as in the Baltic, so elsewhere the merchants of London and Bristol and Plymouth found their activities resented and their efforts blocked and thwarted.

All commerce with the dominions of the King of Spain was carried on with the greatest difficulty. "Our necessitie of oiles and colours for our clothinge trade being so greate," pointed out Hakluyt, "he may arreste almoste the one halfe of our navye, our traficque and recourse beinge so greate in his dominions." The rich trade with the Far East was seriously hampered by the Turks, through whose territories it had to pass, and often a heavy tribute was laid upon it by the Sultan and his minions. Even after the merchants had succeeded in lading their vessels in the eastern Mediterranean with goods from the Orient, they still had to run the gauntlet of the hostile Powers who infested that sea. If they escaped the Knights of Malta, they might be captured by the corsairs of Algeria or Tripoli.

The trade with France had also declined greatly during the closing years of the Sixteenth century. Not only had the religious wars proved a tremendous obstacle, but the government at Paris discriminated against the woolens from England by means of custom duties, while the French workmen were themselves manufacturing cloth of excellent quality in larger amounts than had hitherto been thought possible. In the Low Countries the long and bitter struggle of the people against the bloody bands of Alva had wrought such destruction and had so ruined industry that all foreign commerce had greatly declined.[9]

There can be no surprise, then, that many English economists felt that a crisis had been reached, that nothing save the immediate establishment of colonies would prevent disaster. With the woolen industry declining, with the shipbuilding centres almost idle, with able mariners deserting the service, with the foreign market gradually closing to English wares, with the country overrun with idle and starving laborers, with some of her chief natural resources nearly exhausted and the trade by which her needs were replenished in constant danger, England turned to America as her hope for salvation. Upon securing a foothold in the New World, hitherto monopolized by Spain and Portugal, depended Albion's future greatness and prosperity.

It is this which gave to the London Company its national character, and made its efforts to establish a colony across the Atlantic a crusade, a movement in which every Englishman was vitally concerned. The great lords and wealthy merchants who comprised the Company knew well enough that there was little hope of immediate returns upon the money they subscribed so liberally. They expected to receive their reward in another way, in the revival of English industrial life and the restoration of English economic independence. It is a singular perversion of history, an inaccurate interpretation of men and events, which for so many years beclouded our conception of the beginning of the British colonial empire. The settlement at Jamestown was not the product of a selfish, private venture, but the fruition of long years of thought and endeavor, long years of pleading with the English public, of the conscious and deliberate efforts of the nation to expand to the New World, to break the bonds of economic dependence and to restore to England the place in the world which rightfully was hers.

In addition to, but closely associated with, the economic causes of Anglo-Saxon expansion was the realization in England of the need for prompt action in putting a limit to the growing domains of the King of Spain. In the century which had elapsed since Columbus opened a new world to the peoples of Europe, this monarch had seized the richest part of the great prize, and was still reaching forward to the north and to the south. Unless England took advantage of the present opportunity, the vast American continents might be closed to her forever. Anglo-Saxon civilization in that case might well remain permanently cooped up in the little island that had seen its inception, while the Spanish language and Spanish institutions expanded to embrace the garden spots of the world.[10]

There were still other motives for this great movement. The English felt the prime necessity of discovering and controlling a new route to the East, they wished to expand the influence of the Anglican church and convert the Indians, they hoped to seize and fortify strategic points in America which would aid them in their struggles with the Spaniards. But these things, important as they were, paled beside the pressing necessity of national expansion, of rehabilitating English industrial life, restoring the merchant marine and securing economic independence.

Thus, when Captain Newport returned in 1607 to report that the colony of Virginia had been safely launched, many Englishmen were aroused to a high pitch of hope and expectation. Now at last a province had been secured which could supply the raw materials which England so greatly needed. The active supporters of the undertaking were lavish in their promises. Virginia would yield better and cheaper timber for shipping than Prussia or Poland, she would furnish potash in abundance, and since wood could there be had for the cutting, her copper and iron ore could be smelted on the spot. Wine could be made there, as excellent as that of the Canaries, they boasted, while it was hoped soon to manufacture silk rivalling in fineness that of Persia or of Turkey. The waters of the colony were full of "Sturgion, Caviare and new land fish of the best," her fields could produce hemp for cordage and flax for linen. As for pitch, tar, turpentine and boards, there was a certainty of a rich return.[11] In February 1608, the Council of Virginia wrote to the corporation of Plymouth: "The staple and certain Comodities we have are Soap-ashes, pitch, tar, dyes of sundry sorts and rich values, timber for all uses, fishing for sturgeon and divers other sorts . . . making of Glass and Iron, and no improbable hope of richer mines."[12]

And no sooner had the infant colony been established than the Company turned with enthusiasm to the production of these highly desired commodities. A number of foreigners, Dutchmen and Poles skilled in the manufacture of ship-stores, were sent over to make a start with pitch, tar, turpentine and potash. They were to act as instructors, also, and it was expected that within a few years the Virginia forests would be filled with workers in these trades. Unfortunately their efforts met with ill success, and save for a few small samples of pitch and tar which were sent to England, nothing of value was produced.

For this failure the reason is apparent. All the able economists and statesmen who had predicted that the colony would become an industrial center had overlooked one vitally important factor—the lack of cheap labor. No matter how rich in natural resources, Virginia could not hope to compete with the long-established industries of Europe and Asia, because she lacked the abundant population requisite to success. It had been imagined by Hakluyt and others that the colony could avail herself of the surplus population of England, could drain off the upper stratum of the idle and unemployed. What more feasible than to set these men to work in the forests of the New World to produce the raw materials the want of which was responsible for unemployment in England itself!

But the voyage across the Atlantic was so long and costly, that it proved impossible to transport in any reasonable length of time enough workers to Virginia to supply her needs. And the few thousand that came over in the early years of the Seventeenth century were in such great demand that they could secure wages several times higher than those in vogue throughout Europe. Thus the London Company, from the very outset, found itself face to face with a difficulty which it could never surmount. Virginia could not compete with the ship-stores of the Baltic nations because her labor, when indeed it was found possible to secure labor at all, was far more expensive than that of Poland or Sweden or Russia. It mattered not that the Company sent over indentured servants, bound by their contracts to work for a certain number of years; the effect was the same. The cost of transportation swallowed up the profits from the servant's labor, when that labor was expended upon industries which had to face the competition of the cheap workers of the Old World.

It speaks well for the acumen of Captain John Smith that

he seems to have been the first to grasp clearly this truth. He wrote that the workingmen had made a beginning of "Pitch and Tarre, Glass, Sope-ashes and Clapboard," but that little had been accomplished. "If you rightly consider what an infinite toyle it is in Russia and Swetland, where the woods are proper for naught else, and though there be the helpe both of man and beast in those ancient Common-wealths, which many a hundred years have used it, yet thousands of those poor people can scarce get necessaries to live . . . you must not expect from us any such matter."[13]

The attempt to produce iron in Virginia was pursued even more vigorously, but with equally poor success. The early settlers, eager to assure the Company that the venture they had entered upon would soon yield a rich return, spoke enthusiastically of the numerous indications of the presence of iron ore. In 1609 Captain Newport brought with him to England a supply of ore from which sixteen or seventeen tons of metal were extracted of a quality equal or superior to that obtained from any European country. The iron was sold to the East India Company at the rate of £4 a ton.[14] Immediately plans were launched for taking advantage of what seemed to be a splendid opportunity. In the course of the first three years machinery for smelting and manufacturing iron was sent over and men were set to work to operate it. But the difficulties proved too great and ere long the attempt had to be abandoned.

The Company had no idea of relinquishing permanently its quest for staple commodities, however, and soon a new and far more ambitious project was set on foot for extracting the ore. The spot selected was at Falling Creek, in the present county of Chesterfield, a few miles below the rapids of the James river. George Sandys had noted with satisfaction some years before that the place was in every respect suited for iron smelting, for in close proximity to the ore was wood in abundance, stones for the construction of the furnace and deep water for transportation. To him it seemed that nature itself had selected the site and endowed it with every facility which the enterprise could require.[15]   Here the London Company spent from £4,000 to £5,000 in a supreme effort to make their colony answer in some degree the expectations which had been placed in it.   A Captain Blewit, with no less than 80 men, was sent over to construct the works, upon which, they declared, were fixed the eyes of "God, Angels and men."   But Blewit soon succumbed to one of the deadly epidemics which yearly swept over the little colony, and a Mr. John Berkeley, accompanied by 20 experienced workers, came over to take his place.

At first things seem to have gone well with this ambitious venture.   Soon the Virginia forests were resounding to the whir of the axe and the crash of falling trees, to the exclamations of scores of busy men as they extracted the ore, built their furnace and began the work of smelting.   Operations had progressed so far that it was confidently predicted that soon large quantities of pig iron would be leaving the James for England, when an unexpected disaster put an abrupt end to the enterprise.   In the terrible massacre of 1622, when the implacable Opechancanough attempted at one stroke to rid the country of its white invaders, the little industrial settlement at Falling Creek was completely destroyed.   The furnace was ruined, the machinery thrown into the river, the workmen butchered.   This project, which had absorbed so much of the attention and resources of the Company, is said to have yielded only a shovel, a pair of tongs and one bar of iron.[16]

The history of the attempts to establish glass works in Virginia is also a story of wasted energy and money, of final failure.   The Dutch and Polish workers who came in 1608 set up a furnace at Jamestown,[17] but nothing more is heard of them, and it is clear that they met with no success. Nor did Captain William Norton, who arrived in 1621 with a number of skilled Italian glass workers fare any better.[18] In 1623 George Sandys wrote: "Capt. Norton dyed with all save one of his servants, the Italians fell extremely sick yet recovered; but I conceave they would gladly make the work to appear unfeasable, that they might by that means be dismissed for England. The fier hath now been for six weeks in ye furnace and yet nothing effected. They claim that the sand will not run." Shortly after this the workmen brought matters to an end by cracking the furnace with a crowbar.[18]

Thus ended in complete failure the efforts of England to reap what she considered the legitimate fruits of this great enterprise. The day of which her farseeing publicists had dreamed had arrived; she had at last challenged the right of Spain to all North America, her sons were actually settled on the banks of the James, a beginning had been made in the work of building a colonial empire. But the hope which had so fired the mind of Hakluyt, the hope of attaining through Virginia British economic independence, was destined never to be fulfilled. However lavishly nature had endowed the colony with natural resources, however dense her forests, however rich her mines, however wide and deep her waterways, she could not become an industrial community. Fate had decreed for her another destiny. But England was reluctant to accept the inevitable in this matter. Long years after Sir Edwin Sandys and his fellow workers of the London Company had passed to their rest, we find the royal ministers urging upon the colony the necessity of producing pig iron and silk and potash, and promising every possible encouragement in the work. But the causes which operated to bring failure in 1610 or 1620 prevented success in 1660 and 1680. Virginia had not the abundant supply of labor essential to the development of an industrial community and for many decades, perhaps for centuries, could not hope to attain it. Her future lay in the discovery and exploitation of one staple commodity for which she was so preëminently adapted that she could, even with her costly labor, meet the competition of other lands. The future history of Virginia was to be built up around the Indian plant tobacco.

CHAPTER II

THE INDIAN WEED

History is baffling in its complexity. The human mind instinctively strives for simplicity, endeavors to reproduce all things to set rules, to discover the basic principles upon which all action is based. And in various lines of research much success has attended these efforts. We know the laws underlying the movements of the planets, of various chemical reactions, of plant and animal life. It is inevitable, then, that attempts should be made to accomplish similar results in history, to master the vast multitude of facts which crowd its pages, many of them seemingly unrelated, and show that after all they obey certain fundamental laws. Despite the vaunted freedom of the human will, it is maintained, mankind like the planets or the chemical agents, cannot escape the operation of definite forces to which it is subjected. And if these forces are studied and understood, to some extent at least, the course of future events may be predicted.

Thus it may be accepted as practically established that in any country and with any people a condition of continued disorder and anarchy must be succeeded by one of despotism. History records, we believe, no exception to this rule, while there are many instances which tend to confirm it. The absolute rule of the Caesars followed the anarchy of the later Roman republic, the Oliverian Protectorate succeeded the British civil wars, the first French Empire the Reign of Terror, the Bolshevik despotism the collapse of the old regime in Russia. Such will always be the case, we are told, because mankind turns instinctively to any form of government in quest of

protection from anarchy, and the easiest form of government to establish and operate is despotism.

Not content with generalizations of this kind, however, certain historians have undertaken to reduce all human action to some one great fundamental principle. The Freudian view emphasizes the influence of sex; Buckle maintains that the effect of climate is all-powerful. In recent years many students, while not agreeing that the solution of the problem is quite so simple, yet believe that underlying all social development will be found economic forces of one kind or another, that in commerce and industry and agriculture lies the key to every event of moment in the history of mankind. Often these forces have been obscured and misunderstood, but close study will always reveal them. It is folly to waste time, they say, as writers have so long done, in setting forth the adventures of this great man or that, in dwelling upon the details of political struggles or recounting the horrors of war. All these are but surface indications of the deeper movements underneath, movements in every case brought about by economic developments.

But this interpretation of history is by no means universally accepted. While admitting readily that the conditions surrounding the production and exchange of useful commodities have affected profoundly the course of events, many historians deny that they give the key to every important movement. We must study also the progress of human thought, of religion, of politics, or our conception of history will be warped and imperfect. How is it possible to explain the French religious wars of the Sixteenth century by the theory of economic causes? In what way does it account for the rebellion of Virginia and North Carolina and Maryland against the British government in 1775? How can one deny that the assassination of Abraham Lincoln affected profoundly the course of American history?

These efforts to simplify the meaning of human events have often led to error, have stressed certain events too strongly, have minimized others. The complexity of history is self-evident; we must for the present at least content ourselves with complex interpretations of it. If there be any great underlying principles which explain all, they have yet to be discovered.

Thus it would be folly in the study of colonial Virginia to blind ourselves to the importance of various non-economic factors, the love of freedom which the settlers brought with them from England, their affection for the mother country, the influence of the Anglican church. Yet it is obvious that we cannot understand the colony, its social structure, its history, its development unless we have a clear insight into the economic forces which operated upon it. These Englishmen, finding themselves in a new country, surrounded by conditions fundamentally different from those to which they had been accustomed, worked out a new and unique society, were themselves moulded into something different.

And in colonial Virginia history there is a key, which though it may not explain all, opens the door to much that is fundamental. This key is tobacco. The old saying that the story of Virginia is but the story of tobacco is by no means a gross exaggeration. It was this Indian plant, so despised by many of the best and ablest men of the time, which determined the character of the life of the colony and shaped its destinies for two and a half centuries. Tobacco was the chief factor in bringing final and complete failure to the attempts to produce useful raw materials, it was largely instrumental in moulding the social classes and the political structure of the colony, it was almost entirely responsible for the system of labor, it even exerted a powerful influence upon religion and morals. In a word, one can understand almost nothing of Virginia, its infancy, its development, its days of misfortune, its era of prosperity, its peculiar civilization, the nature of its relations to England, unless one knows the history of tobacco.

As though they had a prophetic vision of its future importance, the Virginia Indians revered the plant. To them it was an especial gift direct from the Great Spirit, and as such was endowed with unusual properties for doing good. When the fields of maize were dried and parched for lack of rain they powdered the tobacco and cast it to the winds that the evil genii might be propitiated; their priests on great occasions fed it to the sacrificial fires; when the usual catch of fish failed it was scattered over the water.[1] Smoking was considered a token of friendship and peace. When the white men first visited the native villages they soon found that to reject the proffered pipe was to offend their savage hosts and incur their hostility.

It was John Rolfe, celebrated as the husband of Pocahontas, who first experimented with the native leaf. This gentleman was himself fond of smoking, but he found the Virginia tobacco as it came from the hands of the savages, decidedly inferior to that of the West Indies. The leaf itself was small, and although the flavor was weak it was biting to the tongue.[2] Rolfe's efforts proved entirely successful. In 1614, two years after his first attempt, he had obtained a product which Ralph Hamor declared to be as "strong, sweet and pleasant as any under the sun."[3]

Thus, early in its history, Virginia had found a commodity for which she was preëminently suited, in the production of which she could compete successfully with any country in the world. And for her tobacco she had a ready market. During the reign of Queen Elizabeth the habit of smoking had spread rapidly among the upper classes of English, until at the end of the sixteenth century, it was almost universal. When

James I ascended the throne, although feeling a strong aversion to tobacco, he was forced to take up its use in order not to appear conspicuous among his courtiers, for the dictates of custom seem to have been as strong three hundred years ago as at present.[4] At the time that Rolfe was making his experiments England was spending yearly for the Spanish product many thousands of pounds.

It is not surprising, then, that the colonists turned eagerly to tobacco culture. The news that Rolfe's little crop had been pronounced in England to be of excellent quality spread rapidly from settlement to settlement, bringing with it new hope and determination. Immediately tobacco absorbed the thoughts of all, became the one topic of conversation, and every available patch of land was seized upon for its cultivation. The fortified areas within the palisades were crowded with tobacco plants, while even the streets of Jamestown were utilized by the eager planters.[5] In 1617 the George set sail for England laden with 20,000 pounds of Virginia leaf, the first of the vast fleet of tobacco ships which for centuries were to pass through the capes of the Chesapeake bound for Europe.[6] By 1627, the tobacco exports amounted to no less than half a million pounds.[7]

The London Company, together with the host of patriotic Englishmen who had placed such great hopes in the colony, were much disappointed at this unexpected turn of events. They had sought in the New World those "solid commodities" which they realized were fundamental to the prosperity of their country, commodities upon which English industrial life was founded. And they had found only the Indian weed— tobacco. This plant not only contributed nothing to the wealth of the kingdom, it was felt, but was positively injurious to those who indulged in its use. Surely, declared one writer, men "grow mad and crazed in the brain in that they would adventure to suck the smoke of a weed." James I thought there could be no baser and more harmful corruption, while Charles I expressed himself with equal emphasis. So late as 1631 the latter protested against the growing use of tobacco, which he termed "an evil habit of late tymes."[8]

Yet England soon learned to welcome the colonial tobacco as far better than no product at all. Hitherto the leaf in use had been raised in the Spanish colonies, and England's annual tobacco bill was becoming larger and larger. It seemed calamitous that British industry should be drained of good and useful commodities in exchange for a plant the consumption of which was harmful rather than beneficial. It was at least some satisfaction to know, then, that England could substitute for the Spanish leaf the growth of their own colonies. Apparently it was only later, however, that there came a full realization of the opportunity afforded for enriching England and building up her merchant marine by exporting tobacco to foreign countries. For the present they accepted this one product of their experiment in colonial expansion, reluctantly and with keen disappointment, as the best that could be obtained.

Yet it was obvious to the London Company that tobacco held out the only prospect, not only of securing a profit from their venture, but of bringing to Virginia some measure of prosperity. The first consignment of leaf which came from the colony sold for no less than 5s. 3d. a pound, a price which promised a rich return to the planters on the James and their backers in England.[9] And they much preferred to have a prosperous colony, even when prosperity was founded on tobacco, than a weak, impoverished settlement, which would be a drain upon their personal resources and of no value to the nation. Thus they accepted the inevitable, gave what encouragement they could to the new product, and sought to

use it as a means for building up the British empire in
America. When once England had established herself firmly
in the New World, it would be time enough to return to the
attempt to secure from the colony ship-stores, potash, iron
and silk.

With the overthrow of the Company, however, the Crown
made repeated efforts to direct the energies of Virginia away
from the all-absorbing cultivation of tobacco. In 1636
Charles I wrote to the Governor and Council bidding them
moderate the excessive quantities of the plant laid out each
year and to endeavor to produce some other staple commodities.[10] "The King cannot but take notice," he reiterated the
next year, "how little that colony hath advanced in Staple commodities fit for their own subsistence and clothing," and he
warned the planters to emulate the Barbados and Caribee
Islands, where a beginning had been made in cotton, wool
and other useful things.[11] But the colonists paid no heed to
these repeated warnings. The King's commands were no
more effective in establishing new industries than had been
the first attempts of the Company. Virginia was not prepared
to compete with the workers of Europe in their own chosen
fields, and persisted, had to persist, in the production of the
one commodity for which she possessed unsurpassed natural
advantages.

It is remarkable how universally the plant was cultivated
by all classes of Virginians throughout the colonial period.
It was difficult to find skilled artisans in any line of work,
since those who had pursued in England the various trades
usually deserted them, when they landed in the colony, in
order to turn to the raising of tobacco. And the few who
continued to pursue their old vocations usually rented or purchased a small tract of land and devoted a part of their time
to its cultivation. Blacksmiths, carpenters, shipwrights,

coopers all raised their little tobacco crop and sold it to the British merchants,[12] while even the poor minister sought to make ends meet by planting his glebe with Orinoco or Sweet-scented. The Governor himself was not free from the all-prevailing custom, and frequently was the possessor of a farm where his servants and slaves, like those of other gentlemen in the colony, were kept busy tending the tobacco crop.

It is doubtful whether the members of the London Company, even Sir Edwin Sandys himself, ever attempted to visualize the social structure which would develop in the Virginia they were planning. If so, they unquestionably pictured a state of affairs very different from that which the future held in store. They took it for granted that Virginia would to a large extent be a duplicate of England. In the forests of the New World would grow up towns and villages, centers of industry and centers of trade. The population would be divided into various classes—well-to-do proprietors boasting of the title of gentleman; professional men, lawyers, physicians, ministers; skilled artisans of all kinds; day laborers.

We catch a glimpse of the Virginia of their minds from a Broadside issued in 1610, appealing for volunteers for service in the colony.[13] We can see the shipwrights at work in the busy yards of thriving ports; the smelters caring for their iron and copper furnaces; the "minerall-men" digging out the ore; saltmakers evaporating the brackish waters for their useful product; vine-dressers tending their abundant crops of grapes and coopers turning out the hogsheads in which to store the wine which came from the presses; bricklayers and carpenters fashioning substantial houses; fishermen bringing in the plentiful yield of the day and dressers preparing the fish for foreign shipment; joiners, smiths, gardeners, bakers, gun-founders, ploughwrights, brewers, sawyers, fowlers, each plying his trade in the New Brittania.

But how different was the reality.   Virginia became, not an industrial, but a distinctly agricultural community.   For more than a century it could boast not a single town worthy of the name.[14]   It was but a series of plantations, not large in extent, but stretching out for miles along the banks of the rivers and creeks, all devoted to the raising of tobacco.   The population of the colony was but the aggregate of the population of the plantation—the owner, the wage earners, the indentured servant, a few slaves.   Virginia in the Seventeenth century, despite the design of its founders, developed a life of its own, a life not only unlike that of England, but unique and distinct.

Immigration, like everything else in the colony, was shaped by the needs of tobacco.   For its successful production the plant does not require skilled labor or intensive cultivation. The barbarous natives of Africa, who later in the century were imported in such large numbers, eventually proved quite adequate to the task.   But it does require the service of many hands.   For decades after Rolfe's discovery had opened a new vista of prosperity for Virginia, fertile land was so cheap that a person even of moderate means might readily purchase an extensive plantation,[15] but it would be of little service to him unless he could find hands for clearing away the forests, breaking the soil, tending and curing the plants.

Of the three requirements of production—natural resources, capital and labor—the fertile soil furnished the first in abundance, the second could readily be secured, but the last remained for a full century the one great problem of the planters. From the days of Sir George Yeardley to those of Nicholson and Andros there was a persistent and eager demand for workers.   Of this there can be no better evidence than the remarkably high wages which prevailed in the colony, especially in the years prior to the Restoration.   In fact, it is probable that the laborer received for his services four or five times the

amount he could earn in England.   Even during the time of
the London Company we find George Sandys writing to a
friend in London to procure indentured servants for the colony
as the wages demanded were intolerable.   A day's work
brought, in addition to food, a pound of tobacco valued at one
shilling, while in England the unskilled worker considered himself fortunate if he could earn so much in a week.[16]

In his efforts to solve this acute problem the planter found
little hope in the aborigines.   The Spaniards, it is true, had
made use of the Indians to till their fields or work in the gold
and silver mines, but the Pamunkey and the Powhatan were
cast in a different mold from the Aztec and the Peruvian.   To
hunt them out of their native lairs and bind them to arduous
and ignominious servitude was hardly to be thought of.   Their
spirit was too proud to be thus broken, the safe refuge of the
woods too near at hand.   One might as well have attempted to
hitch lions and tigers to the plough shaft, as to place these
wild children of the forest at the handles.   At times it proved
practicable to make use of Indian children for servants, and
there are numerous instances on record in which they are
found in the homes of the planters.[17]   But this, of course,
could be of little service in solving the pressing labor problem,
in clearing new ground or tilling the idle fields.   The Virginia landowner was forced to turn elsewhere for his helpers.

In 1619 a Dutch privateer put into the James river and dis-
embarked twenty Africans who were sold to the settlers as
slaves.   This event, so full of evil portent for the future of
Virginia, might well have afforded a natural and satisfactory solution of the labor problem.   Slaves had long been
used in the Spanish colonies, proving quite competent to
do the work of tending the tobacco plants, and bringing handsome returns to their masters.   But it was impossible at
this time for England to supply her plantations with this type

of labor. The slave trade was in the hands of the Dutch, who had fortified themselves on the African coast and jealously excluded other nations. Thus while the demand for negro slaves remained active in the colony, they increased in numbers very slowly. The muster of 1624-25 shows only 22.[18] During the following half century there was a small influx of negroes, but their numbers were still too small to affect seriously the economic life of the colony.[19]

The settlers were thus forced to look to England itself to supply them with hands for their tobacco fields. They knew that in the mother country were many thousands of indigent persons who would welcome an opportunity to better their lot by migrating to the New World. And the English statesmen, feeling that there was need for blood letting, welcomed an opportunity to divert the surplus population to the new colony in America.[20] The decline in English foreign trade and the stagnation of home industry had brought unemployment and suffering to every class of workers. Wages were so low that the most industrious could not maintain themselves in comfort, while to provide against want in case of sickness or old age was hardly to be thought of. Every parish, every town swarmed with persons stricken with abject poverty. In some parts of the country no less than 30 per cent of the population were dependent in part upon charity for their daily bread, while many were driven into vagabondage and crime, becoming an element of danger rather than of strength to the nation.[21] It seemed to the planters that the mother country constituted an abundant reservoir of labor, a reservoir already overflowing and capable of supplying indefinitely their every need.

The only drawback was the long and expensive voyage across the Atlantic. The fare, even for the poorest and most crowded accommodations, was no less than six pounds sterling, a sum far beyond the means of the thriftiest laborer.[22] Obviously some scheme had to be evolved to overcome this difficulty before Virginia could make use of English labor. And so the planters turned to the simple expedient of advancing the passage money to the immigrant and of placing him under strict legal bonds to work it out after reaching the colony.

This system, around which the economic life of Virginia centered for a full century, proved satisfactory to all concerned. The credit advanced to the immigrant made it possible for him to earn his ocean fare, not in England where labor was cheap, but in America where it was dear. In other words, he was enabled without delay to enjoy the full benefits of selling his services in the best market. The necessity for placing him under a stringent contract or indenture is evident. Had this not been done the immigrant, upon finding himself in Virginia, might have refused to carry out his part of the bargain. But the indenture was in no sense a mark of servitude or slavery. It simply made it obligatory for the newcomer, under pain of severe penalties, to work out his passage money, and until that was accomplished to surrender a part of the personal liberty so dear to every Englishman.

It is erroneous to suppose that most of the servants were degenerates or criminals. It is true that the English Government from time to time sought to lessen the expense of providing for convicted felons by sending some of them to the colonies, among them on rare occasions a few decidedly objectionable characters. More than once the Virginians protested vigorously against this policy as dangerous to the peace and prosperity of the colony.[23] By far the larger part of these penal immigrants, however, were but harmless paupers, driven perhaps to theft or some other petty offense by cold and hunger. Often they were sentenced to deportation by merciful judges in order that they might not feel the full weight of the harsh laws of that day.[24]

And of the small number of real criminals who came in, few indeed made any lasting imprint upon the social fabric of the colony. Many served for life and so had no opportunity of marrying and rearing families to perpetuate their degenerate traits. Those who escaped fled from the confines of settled Virginia to the mountains or to the backwoods of North Carolina. Many others succumbed to the epidemics which proved so deadly to the newcomers from England. In fact the criminal servant was but a passing incident in the life and development of England's greatest and most promising colony.[25]

An appreciable proportion of the so-called criminal laborers were no more than political prisoners taken in the rebellions of the Seventeenth century. These men frequently represented the sturdiest and most patriotic elements in the kingdom and were a source of strength rather than of weakness to the colony. When Drogheda was captured by Cromwell's stern Puritan troops in 1649, some of the unfortunate rebels escaped the firing squad only to be sent to America to serve in the sugar or tobacco fields. Just how many of these Irishmen fell to the share of Virginia it is impossible to say, but the number rises well into the hundreds, and the patent books of the period are full of headrights of undoubted Irish origin.[26]

When Charles II was restored to the throne in 1660 it became the turn of the Puritans to suffer, and many non-conformists and former Oliverian soldiers were sent to Virginia. In fact so many old Commonwealth men were serving in the tobacco fields in 1663 that they felt strong enough to plot, not only for their own freedom, but for the overthrow of the colonial government.[27] In 1678, after the suppression of the Scottish Covenanters by the Highland Host, a new batch of prisoners were sent to the plantations.[28] Seven years later many of Monmouth's followers taken at Sedgemour, who were fortunate enough to escape the fury of Jeffreys and Kirk, were forced to work in the plantations.

But the bulk of the servants were neither criminals nor political prisoners, but poor persons seeking to better their condition in the land of promise across the Atlantic. They constituted the vanguard of that vast stream of immigrants which for three centuries Europe has poured upon our shores. The indentured servant differed in no essential from the poor Ulsterite or German who followed him in the Eighteenth century, or the Irishman, the Italian or the Slav in the Nineteenth. Like them he found too severe the struggle for existence at home, like them he sought to reach a land where labor, the only commodity he had to sell, would bring the highest return. The fact that his passage was paid for him and that he was bound by contract to work it out after reaching America, in no wise differentiates him from the newcomers of later days. In 1671 Sir William Berkeley reported to the Board of Trade that the colony contained "6,000 Christian servants for a short tyme," who had come with the "hope of bettering their condition in a Growing Country."[29]

Virginia is fortunate in having preserved a record of this, the first great migration to the English colonies, which in some respects is remarkably complete. In fact, the names of fully three-fourths of all the persons who came to the colony, whether as freemen or servants during the first century of its existence, are on record at the Land Office at Richmond, and at all times available to the student of history. In the early days of the settlement a law was passed designed to stimulate immigration, by which the Government pledged itself to grant fifty acres of land to any person who would pay the passage from Europe to Virginia of a new settler. Thus if one brought over ten indentured servants he would be entitled to

500 acres of land, if he brought 100, he could demand 5,000 acres. But the headright, as it was called, was not restricted to servants; if one came over as a freeman, paying his own passage, he was entitled to the fifty acres. Should he bring also his family, he could demand an additional fifty acres for his wife and fifty for each child or other member of the household.[30]

When the Government issued a grant for land under this law, the planter was required to record with the clerk of the county court the names of all persons for whose transportation the claim was made. Some of these lists have been lost, especially for the period from 1655 to 1666, but most of them remain, constituting an inexhaustible storehouse of information concerning the colony and the people who came to its shores.[31] How the papers escaped destruction during the fire which did so much damage in the Secretary's office at the time of Andros, it is impossible to say. The explanation is to be found perhaps in the fact that copies of the records were kept, not only at Williamsburg, but in the several counties, so that in case of loss by fire new entries could be made.

Immigration to Virginia continued in unabated volume throughout the Seventeenth century. The needs of the tobacco plantations were unceasing, and year after year the surplus population of England poured across the Atlantic in response. An examination of the list of headrights shows that the annual influx was between 1500 and 2000. Even during the Civil War and Commonwealth periods this average seems to have been maintained with surprising consistency. Apparently the only limit which could be set upon it was the available space on board the merchant fleet which each year left England for the Chesapeake bay. Thus in the year ending May 1635 we find that 2000 landed in the colony,[32] while in 1674 and again in 1682 the same average was maintained.[33]

At times the numbers dropped to 1200 or 1300, but this was the exception rather than the rule. All in all, considerably more than 100,000 persons migrated to the colony in the years that elapsed between the first settlement at Jamestown and the end of the century.[34]

This great movement, which far surpassed in magnitude any other English migration of the century, fixed for all time the character of the white population of tidewater Virginia. The vast bulk of the settlers were English. An examination of the headright lists shows here and there an Irish or a Scotch name, and on very rare occasions one of French or Italian origin, but in normal periods fully 95 per cent were unmistakably Anglo-Saxon. In fact, such names as Dixon, Bennett, Anderson, Adams, Greene, Brooke, Brown, Cooper, Gibson, Hall, Harris, King, Jackson, Long, Martin, Miller, Newton, Philips, Richards, Turner, White, appear with monotonous repetition. Except in the years 1655 and 1656, after the Drogheda tragedy when one sees such names as O'Lanny, O'Leaby, O'Mally, and Machoone, or in 1679 when there was a sprinkling of Scottish names, the entire list is distinctly English.

It must not be supposed that immigration to Virginia in the Seventeenth century was restricted to indentured servants. Some of the settlers were freemen, paying their own passage and establishing themselves as proprietors immediately after arriving in the colony. But the conditions which attracted them were the same as those which brought over the servants. In both cases it was tobacco, the rich returns which it promised and the urgent need it had of labor, which impelled them to leave their homes in England to seek their fortunes in the strange land beyond the seas.

Having seen the character of the immigration to Virginia, it remains to determine what was the fate of the settler after he reached the colony, what rôle lay before him in its social and economic life. Would he remain permanently in the status of a servant, entering into a new agreement with his master after the expiration of the old? Would he eventually become a day laborer, working for wages upon the estates of the wealthy? Would he become a tenant? Could he hope to become a freeholder, making of Virginia, like Rome in the early days of the republic, the land of the small proprietor?

CHAPTER III

THE system of indentured labor differed vitally from negro slavery. The servant usually was bound to his master for a limited period only, and at the expiration of four or five years was a free man, to go where he would and pursue what employment seemed most lucrative. And of tremendous importance to the future of Virginia was the fact that he was of the same race and blood as the rest of the population. There was no inherent reason why he might not take up land, marry and become a part of the social structure of the colony.

When races of marked physical differences are placed side by side in the same territory, assimilation of one or the other becomes difficult, and an age long repugnance and conflict is apt to result. Perhaps the greatest crime against the southern colonies was not the introduction of slavery, but the introduction of negroes. It was inevitable that eventually slavery would be abolished. But the negro race in America cannot be abolished, it cannot be shipped back to Africa, it cannot well be absorbed into the white population. Today California is struggling to avoid a like problem by excluding the Japanese, while Canada, Australia and New Zealand are closing their doors to Orientals of all kinds.

Thus Virginia, during its century of white immigration, was storing up no perplexing difficulties for the future, was developing slowly but surely into an industrious, democratic, Anglo-Saxon community. Not until the black flood of slaves was turned loose upon her, strangling her peasantry and revolutionizing her industrial and social life, was her future put in pawn. The white servants, so far as they remained in the colony, became bone of her bone, flesh of her flesh, promised her a homogeneous race, a sound economic and political development.

When the alien newcomer to the United States sees from the deck of his steamer the Statue of Liberty and the ragged sky line of lower Manhattan, he feels that the goal of his ambition has been reached, that the land of opportunity lies before him. But to the indentured settler of the Seventeenth century, his arrival in the James or the York was but the beginning of his struggles. Before he could grasp the riches of the New World, he must pay the price of his passage, must work out through arduous years the indenture to which he had affixed his signature.

And these years were filled not only with toil, perhaps with hardship, but with the greatest peril. He might account himself fortunate indeed if during the first twelve months he escaped the so-called Virginia sickness. Tidewater Virginia for the English settlers was a pest-ridden place. The low and marshy ground, the swarming mosquitoes, the hot sun, the unwholesome drinking water combined to produce an unending epidemic of dysentery and malaria. And at frequent intervals, especially in the early years, yellow fever, scurvy and plague swept over the infant colony, leaving behind a ghastly train of suffering and death.[1] At one time the mortality among the settlers upon the James ran as high as 75 per cent and for a while it seemed that this attempt of the British nation to secure a foothold upon the American continent must end in failure.[2]

But as the years wore on better conditions prevailed. Governor Berkeley testified in 1671, "there is not oft seasoned hands (as we term them) that die now, whereas heretofore not one of five escaped the first year."[3] This improvement was brought about by the use of Peruvian bark, a clearer understanding of sanitary matters and the selection of more healthful sites for plantations. At the time when Sir William wrote it is probable that 80 per cent or more of the indentured servants survived the dangers of the tobacco fields, completed their terms of service and, if they remained in the colony, became freedmen with the full rights of Englishmen and Virginians.

In the period from 1660 to 1725 there was, as we shall see, an exodus of poor whites from Virginia. This, however, was chiefly the result of the influx of slaves which marked the end of the century, and it is safe to assume that prior to the Restoration there was no extensive movement from Virginia to other colonies. The servant, upon attaining his freedom, usually remained in the colony and sought to establish himself there.

Although it is impossible to determine accurately the average length of service required by the indentures, there is reason to believe that it did not exceed five years. In cases of controversy between masters and servants who had come in without written contracts as to when their terms should expire, it was at first required by law that the period be fixed at five years if the age was in excess of twenty-one.[4] In 1654, however, a new act was passed by the Assembly, making it necessary for those who had no indentures, if over sixteen to serve six years, if less than sixteen until the twenty-fourth year had been reached.[5] This was found to work to the disadvantage of the colony by discouraging immigration, and in 1662 the law was changed so that in all doubtful cases the legal term should be five years for persons over sixteen.[6] Since the Assembly, which was so largely made up of persons who themselves held servants, would certainly not fix the legal term for a period shorter than that normally provided for in the indentures, we may assume that usually the servant secured his freedom within four or five years after his arrival in the colony.

Thus it is evident that the bulk of the population could not have been, as is so often supposed, made up of large landed proprietors with their servants and slaves. Such a conception takes no account of the annual translation of hundreds of men and women from bondsmen into freedmen. The short duration of the average term of service, together with the fact that the servants were usually still young when freed, made it inevitable that in time the freedmen would outnumber those in service. The size of the annual immigration could in no wise alter this situation, for the greater the influx of servants, the greater would be the resulting graduation into the class of freedmen.

The average number of headrights, as we have seen, was probably not less than 1750 a year. If it is assumed that 1500 of these were servants, five per cent of whom served for life and 20 per cent died before the expiration of their terms, no less than 1125 would remain to become freedmen. While the number of those under indenture remained practically stationary, the size of the freedman class grew larger with the passing of the years.

Placing the average term at five years, then, and the average mortality at twenty per cent, there would be in service at any given time some 6,000 men and women. In fact, Sir William Berkeley, in his famous report of 1671, estimated the number of servants in the colony at this figure.[7] On the other hand an annual accession of 1125 to the class of freedmen would in five years amount to 5,625, in ten years to 11,250, in fifteen to 16,875, in twenty to 22,500. At the end of half a century no less than 56,250 persons would have emerged from servitude to become free citizens. Although there is every reason to believe that these figures are substantially correct,[8] their accuracy or lack of accuracy in no way affect the principle involved. From its very nature it was impossible that the system of indentured servants should long remain the chief factor in the industrial life of the colony or supply most of the labor.

It is true, of course, that the number of those completing their terms of indenture is not an absolute gauge, at any given date, of the size of the freedman class. To determine this it would be necessary to know the average span of life of the freedman, a thing certainly not worked out at the time and impossible of accomplishment now. We may assume, however, that it was relatively long. The newcomer who had lived through the first terrible year in the tobacco fields had been thoroughly tested, "seasoned" as the planters called it, and was reasonably certain of reaching a mature age. Moreover, the servants were almost universally of very tender years. Seldom indeed would a dealer accept one over twenty-eight, and the average seems to have been between seventeen and twenty-three. The reasons for this are obvious. Not only were young men and women more adaptable to changed conditions, more capable of resisting the Virginia climate, stronger and more vigorous, but they proved more tractable and entered upon the adventure more eagerly.[9] These conclusions are fully borne out by an examination of the lists of servants given in Hotten's *Emigrants to America.* Of the first 159 servants here entered whose ages are attached, the average is twenty-three years.[10] And as many of these persons were brought over as skilled artisans to take part in the industrial life which the Company had planned for the colony, it is probable that they were much older than the average servant of later days who came as an agricultural laborer. There is every reason to believe, then, that the average servant was still in his prime when he completed his term, perhaps not more than twenty-six or twenty-seven, with many years of usefulness and vigor before him.

It must also be remembered that the freedman, by a display of energy and capability, might acquire property, marry and rear a family. While the number of indentured servants was strictly limited to those who were brought in from the outside, the class of poor freemen might and did enjoy a natural increase within itself. Thus it was inevitable that with the passing of the years the servants were more and more outnumbered by the growing group of freemen. In 1649, when the population was but 15,000,[11] 6,000 servants might well have performed most of the manual labor of the tobacco fields, but in 1670, when the inhabitants numbered 40,000,[12] or in 1697 when they were 70,000,[13] they would form a comparatively small proportion of the people, so small in fact that most of the work of necessity had to be done by freemen. In other words the picture so often presented, even by historians of established reputation, of a Seventeenth century Virginia in which the land was divided into large plantations owned by rich proprietors and tilled chiefly by indentured servants is entirely erroneous. Such a state of affairs was made impossible by the very nature of the system of indentures itself.

It becomes a matter of prime interest, then, to determine what became of the mass of freedmen, what rôle they played in the social and economic life of the colony. Because the servant who had completed his term was free to follow his own bent, we have no right to assume that he sought at once to establish himself as an independent proprietor. He might seek service with the large planters as a hired laborer, he might become a tenant. In either case the population would have been divided into two classes—the wealthy landowner and those who served him.

We know that at all periods of Virginia history there were a certain number of persons employed as wage earners. The colonial laws and the county records contain many references to them. Payment of wages was not unusual even under the Company, and we are told by George Sandys that hired laborers received one pound of tobacco a day in addition to their food.[14] In later years we have from time to time references to wage rates, and in some cases copies of contracts entered into between employer and wage earner. But such cases are comparatively rare, and it is evident that the use of hired labor throughout the colonial period was the exception rather than the rule. In fact it would seem that few save servants newly freed and lacking in the funds necessary for purchasing and equipping little farms of their own ever sought employment upon the large plantations. And even in such cases the contracts were for comparatively short periods, since it often required but a year or two of labor for the freedman to save enough from his wages to make a beginning as an independent proprietor.

When once established, there was no reason, in the days prior to the introduction of slavery, why he should not hold his own in competition with his wealthy neighbor. In the production of tobacco the large plantation, so long as it was cultivated only by expensive white labor, offered no marked advantage over the small. With the cost of land very low, with the means of earning the purchase price so readily in hand, with the conditions for an independent career all so favorable, it was not to be expected that the freedman should content himself permanently with the status of a hired laborer.

Nor was there any reason why he should become a tenant. Had all the fertile land been preëmpted, as was the case on the banks of the Hudson, the poor man might have been compelled to lease the soil upon which he expended his efforts or do without entirely. But such was not the case. It is true that at the end of the Seventeenth century certain wealthy men got possession of large tracts of unsettled land, but their monopoly was so far from complete that they gladly sold off their holdings in little parcels to the first purchasers who presented themselves. Apparently they made no attempts to establish themselves in a position similar to that of the great landlords of England.

The records afford ample evidence that the leasing of property was by no means unknown in colonial Virginia, but the custom was comparatively rare. Hugh Jones, writing in 1721, declared that the tenant farmers constituted but a small fraction of the population, a fact which he explained by the unusual facilities for acquiring property in fee simple.[15] It would have been folly for the tobacco planter to expend his labor upon another man's property, perhaps erecting barns and fences and otherwise improving it, when he could for so small an outlay secure land of his own.

Thus we are led to the conclusion that the average Virginia plantation must have been comparatively small in extent. The development of large estates was narrowly limited by the various factors which made it impossible to secure an adequate labor supply—the restrictions upon the slave trade, the insufficient number of indentured servants and the shortness of their terms, the unwillingness of freedmen and others to work for wages. On the other hand, it would be expected that the servants upon securing their freedom would purchase land of their own, and cover all tidewater Virginia with little farms.

Turning to the various records of the time that deal with the distribution of land—deeds, wills, transfers, tax lists, inventories—we find that these conclusions are fully borne out. All reveal the fact that the average plantation, especially in the Seventeenth century, so far from vieing with the vast estates in existence in certain parts of America, was but a few hundred acres in extent.

The land transfers of Surry county afford an interesting illustration. In thirty-four instances mentioned during the years from 1684 to 1686, for which the exact number of acres is given, the largest is 500 acres, the smallest twenty. The aggregate of all land which changed hands is 6,355 acres, or an average of 187 for each sale. There are eleven transfers of 100 acres or less, twenty-three transfers of 200 or less and only four of more than 300 acres.[16] One can find in this no evidence of the fabled barons of colonial Virginia, but only of a well established class of small proprietors.

The York county books for the years from 1696 to 1701 tell the same story. Here we find recorded forty-one transfers and leases. Twenty-two are for 100 acres or less, 33 for 200 acres or less, and four, one for 1,400, one for 1,210, one for 600 and one for 550, are more than 300 acres in extent. The aggregate is 8,153 acres and the average 199.[17]

In the Rappahannock county records from 1680 to 1688 of fifteen land transfers taken at random from the books, the largest is 400 while the average is 168 acres.[18] Of the forty-eight transfers mentioned in the Essex county books for the years from 1692 to 1695, the largest is 600 acres and the smallest 50. Twenty are for 100 acres or less, 31 for 200 or less and only four for over 300.[19]

That conditions not fundamentally different prevailed in the early days of the colony is shown by the census taken of the landowners in 1626. Of the holdings listed no less than 25 were for 50 acres or less, 73 for 100 and most of the others for less than 300 acres. The total number of proprietors listed is 224 and the total acreage 34,472, giving an average for each plantation of 154 acres.[20]

It has been assumed by certain writers that the land grants

preserved in the Registrar's Office in Richmond tend to con-
tradict this evidence. Although the average patent is by no
means large, it is much more extensive than the typical land
transfer. In 1638 this average was 423 acres, in 1640 it was
405, in 1642 it was 559, in 1645 it was 333, in 1648 it was
412, in 1650 it was 675. During the entire period from 1634
to 1650 inclusive the size of the average land grant was 446
acres. From 1650 to 1655 the average was 591 acres, from
1655 to 1666 six hundred and seventy-one, from 1666 to 1679
eight hundred and ninety acres, from 1679 to 1689 six hundred and seven acres, from 1689 to 1695 six hundred and one
acres, from 1695 to 1700 six hundred and eighty-eight acres.[21]
In the course of the entire second half of the Seventeenth
century the average size of the patent was 674 acres.

Yet these facts have little direct bearing upon the extent of
the plantations themselves. The system of granting land, as
we have seen, was not based upon the individual needs of the
planters, but upon the number of headrights presented to the
Government. Obviously it was the question of the most economical method of transporting immigrants which would determine the average size of the grant. If it proved best to
bring in servants in small groups, distributed among vessels
devoted chiefly to merchandise, the patents would be small; if
they came in on immigrant vessels, in numbers ranging from
50 to 200, the patents would be large.

Apparently both methods were in vogue. There are grants
recorded varying in size from 50 acres to 10,000 acres.[22] Beyond doubt many merchants, finding that their vessels on the
western voyage were not fully laden, from time to time took
on a few indentured servants. If they furnished accommodation for from ten to twenty immigrants, they could demand,
in addition to the sale of the indentures, 500 to 1,000 acres of
land. It was a frequent practice, also, for planters in Vir-

ginia to send orders to their agents in England to procure and
ship one or more servants as need for them arose.[23] "Your
brother George hath moved you in his letters to send him over
some servants the next year," wrote Richard Kemp to Robert
Read in 1639.[24] Undoubtedly in cases of this kind the servants
usually sailed in small parties upon the regular merchant
vessels.

On the other hand it would appear that large numbers of
persons arrived on strictly immigrant vessels, in which they
made the chief if not the only cargo. Some of the best
known men in the colony were dealers in servants and reaped
from the business very large profits. Of these perhaps
the best known in the earlier period was William Claiborne,
celebrated for his dispute with the Maryland proprietors over
the possession of Kent Island. Peter Ashton was another extensive dealer in servants, at one time receiving 2,550 acres
for his headrights, at another 2,000. Isaac Allerton, Lewis
Burwell, Giles Brent, Joseph Bridger and many others of like
prominence are upon the patent rolls for large grants. The
most inveterate dealer in servants, however, was Robert Beverley. This well known planter, so famous for his part in
Bacon's Rebellion and in the political contests which grew out
of it, is credited with patents aggregating 25,000 or 30,000
acres.[25]

Often partnerships were formed for the importation of servants, in which cases the patents were made out jointly.
Among the more interesting are patents to Robert Beverley
and Henry Hartwell, to Thomas Butt and Thomas Milner, to
William Bassett and James Austin, to Thomas Blunt and
Richard Washington. When associations of three or more
persons were formed for the importation of servants, a not
infrequent occurrence, the number of headrights is unusually
large and the grants patented in consequence extensive. Thus

Edmund Bibbie and others are credited with 3,350 acres, Robert Ambrose and others with 6,000, George Archer and others with 4,000.[26]

It is clear, then, that the size of the average patent in the Seventeenth century is not an indication of the extent of the average plantation. If economic conditions were such as to encourage large holdings, extensive farms would appear regardless of the original patents, for the small proprietors would be driven to the wall by their more wealthy rivals and forced to sell out to them. On the other hand, if the large planters found it difficult to secure adequate labor they would of necessity have to break up their estates and dispose of them to the small freeholders. That the latter development and not the former actually took place in Virginia during the Seventeenth century a careful examination of the country records makes most apparent.

Over and over again in the records of various land transfers it is stated that the property in question had belonged originally to a more extensive tract, the patent for which was granted under the headright law. A typical case is that of John Dicks who purchased for 8,500 pounds of tobacco, "all the remaining part of 900 acres gotten by the transporting of 19 persons."[27] Similarly we find John Johnson in 1653 selling to Robert Roberts half of 900 acres which he had received by patent.[28] In 1693 John Brushood sold to James Grey 200 acres, a part of 5,100 acres originally granted to Mr. Henry Awbrey.[29] Such cases could be multiplied indefinitely.

Perhaps the most instructive instance left us of this development is the break up of a tract of land known as Button's Ridge, in Essex country. This property, comprising 3,650 acres, was granted to Thomas Button in the year 1666.[30] The original patentee transferred the entire tract to his brother Robert Button, who in turn sold it to John Baker. The lat-

ter, finding no doubt that he could not put under cultivation
so much land, cut it up into small parcels and sold it off to
various planters. Of these transactions we have, most fortunately, a fairly complete record. To Captain William Moseley he sold 200 acres, to John Garnet 600, to Robert Foster
200, to William Smither 200, to William Howlett 200, to
Anthony Samuell 300, to William Williams 200. It is probable that he sold also a small holding to Henry Creighton, for
we find the latter, in 1695, transferring to William Moseley
100 acres, formerly a part of Button's Ridge.[31]

Important as are these gleanings from the county records,
we have at our disposal even better and more conclusive evidence that colonial Virginia was divided, not into baronial
estates of vast proportions, but into a large number of comparatively small farms. Governor Nicholson's rent roll,
which is published as an appendix to this volume, for the early
years of the Eighteenth century at least, places the matter beyond doubt. Here we have before us an official inventory of
all Virginia save the Northern Neck, giving the name of every
proprietor and the number of acres in his possession.

It will be remembered that in the Crown colonies there was
a perpetual obligation imposed upon all land when first granted
known as the quit-rent. In Virginia this duty amounted to
one shilling for every fifty acres, payable in tobacco at the rate
of a penny per pound.[32] Despite the fact that some 27 per
cent of the returns was consumed by the cost of collection,
and that there were frequent frauds in disposing of the tobacco, the revenue derived from this source was of considerable importance.[33] The amount collected in 1705 was £1,841.
1. 6¾. When James Blair, the Virginia Commissary of the
Bishop of London, petitioned William and Mary for a fund
from the accumulated quit-rents for his proposed college at
Williamsburg, some of the British governmental officials ob-

jected strenuously. "This sum is perhaps the only ready cash in all the plantations," it was declared, "which happens to be by good husbandry and is a stock for answering any emergency that may happen in Virginia."[34]

Throughout the entire Seventeenth century, however, the Governors had experienced great difficulty in collecting this tax. Over and over again they reported in their letters to the Board of Trade that there were large arrears of quit-rents which it was impossible to make the landowners pay.[35] The reason for this was obvious enough. In each county the tax collector was the sheriff. Although this officer was appointed by the Governor, he usually had a wholesome respect for the larger proprietors and in consequence was wary of giving offense by holding them to too strict an account of their estates.[36] At times the sheriffs themselves were the sufferers by this state of affairs, for they were held responsible for the rents upon all land patented in their counties, for which returns had not been made.

Although the Governors from time to time made rather feeble attempts to remedy the prevailing laxness in this matter, nothing of importance was accomplished before the first administration of Francis Nicholson. The chief executive himself had much need of the good will of the richer inhabitants, and he was not over forward in forcing them to bring in accurate returns. Nicholson, however, who prided himself on his executive ability and who was bent on breaking the power of the clique which centered around the Council of State, exerted himself to the utmost to secure full payment for every acre.

So early as 1690 we find him issuing orders to the sheriffs for the drawing up of an accurate rent roll, through an examination of the patent lists and the records of land transfers.[37] May 15, 1691, he took up the matter again, warning the sheriffs that he expected more accurate returns than they had yet made.[38] With the appointment of Sir Edmund Andros as Governor, however, interest in the quit-rents lapsed, and not until his removal and the reappointment of Nicholson was the attempt resumed.

In July, 1699, Nicholson wrote the Commissioners of Trade and Plantations that he was doing his best to improve the quit-rents and that the auditor had been ordered to draw up a scheme for securing a more exact list of land holdings.[39] But for a while the matter still hung fire. The leading men in the Government were ready enough in making suggestions, but they were extensive landholders themselves and apparently rendered no real assistance. "I have considered those papers given me by your Excellency relating to a perfect rent roll," the auditor, William Byrd I wrote Nicholson, Oct. 21, 1703, "notwithstanding I have, according to your repeated directions used my utmost diligence in giving charge to sheriffs and taking their oaths to rolls, I am sensible there is still very great abuse therein."[40]

Despite these discouragements Nicholson persisted and in 1704 succeeded in obtaining the first really accurate rent roll of the colony. These lists have long been missing, and perhaps were destroyed in one of the several fires which have wrought so much havoc with the records of colonial Virginia, but a true copy was made by the clerk, William Robertson, and sent to the Board of Trade. Fortunately the British Government has been more careful of its priceless historical manuscripts than has Virginia, and this copy today reposes in the Public Record Office in London, a veritable treasure trove of information concerning economic and social conditions in the colony.[41]

Even a cursory examination of the rent roll is sufficient to dispel the old belief that Virginia at this time was the land

of the large proprietor. As one glances down the list of plantations he is struck by the number of little holdings, the complete absence of huge estates, the comparative scarcity even of
those that for a newly settled country might be termed extensive. Here and there, especially in the frontier counties is
listed a tract of four or five or even ten thousand acres, but
such cases are very rare. In Middlesex county there is but
one plantation of more than 2,500 acres, in Charles City
county the largest holding is 3,130, in Nansemond 2,300, in
Norfolk county 3,200, in Princess Anne 3,100, in Elizabeth
City county 2,140, in York 2,750, in Essex 3,200.

On the other hand the rolls reveal the existence of thousands
of little proprietors, whose holdings of from 50 to 500 acres
embraced the larger part of the cultivated soil of the colony.
Thus we find that in Nansemond, of 376 farms 26 were
of 50 acres or less, 66 were between 50 and 100 acres, 110
between 100 and 200 acres, 88 between 200 and 400 acres, 78
between 400 and 1,000 acres, and only eight over 1,000 acres.
In Middlesex county out of 122 holdings eleven were of 50
acres or less, 33 between 50 and 100 acres, 32 between 100
and 200 acres, 25 between 200 and 500 acres, 19 between 500
and 2,500 acres, one of 4,000 acres and one of 5,200 acres. Of
the 94 plantations in Charles City county 26 were of 100
acres or less, 21 between 100 and 200 acres, 25 between 200
and 500 acres, 19 between 500 and 2,500 acres and three more
than 2,500 acres.[42]

Although the average size of the plantations varied considerably in different counties it was everywhere comparatively
small, far smaller than the average land grant of the time, far
smaller than has been imagined by some of the closest students of the period. For Nansemond the rolls reveal the average holding as 212 acres, for James City county 400, for
York 298, for Warwick 308, for Elizabeth City county 255,

for Princess Anne 459, for Gloucester 395, for Middlesex 406, for Charles City county 553.[43]

In the past few decades much has been written of the social life and customs of the people of colonial Virginia. But except in the able works of Dr. Philip Alexander Bruce little has been said concerning the small planter class, the men who made up the vast bulk of the population, the true Seventeenth century Virginians. We have long and detailed descriptions of the residences of the small group of the well-to-do, their libraries, their furniture, their table ware, their portraits, their clothing, their amusements. The genealogy of the leading families has been worked out with minute care, their histories recorded, some of their leading members idealized by the writers of fiction. The mention of colonial Virginia brings instantly to mind a picture of gay cavaliers, of stately ladies, of baronial estates, of noble manors. And the sturdy, independent class of small farmers who made up a full 90 per cent of the freeholders at the time the rent roll was taken, have been relegated into undeserved obscurity.

It is to be noted that the roll does not include the names of proprietors residing in the Northern Neck, as the peninsula between the Potomac and the Rappahannock is called. This territory, although acknowledging the jurisdiction of the Government at Williamsburg in most matters and sending representatives to the House of Burgesses, paid its quit-rents, not to the Crown but to a proprietor. Nicholson, therefore, was not concerned in their collection and took no steps to list its landholders in his new roll. There is no reason to believe, however, that conditions in that part of the colony were fundamentally different.

Nor can the accuracy of the rent roll be challenged. There existed always the incentive to make false returns, of course, in order to escape the payment of taxes, and not many sheriffs were so diligent as the one in Henrico who unearthed 1,669 acres that had been "concealed."[44] Yet it must be remembered that the Governor brought to bear all the pressure at his disposal to make this particular roll accurate, that the sheriffs were his appointees, that they could not lightly defy him in so important a matter. And even though in isolated cases they may have winked at false returns from men of wealth and rank, from the mass of small proprietors they must have insisted upon reports as accurate as the records or actual surveying could make them. No doubt certain uncultivated tracts in the frontier counties were omitted, but with these we are not immediately concerned. For conditions in the older parts of the colony, where the slow evolution of economic factors had been at work for a century, the roll presents unimpeachable evidence that the bulk of the cultivated land was divided into small plantations.

But it still remains to prove that their owners were men of meagre fortunes, men who tilled the soil with their own hands. After all a farm of two or three hundred acres might give scope for large activities, the employment of many servants and slaves, the acquisition of some degree of wealth. Might it not be possible that though the acres of the planter were limited, his estate after all corresponded somewhat with the popular conception?

This leads us to a study of the distribution of servants and slaves among the planters. At the outset we are faced with convincing evidence that at the end of the Seventeenth century the average number for each farm was very small. This is shown by a comparison of the number of plantations listed in the rent roll of 1704 with the estimated number of workers. In the counties for which the sheriffs made returns for Governor Nicholson there were some 5,500 landholders. When to these is added the proprietors of the Northern Neck the number must have approximated 6,500. If at this time the servants numbered 4,000, as seems probable,[45] and the slaves 6,000, together they would have averaged but 1.5 workers for each plantation. A decade earlier, when the use of slaves was still comparatively infrequent, the figure must have been still lower.

Fortunately we have even more direct and detailed evidence. Throughout almost all of Virginia colonial history one of the chief methods of raising revenue for the Government was the direct poll tax. This levy was laid, however, not only on every freeman over sixteen years of age, but upon male servants over 14, female servants who worked in the fields, and slaves above 16 of either sex, all of whom were officially termed tithables.[46] The tax rolls in which these persons were listed, some of which have been preserved among the county records, throw much light upon social and economic conditions in the colony.

In one district of Surry county we find in the year 1675 that there were 75 taxpayers and only 126 tithables. In other words only 51 persons in this district had this duty paid for them by others, whether parents, guardians or masters. And of the taxpayers, forty-two were liable for themselves alone, having no servants, slaves or dependent sons over 16; fifteen were liable for one other person, eight for two others, and only one, Lieutenant-Colonel Jordan, for so many as seven.[47]

In other districts the story is the same. In one there were forty taxpayers, 75 tithables and 25 persons who paid for themselves alone; in another 28 taxpayers, 62 tithables, fifteen who had no servants or slaves; in a third 48 taxpayers, 83 tithables, 28 who paid only for themselves, eleven who paid for two, five who paid for three; in a fourth district 29 taxpayers, 63 tithables, fourteen who had no servants or slaves; in a fifth 25 taxpayers, 45 tithables, 12 who paid only for themselves.[48] Thus in Surry county in the year 1675 there were in all 245 taxpayers and 434 tithables. In other words the men who paid their own tax outnumbered all those whose tax was paid for them, whether servants, slaves or relatives, at the ratio of about 4 to 3.

A study of the records of the same county ten years later leads to almost identical results. At that time Surry seems to have been divided into four districts. In the first there were 78 taxpayers, 132 tithables, 30 persons who paid only for themselves; in the second, 63 taxpayers, 133 tithables, 33 persons who paid for themselves alone; in the third there were 38 taxpayers, 74 tithables and 22 persons paying only for themselves; in the fourth 125 taxpayers, 201 tithables and 81 persons having no dependents to pay for. Thus there were 540 tithables in all and 304 taxpayers. In the entire county there were about 122 persons who paid the poll tax for others. The largest holders of servants or slaves were Mr. Robert Randall with seven, Lieutenant-Colonel William Browne with nine, Mr. Robert Canfield with seven, Mr. Arthur Allen with six, Mr. William Edwards with six, Mr. Francis Mason with seven and Mr. Thomas Binns with eight.[49]

Here again is proof that the popular conception of the Virginia plantation life of the Seventeenth century is erroneous. Instead of the wealthy planter who surrounded himself with scores of servants and slaves, investigation reveals hundreds of little farmers, many of them trusting entirely to their own exertions for the cultivation of the soil, others having but one or two servants, and a bare handful of well-to-do men each having from five to ten, or in rare cases twenty or thirty, servants and slaves.

A further confirmation of these conclusions is to be had by comparing the number of plantations listed in the rent roll of 1704 with the official returns of tithables for 1702.[50] Thus in

Nansemond there were 375 plantations and 1,030 tithables, Henrico with 162 plantations had 863 tithables, Middlesex with 122 plantations had 814 tithables, Gloucester with 381 plantations had 2,626, James City with 287 plantations had 1,193, York with 205 plantations had 1,180, Warwick with 122 plantations had 505, Elizabeth City with 116 plantations had 478, Princess Anne with 215 plantations had 727, Surry with 273 plantations had 739, Isle of Wight with 262 plantations had 896, Norfolk with 303 plantations had 693, New Kent with 497 plantations had 1,245, King William with 217 plantations had 803, King and Queen with 403 plantations had 1,848, Essex with 376 plantations had 1,034, Accomac with 392 plantations had 1,041, Northampton with 258 plantations had 693, Charles City and Prince George together with 420 plantations had 1,327.[51]

In Nansemond the average number of tithables as compared with the number of plantations was 2.7, in Henrico 5.1, in Middlesex 6.7, in Gloucester 6.9, in James City 4.2, in York 5.7, in Warwick 4.1, in Elizabeth City 4, in Princess Anne 3.4, in Surry 2.7, in Isle of Wight 3.3, in Norfolk 2.3, in New Kent 2.5, in King William 3.7, in King and Queen 4.6, in Essex 2.8, in Accomac 2.6, in Northampton 2.3, in Charles City and Prince George combined 3.1. In all Virginia, with the exclusion of the Northern Neck, there were 19,715 tithables and some 5,500 plantations, an average of 3.6 tithables for each plantation. If we deduct from the tithables all the male freeholders included in the rent roll, there remains only some 14,700 persons south of the Rappahannock to make up the list, not only of servants and slaves, but of professional men, wage earners, artisans and dependent sons of landholders over 16 years of age.

Another invaluable source of information concerning the distribution of servants and slaves is provided by the numer-

ous inventories, deeds, and wills which have been preserved
in the records. Thus in Surry during the years from 1671 to
1686 we find listed the estates of fifty-nine persons. Of these
no less than fifty-two were apparently without servants or
slaves; two, William Rooking and Captain Robert Spencer,
had five each; one, Mr. William Chambers, had three; and
four, Captain William Corker, John Hoge, Mr. John Goring
and Samuel Cornell, had one each.[52]

In Elizabeth City of twenty-seven estates recorded during
the years from 1684 to 1699 sixteen were without servants or
slaves; of twenty-six recorded in York during the period from
1694 to 1697 thirteen had no servants or slaves; of twenty-
three recorded in Henrico from 1677 to 1692 fourteen were
without servants or slaves.[53]   It is true that these inventories
and wills, since they would usually pertain to persons of advanced age, perhaps do not furnish an absolutely accurate
gauge of the average number of servants held by each planter.
On the other hand, it is equally probable that a larger proportion of big estates than of the small found their way into the
records.   At all events it is evident that a goodly proportion of
the landholders, perhaps sixty or sixty-five per cent possessed
no slaves or indentured servants, and trusted solely to their
own exertions for the cultivation of their plantations.

Thus vanishes the fabled picture of Seventeenth century
Virginia.   In its place we see a colony filled with little farms
a few hundred acres in extent, owned and worked by a sturdy
class of English farmers.   Prior to the slave invasion which
marked the close of the Seventeenth century and the opening
of the Eighteenth, the most important factor in the life of the
Old Dominion was the white yeomanry.

CHAPTER IV

FREEMEN AND FREEDMEN

It is obvious that the small planter class had its origin partly in the immigration of persons who paid their own passage, partly in the graduation into freedmen of large numbers of indentured servants. But to determine accurately the proportion of each is a matter of great difficulty. Had all the records of Seventeenth century Virginia been preserved, it would have been possible, by means of long and laborious investigation, to arrive at strictly accurate conclusions. But with the material in hand one has to be satisfied with an approximation of the truth.

It must again be emphasized that the indentured servants were not slaves, and that at the expiration of their terms there was no barrier, legal, racial or social to their advancement. The Lords of Trade and Plantations, in 1676, expressed their dissatisfaction at the word "servitude" as applied to them, which they felt was a mark of bondage and slavery, and thought it better "rather to use the word service, since those servants are only apprentices for years."[1] "Malitious tongues have impaired it (Virginia) much," Bullock declared in 1649, "for it hath been a constant report among the ordinary sort of people that all those servants who are sent to Virginia are sold into slavery, whereas the truth is that the merchants who send servants and have no plantations of their own doe not only transferre their time over to others, but the servants serve no longer than the time they themselves agreed for in England, and this is the ordinary course in England, and no prejudice or hurt to the servant."[2]

60

The terms of indenture not only took for granted that the servant, upon completing his contract, would establish himself as a proprietor, but usually made it obligatory for the master to furnish him with the equipment necessary for his new life. With rare exceptions he received a quantity of grain sufficient to maintain him for one year; two suits, one of Kersey, the other of cotton; a pair of canvas drawers; two shirts; and one felt hat.[3] The historian Beverley states that to this outfit was added a gun worth twenty shillings.[4] Another writer tells us that the freedman received "a year's provision of corne, double apparel" and a supply of tools.[5]

There existed in England a widespread impression that the servant, upon securing his freedom, was entitled by law to fifty acres of land. This appears to have been a mistake arising from a misapprehension of the nature of the headright, which belonged not to the servant himself, but to the person who paid for his transportation. In many cases the indentures do not state the exact rewards to be received by the new freedman, but only that they are to accord with "the custom of the country," a very elastic term which could be construed by the master to suit his own interest.[6] John Hammond, in his *Leah and Rachel,* strongly advised the immigrant before affixing his signature to the indenture to insist upon the inclusion of a clause specifically providing for the payment of the fifty acres.[7] But the importance which attaches to this matter lies as much in the servant's expectation as in its fulfilment. Whether or not he received his little plantation, he believed that he was to get a tract of land, a very extensive tract it must have seemed to him, which would assure him a good living and make it possible for him to rise out of the class to which he belonged.[8]

In 1627 the Virginia General Court issued an order which is significant of the attitude of the colony itself to the freedmen. "The Court, taking into consideration that the next ensueing year there will be many tenants and servants freed unto whom after their freedom there will be no land due, whereby they may without some order taken to the contrary settle and seat themselves . . . have ordered that the Governor and Council may give unto the said servants and tenants leases for terms of years such quantities of land as shall be needful."[9] Thus, at this period at least, not only was it expected in the colony that servants would become land holders, but it was felt that for them not to do so was a matter of such grave concern as to require the special attention of the Government.

After all, however, the key to the situation must be sought in the history of tobacco culture and the tobacco trade. Tobacco was the universal crop of the colony and upon it every man depended for his advancement and prosperity. If the market was good and the price high, the planters flourished; if sales fell off and the price was low, they suffered accordingly. It is evident, then, that the ability of the freedman to secure a position of economic independence hinged upon the profit to be derived from his little tobacco crop. It does not matter whether he worked as a wage earner, tenant or freeholder, in the end the result would be the same. If the returns from his labor greatly exceeded his expenses, his savings would make it possible for him to establish himself firmly in the class of the colonial yeomanry. On the other hand, if he could wring from the soil no more than a bare subsistence, he would remain always a poor laborer, or perhaps be forced to seek his fortune in some other colony. Thus if we are to understand the status of the freed servant and the hope which he could entertain of advancement, it is necessary to turn our attention once more to economic conditions in the colony. First, we must determine the amount of tobacco the freedman could produce by his unassisted labor; second, the price he received for it; third, how much he had to give the merchants in exchange for their wares; and finally, the margin of profit left after all expenses had been paid.

Despite a marked divergence of testimony regarding the amount of tobacco one man could cultivate, we are able to determine this matter with some degree of exactness. In 1627 the King, in outlining a plan to take into his own hands the entire tobacco trade, proposed to limit the imports to 200 pounds for each master of a family and 125 for each servant.[10] To this, however, the planters entered a vigorous protest, claiming that the quantity was "not sufficient for their maintenance." They in turn suggested that the King take a total of 500,000 pounds a year, which for a population of 3,000 meant 167 pounds for each inhabitant, or perhaps about 500 pounds for each actual laborer.[11] Again in 1634 it was proposed that the Crown purchase yearly 600,000 pounds of Virginia tobacco.[12] As the population of the colony at that date was about 5,000, this would have allowed only 120 pounds for each person, and once more the planters protested vigorously.[13] It would seem that both of these offers were based not so much upon the amount that one man could raise as upon the quantity which could be sold in England at a certain price. In fact it is probable that even so early as 1628 the average output of one freedman was not less than 1,000 pounds. It is interesting to note that in 1640, soon after Governor Francis Wyatt's arrival from England, it was found that the excessive crop of the previous year had so clogged the market that upon the advice of the merchants the Government was "forced to a strict way of destroying the bad and halfe the goode."[14]

The author of *A New Description of Virginia,* published in 1649, claims that one man could plant from 1,600 to 2,000 pounds a year.[15] As the pamphlet presents a somewhat optimistic picture of affairs in general in the colony, this estimate must be taken with some reserve.   More trustworthy is the statement of Secretary Thomas Ludwell in 1667 that 1,200 pounds was "the medium of men's yearly crops."[16]

At all events, it is evident that the planter, even when entirely dependent upon his own exertions, could produce a goodly crop.   It is now necessary to ascertain what he got for it.   In the second and third decades of the Seventeenth century the price of tobacco was very high.   The first cargo, consisting of 20,000 pounds consigned in the George, sold for no less than £5,250, or 5s. 3d. a pound.[17]   No wonder the leaders of the London Company were pleased, believing that in the Indian weed they had discovered a veritable gold mine!   No wonder the settlers deserted their pallisades and their villages to seek out the richest soil and the spots best suited for tobacco culture!   The man who could produce 200 pounds of the plant, after all freight charges had been met, could clear some £30 or £35, a very tidy sum indeed for those days.   It was the discovery that Virginia could produce tobacco of excellent quality that accounts for the heavy migration in the years from 1618 to 1623.   In fact, so rich were the returns that certain persons came to the colony, not with the intention of making it their permanent residence, but of enriching themselves "by a cropp of Tobacco," and then returning to England to enjoy the proceeds.[18]

But this state of affairs was of necessity temporary.   Very soon the increasing size of the annual crop began to tell upon the price, and in 1623 Sir Nathaniel Rich declared that he had bought large quantities of tobacco at two shillings a pound.[19]   This gentleman felt that it would be just to the planters were they to receive two shillings and four pence for the best varieties, and sixteen pence for the "second sort."   In the same year Governor Wyatt and his Council, in a letter to the Virginia Company, placed the valuation of tobacco at eighteen pence a pound.[20] Three years later, however, the Governor wrote the Privy Council advising the establishment in Virginia of a "magazine" or entrepot, where the merchants should be compelled to take the tobacco at three shillings a pound.[21] This proposal did not seem reasonable to the King, and when Sir George Yeardley came over as Governor for the second time he was instructed to see to it that "the merchant be not constrained to take tobacco at 3. P. Pound in exchange for his wares," and to permit him to "make his own bargain."[22]

Apparently not discouraged by this rebuff, in 1628 the Governor, Council and Burgesses petitioned the King, who once more was planning to take the trade into his own hands, to grant them "for their tobacco delivered in the colony three shillings and six pence per pound, and in England four shillings."[23] This valuation undoubtedly was far in advance of the current prices, and King Charles, considering it unreasonable would not come to terms with the planters. In fact, it appears that for some years the price of tobacco had been declining rapidly. In May, 1630, Sir John Harvey wrote the Privy Council that the merchants had bought the last crop with their commodities at less than a penny per pound,[24] and two years later, in a statement sent the Virginia Commissioners, he claimed that the price still remained at that figure.[25]

It may be taken for granted, however, that this estimate was far below the actual price. The planters showed a decided tendency to blow hot or cold according to the purpose in view, and in these two particular statements Sir John was pleading for better treatment from the merchants. Yet it is reasonably certain that tobacco was at a low ebb in the years from 1629 to 1633, and sold at a small fraction of the figures of the preceding decade.[26] The Governor repeatedly wrote asking for relief, while in the Assembly attempts were made to restore the market by restricting the size of the annual crop.[27]

Yet things must have taken a favorable turn soon after, for in 1634 the planters informed the King's Commissioners that they would not sell him their tobacco at less than six pence in Virginia and fourteen pence delivered in England.[28]   Later the King wrote to the Governor and Council that the rate had recently "doubly or trebly advanced."[29]   This is substantiated by the fact that the Commissioners, in 1638, allowed the planters "4d. a pound clear of all charges," despite which they complained that in an open market they could do better.[30]

In 1638 several prominent Virginians estimated that on an average during the preceding eleven years they had received not more than two pence for their tobacco, but here again it is probable that there was some exaggeration.[31]   In 1649 the author of *A New Description of Virginia* stated that tobacco sold in Virginia for three pence a pound.[32]   All in all it seems that prices in the early years of the settlement varied from five shillings to a few pence, that a disastrous slump occurred at the end of the third decade, followed by a rapid recovery which brought the rate to about three pence, at which figure it remained fairly constant for twenty-five years or more throughout the Civil War and most of the Commonwealth periods.

The return which the Virginia farmer received from his one staple crop was determined by a number of factors over which he himself had but little control.   Had he been permitted to seek his own market and drive his own bargain free from the restraining hand of the British Government, no doubt he would have secured a much better price.   But from the moment it became apparent that the Virginia tobacco rivalled in flavor that of the Spanish colonies and could command as ready a sale throughout Europe, the trade was subjected to various regulations and restrictions which proved most vexatious to the colony and elicited frequent and vigorous protests. Neither James nor Charles had any idea of permitting free trade. In their prolonged struggle with the liberal party both saw in tobacco a ready means of aiding the Exchequer, and so of advancing toward the goal of financial independence. These monarchs were by no means hostile to Virginia. In fact, both took great interest in the tiny settlement upon the James, which they looked upon as the beginning of the future British colonial empire. Yet they lent too willing an ear to those who argued that tobacco might be made to yield a goodly revenue to the Crown without injury to the planters.

The policy adopted by the early Stuart kings and adhered to with but minor changes throughout the colonial period consisted of four essential features. First, the tobacco raised in the plantations should be sent only to England; second, upon entering the mother country it must pay a duty to the Crown; third, Spanish tobacco should be excluded or its importation strictly limited; lastly, the cultivation of the plant in England itself was forbidden.

In the years when the colony was still weak and dependent upon the mother country this program was not unfair. The prohibition of tobacco growing in England, however unnecessary it would have been under conditions of free trade, was felt by the planters to be a real concession, while the restrictions upon foreign importations saved them from dangerous competition at the very time when they were least able to combat it. Nor were they seriously injured by the imposition of the customs duties. The planters themselves imagined that the incidence of this tax fell upon their own shoulders and that they were impoverished to the full extent of the revenues derived from it. But in this they were mistaken. The duty, in the last resort, was paid not by the planters but by the British consumers. The colonists were affected adversely only in so far as the enhanced price of tobacco in England restricted the market.

On the other hand, the prohibition of foreign trade was a very real grievance and elicited frequent protests from the planters. Dutch merchants paid high prices for the Virginia tobacco and offered their manufactured goods in return at figures far below those of the British traders. The Virginians could not understand why they should not take advantage of this opportunity. "I humbly desire to be informed from your honors," wrote Governor Harvey to the Virginia Commissioners in 1632, "whether there be any obstacle why we may not have the same freedome of his Majesties other subjects to seek our best market."[33]

But Harvey was attacking what already had become a fixed policy of the Crown, a policy which was to remain the cornerstone of the British colonial system for centuries. The Government had, therefore, not the slightest intention of yielding, and from time to time issued strict orders that all colonial tobacco, whether of Virginia or the West Indies, be brought only to England or to English colonies. When Sir William Berkeley was appointed Governor in 1642 he was instructed to "bee verry careful that no ships or other vessels whatsoever depart from thence, freighted with tobacco or other commodities which that country shall afford, before bond with sufficient securities be taken to his Majesty's use, to bring the same directly into his Majesty's Dominions and not elsewhere."[34]

Despite the insistence of the British Government in this matter, there is abundant evidence to show that the Virginians continued to indulge in direct trade with the continent for many years after the overthrow of the Company. In 1632 Governor Harvey wrote that "our intrudinge neighbours, the

Dutch, doe allow us eighteen peance p. pound" for tobacco, while a few months later we find him reporting the attempt of John Constable and others "to defraud his Majesty of his duties by unloading in the Netherlands."[35]

With the advent of the English Civil War and throughout the Commonwealth period Virginia enjoyed a large degree of independence and found it possible to trade with the Dutch almost with impunity. Even the strict Berkeley seems to have felt it no disloyalty for the planters to seek foreign markets for their staple while the mother country was torn by the contending armies of King and Parliament. And so the merchantmen of Flushing and Amsterdam pushed their prows into every river and creek in Virginia and Maryland, taking off large quantities of tobacco and giving in return the celebrated manufactured goods of their own country. At Christmas 1648, if we may believe the testimony of the author of *A New Description of Virginia,* there were trading in the colony ten ships from London, two from Bristol, seven from New England and twelve from Holland. In 1655 the statement was made that "there was usually found intruding upon the plantation divers ships, surruptitiously carrying away the growth thereof to foreign ports to the prejudice of this Commonwealth."[36]

Thus in the years prior to the Restoration Virginia was never fully subjected to the operation of the British colonial system. When the price of tobacco in the London market fell lower and lower, the planters might and often did find relief by defying the King's commands and trading directly with the Dutch.[37] And this benefitted them doubly, for not only did they strike a better bargain with the foreign traders, but every cargo of tobacco diverted from England tended to relieve the market there and restore prices. In fact there can be little doubt that the frequent violations of the trade restrictions of this period alone saved the colony from the poverty and distress of later days and made possible the prosperity enjoyed by the planters.

It must be noted also that of the tobacco sent to England itself, a part was reshipped to foreign countries. In 1610 a law was enacted for the refunding of all import duties upon articles that were re-exported. This drawback applied also to colonial products, but under Charles I an exception was made in their case and the privilege withdrawn. In consequence the importers made a vigorous protest in Parliament, and the King, in 1631, modified his policy by ordering that of the nine pence duty then in operation, six pence should be refunded when the tobacco was shipped abroad. In 1632 the drawback was increased to seven pence leaving the total duty paid by the merchants who traded through England to foreign countries two pence a pound only.[38] Although this constituted a most serious obstacle to trade and at times aroused the merchants to bitter protest, it by no means completely blocked re-exportation. So great were the natural qualifications of Virginia for producing tobacco, that it was possible to purchase a cargo from the planters on the James, proceed with it to London, pay there the two pence a pound duty, reship it to the continent and sell it there at a profit.[39] Although this trade was not extensive, it must have had an important influence in maintaining prices and in bringing prosperity to all classes in the colony.

Thus Virginia, contrary to the wishes of the mother country and in defiance of her regulations, enjoyed for its staple product in the years prior to 1660, a world market. Whether by direct trade or by re-exportation from England a goodly share of the annual crop was consumed in foreign countries, a share which had it been left in England to clog the market, would have reacted disastrously upon all concerned.

It is apparent, then, that in the first half century of its existence Virginia was the land of opportunity. The poor man who came to her shores, whether under terms of indenture or as a freeman, found it quite possible to establish himself as a person of some property and consideration. We may imagine the case of the servant who had completed his term and secured his freedom at any time during the third decade of the Seventeenth century. As we have seen, it was an easy matter for him to secure a small patch of land and the tools with which to cultivate it. By his unassisted efforts, if he applied himself steadily to the task, he could produce a good crop of tobacco, consisting perhaps of some 400 pounds. This he could sell to the merchants for from two shillings to six pence a pound, or a total of from £10 to £40.[40]

In the years from 1630 to 1640, when the price of tobacco seems to have stabilized itself at from two to three pence, cases of such extraordinary returns must have been of less frequent occurrence, but to some extent lower prices were offset by larger crops. If our freedman in 1635 could raise 800 pounds of leaf and dispose of it for four pence, his income would be £13.6.8; in 1649, by producing 1,000 pounds, he could sell it at three pence for £12.10.0. In fact, it is not too much to say that the average annual income from the labor of one able worker at any time prior to 1660 was not less than £12. When we take into consideration the fact that the planter produced his own food, and that out of the proceeds of his tobacco crop he paid only his taxes and his bills to the English importers, it is evident that he had a goodly margin of profit to lay aside as working capital.

It must not be forgotten, however, that this margin was greatly reduced by the high cost of clothing, farm implements and all other articles brought from across the ocean. The long and dangerous voyage from London to the Chesapeake made the freight rates excessive, while the merchants did not scruple to drive a hard bargain whenever possible. The letters of the Governors are filled with complaints against the exactions of these men. "This year the Merchants have bought our tobacco with their commodities at less than a penny the pounde," Harvey wrote in 1630, "and have not shamed to make the planters pay twelve pounds Sterlinge the tunn freight home."[41] Two years later he complained that a certain Captain Tucker had just sailed leaving his stores well stocked with goods, but with "instructions to his factors not to sell but at most excessive rates."[42] In 1628, the Governor, Council and Burgesses, in a petition to the King, declared that for years they had "groaned under the oppression of unconscionable and cruel merchants by the excessive rates of their commodities."[43] Six years later Governor Harvey stated that all things which "come hither" are sold at "thrice the value they cost in England."[44]

It is obvious, however, that after all expenses had been paid, a goodly margin of profit was left, a margin perhaps averaging some three or four pounds sterling. The provident and industrious immigrant, a few years after the conclusion of his term, might well lay aside enough to make it possible for him in turn to secure a servant from England. This accomplished, he at once rose into the class of employers and his future advance was limited only by his capabilities and his ambition.

We would naturally expect to find, then, that during these years a large percentage of those who came to the colony under terms of indenture, sooner or later acquired land, perhaps bought servants, and became persons of some standing in the colony. Certainly the opportunity was theirs. It will be interesting therefore to study the early records in order to glean what evidence we may concerning this matter. If the servants graduated in any appreciable numbers into the planter class, the patents, wills, inventories, land transfers and muster rolls could hardly fail to yield some evidence of the fact.

Turning first to the earliest period, we find that of the laborers who were imported by the London Company to cultivate the public lands, a fair proportion became proprietors and were regarded by later comers with especial esteem as "ancient planters." At the termination of their service they were granted 100 acres and when this was fully cultivated received another tract of the same extent. To the apprentices bound out to tenants even more liberal treatment was accorded, for they were provided with a year's store of corn, a house, a cow, clothing, armor, household utensils, farm tools and as much land as they could till.[45]

The guiding hand of the Company was missed by the freedmen after the revoking of the charter, for the Governors seem to have left them to shift for themselves. Yet this fact did not prevent many from forging ahead, acquiring land, and in some cases positions of trust in the Government itself. In Hotten's *Immigrants* is published a muster roll for the year 1624 of all the settlers in Virginia, in which servants are carefully distinguished from freemen.[46] By following, as well as the imperfect records of the period permit, the after careers of the former, it is possible to determine with a fair degree of accuracy to what extent the small farmer class at this period was recruited from persons coming to the colony under terms of indenture.

Of the forty-four Burgesses who sat in the Assembly of 1629, no less than seven—John Harris, William Allen, William Popleton, Anthony Pagett, Richard Townsend, Adam Thoroughgood and Lionell Rowlston—were listed as servants in the muster of 1624.[47] Thus some sixteen per cent of this important body, the Virginia House of Commons, at this time was made up of men who five years previously had been work-

ing out their passage money. Among the thirty-nine members
of the House of 1632, six appear as servants in the muster—
Thomas Barnett, Adam Thoroughgood, Lionell Rowlston,
Thomas Crump, Roger Webster and Robert Scotchmon.
Whether there were other members who came over under
terms of indenture but secured their freedom before 1624, we
have no means of determining.

The author of *Virginia's Cure,* published in 1662, asserted
that the Burgesses "were usual such as went over as servants
thither; and though by time, and industry, they may have obtained competent estates, yet by reason of their poor and mean
condition, were unskilful in judging of a good estate, either
of church or Commonwealth."[48]   This statement is a gross
exaggeration both as to the composition of the Burgesses and
their abilities.   Instances of the election of freedmen to the
House, fairly frequent in the early years of the colony, became rarer as the century advanced and the field of selection
widened.   Yet in the Assembly of 1652, of the thirty-five
members, eight or nine appear on the patent rolls as headrights
brought over by others.[49]   It is evident that even so late as the
middle of the century the door of opportunity was still open
to the freedmen.

In the absence of a complete census for the decades after
1624, it is very difficult to determine what proportion of the
servants listed in the muster roll of that year subsequently became landowners.   Some light is thrown on the matter by a
search through the patent books.   Here are found a surpris-
ingly large number of persons who in 1624 were servants.
Among these are Anthony Jones, John Sparkes, John Cooke,
Roger Delk, John Trussell, William Woolritch, Pettyplace
Cloyse, Edward Sparshott, William Dawson, Richard Bell,
Robert Browne, Nicholas Browne, John Chandler, Lionell
Rowlston, Thomas Savadge, Samuel Bennett, Daniel Shurley,

James Hatfield, Adam Thoroughgood, John Robinson, John Hill, John Seaward, William Ramshaw, Samuel Weaver, John Upton, John Watson, Thomas Crompe and John Russell.[50]

Of these persons several acquired a fair degree of wealth and became of importance in the early life of the colony. It is interesting to note also, that some were men of good condition in England, the case of Adam Thoroughgood, whose brother Sir John Thoroughgood was at one time secretary to the Earl of Pembroke, is notable in this respect. John Hill, before coming to Virginia, had been a book binder in Oxford university, and his father had been a fletcher.[51] The patents of Thomas Crompe and John Russell state that fifty acres was due in each case for the "personal adventure" of the patentee, but since they are distinctly listed as servants in 1624 it seems probable that subsequently each made a visit to England and put in claims for the headright for the return voyage.[52]

Thus it is evident that a large proportion of the landholders during and prior to 1635 had come to the colony under terms of indenture, either under the Company or with private individuals. Perhaps it would not be unfair to estimate this proportion at from thirty to forty per cent, but it must be distinctly understood that the matter cannot be determined with any degree of accuracy or finality. Some years later Governor Berkeley in an address before the Assembly, stated that hundreds of examples testified to the fact that no man in Virginia was denied the opportunity to rise and to acquire both property and honor.[53] Careful research tends to corroborate this assertion but it does not and cannot show whether the bulk of the early planters came to the colony as freemen or as indentured servants.

During the years from 1635 to 1660 the process of building up a class of small farmers in large part from freedmen continued unabated. But the difficulties of the investigator in studying this period are also very great. Yet it is possible, by examining the names that appear in the land patents and wills, and comparing them with the list of headrights, to arrive at fairly satisfactory results. We find that of the 131 persons listed in the York county wills from 1646 to 1659 no less than twenty-five appear as headrights for others. Of these the major part became landowners, some of them men of influence in Virginia.[54] The Rappahannock wills for the years from 1656 to 1664 show a like result. Thirty-nine persons appear in the records, of whom seven came in as headrights.[55]

There is always the possibility of error in identifying these persons for the recurrence of such names as Smith, Jones, Turner, Davis, Hall, the monotonous repetition of a few common given names, and the universal omission of middle names add greatly to our difficulties. Moreover, mistakes are apt to occur because of the transfer of headrights by sale. The free immigrant to whom was due fifty acres for his "personal adventure" might not care to settle on the frontier where alone unpatented land could usually be found. At times he sold his right and purchased a plantation in some one of the older and more advanced counties. It is not conclusively proved, then, that a certain person came as a servant merely because he is listed as a headright. On the other hand, the fact that it was the custom to set forth such transfers clearly in the patent itself, justifies the conclusion that in the cases where no statement of the kind is made, the headright for which the land was granted usually came in under terms of indenture.

In Volume III of the land patents are listed in the years from 1635 to 1653 patents to fifty-seven persons in James City county.[56] Of these no less than thirty-one are found also as headrights belonging to others, although a duplication of names in several cases makes identification uncertain. One person only claimed the fifty acres for having paid his own passage to Virginia. When all possible allowance is made for transfers of rights it is obvious that at this time freedmen were still entering freely into the class of landowners.

An examination of the James City county patents in Volume IV, covering the years from 1653 to 1663, leads to similar results, for of the eighty-five names which appear there, forty-five are listed as headrights belonging to others. And although the tracts granted these men were usually small in size, in certain cases they were far in excess of the average plantation. Thus Edward Cole, who appears as a headright in 1642, patented 900 acres in 1655;[57] Thomas Warburton patented 1,664 acres;[58] George Gilbert 1,000 acres; Francis Burwell 1,000 and John Underwood 2,000 acres.[59] The number of years which elapsed between the listing of the headrights and the granting of the patents varied from two to twenty-eight. The average for the thirty-five cases in which the dates are given is twelve years. As the claims for headrights were often made long after the actual arrival of the servant, it may be assumed that the average was even greater than this. Once more, however, it must be remembered that these lists do not record personal transfers of land, while it is quite certain that many freedmen, instead of patenting unoccupied tracts, secured their little farms by purchase. Some probably became proprietors in the very first year of their freedom and set to work with hoe and plow to wrest their living from the soil.

In the patent rolls the bulk of the headrights are alluded to simply as "persons," leaving it undecided whether those included in the various lists are freemen or servants. But occasionally the newcomers are specifically described as "servants," in which case, of course, there can be no doubt whatever as to their status. By selecting at random a number of names from those so termed, avoiding for convenience sake all Smiths, Joneses and others the frequent recurrence of whose names would make identification difficult, it is possible to arrive at definite conclusions by following, as best we can, their careers in after life. With this in view we have made up the following list of servants: Henry Arnetrading, George Archer, Silvester Atkins, Nicholas Atwell, Edward Ames, John Aram, Robert Arnall, Peter Asheley, William Baldwin, Edward Burt, Francis Baile, John Bauchees, John Bishop, John Blackstone, Anthony Box, Michael Brichley, Peter Buck, William Burcher, John Causey, Robert Chesheire, Thomas Chilcott, Thomas Clayton, Annanias Coplestone, James Courtney, Thomas Cropp, Thomas Connagrave, John Day, John Dodman, Jonathan Ellison, Edward Eastwood, James Fletcher, Thomas Foanes, John Fouke, Francis Francklin, Armstrong Foster, Robert Fossett, John Farr, Robert Garsell, George Gilbert, Henry Giles, Hector Godbear, Francis Gray, Reginald Griffin, Thomas Halcock, Thomas Hand, Henry Hartwell, Hugh Hayes, John Hedler, Richard Huett, John Hodgbins, John Holdin, William Hankinson, John Hether, Lazarus Manning, Thomas Pattison, John Pullapin, Sampson Robins, George Walton, Francis Withers, Robert Webstie and Thomas Warden. A search through the patent rolls, wills, tithable lists and other data found in the records of the period, has led to the more or less positive identification of fifteen of these persons.

John Bishop, who was transported by Thomas Gray, became a man of influence and means. He represented Charles City county in the House of Burgesses in the sessions of 1644, 1652 and 1653, and was variously known as Captain Bishop or Mr. Bishop.[60] Although he became a landowner so early as 1638,[61] his family arrived from England only in 1651. Francis Gray, brought to Virginia at the age of fifteen by Joseph Johnson, also became prominent, securing a seat in the Assembly and acquiring a fair estate. In 1653 he took up 750 acres in Charles City county, while ten years later he is credited with 374 acres more in Westmoreland.[62] His will was recorded in 1667.[63]

George Archer became an extensive landowner, patenting 250 acres in 1663, 550 acres in 1665, 784 acres in 1671 and 1,395 acres in 1673.[64] In 1691 he received, in conjunction with others, title to a tract of 2,827 acres in Henrico.[65] John Holding patented in York county 850 acres in 1649 and 389 acres in 1653.[66] William Baldwin, who came in the Plaine Joan when he was twenty-four years of age, received three grants of land, one for 600 acres in York county, one for 67 acres in Isle of Wight, and one, in conjunction with Richard Lawrence, for 300 in Rappahannock.[67]

Thomas Pattison, transported by Francis Epes in 1635, took up in Lancaster two tracts, one for 200 acres and one for 400.[68] He also became part owner of two more tracts, one for 220 acres and the other for 504.[69] John Dodman secured a patent for 350 acres in Westmoreland in the year 1662.[70] Thomas Warden is mentioned as a landowner in James City county in 1643.[71] George Gilbert, transported in 1635 by Joseph Johnson, took up fifty acres in James City county in 1643.[72] In 1663, in partnership with Richard Scruely, he patented 1,000 acres in the same county north of the Chickahominy river.[73] John Blackstone acquired two tracts, one for 100 acres and the other for 151 acres,[74] while William Burcher received a grant for 300 acres.[75]

Several of these men who came as servants to the Eastern Shore are found in succeeding years among the yeomanry of Accomac and Northampton. Henry Arnetrading, Armstrong Foster, William Burcher and Sampson Robins were signers of the Northampton submission to the Commonwealth in 1652.[76] Henry Arnetrading was the owner of 300 acres of land.[77]

Armstrong Foster was the official tobacco viewer for Hungers, a position entailing no little responsibility.[78]   Sampson Robins received a patent for a tract of land in Northampton in 1655.[79] Thomas Clayton is listed among the Northampton tithables of 1666.[80]

In the case of John Day some uncertainty arises.   Apparently there were two men of this name in the colony, one transported by John Slaughter, and the other not only paying for his own passage, but for that of a servant as well.[81]   A John Day later secured 400 acres in Gloucester county,[82] but whether it was the one who had come as a servant or the one who had entered the colony as a freeman, apparently there is no way of ascertaining.

All in all the story of these men tends to confirm the conclusions hitherto arrived at.   It must be remembered that the mortality among the servants in the tobacco fields in the early days of the colony was extremely heavy.   It is not improbable that of our sixty-one servants, twenty or more succumbed before the completion of their first year.   That of the remaining forty-one, fourteen or fifteen established themselves as solid farmers, while several became men of influence in the colony, is a striking proof that at this period many freedmen had the opportunity to advance.   Taking it for granted that the records of some of the sixty-one have been lost, or that our research has failed to reveal them, we once more come to the conclusion that a full thirty or forty per cent of the landowners of the period from 1635 to 1666 came to the colony under terms of indenture.

On the other hand, it is equally positive that the class of poor planters was recruited in part from free immigrants, men who paid their own passage across the ocean and at once established themselves as freeholders.   Of this too, the records furnish ample testimony.   Thus in 1636 we find that

Richard Young was granted 100 acres in Warwick "due him for his personal adventure and for the transportation of his wife Dorothy Young."[83]   A year later Roger Symonds received 100 acres in Charles City "due him for the transportation of his wife, Alice, and one servant, Richard Key."[84] Similarly in May 1636, Thomas Wray was allowed 50 acres for his "personal adventure."   Such cases could be multiplied indefinitely.[85]

A careful analysis of the patent rolls from 1623 to July 14, 1637, published in the *Virginia Magazine of History and Biography* for April, 1901, shows conclusively that the lists contain the names of many persons who at no time were under terms of indenture.   Of the 2,675 names appearing in the records, the editor states that 336 are positively known to have come over as freemen, many of them being heads of families. "There are 245 persons whose names do not occur as headrights and yet of whom it is not positively shown that they were freemen, though the probability seems to be that by far the greater number were.   And there were 2,094 persons whose transportation charges were paid by others.   This last number includes some negroes, all those specifically termed 'servants' and all others. . . . It would probably be a fair estimate to say that of the names represented in the patents cited, there were about 675 free men, women and children who came to Virginia and about 2000 servants and slaves."[86]   Similarly in the issue of the magazine for January, 1902, the editor says that "for some years, about this period, it is probable (from the best calculations which can be made) that seventy-five per cent of the emigrants to Virginia were indentured servants."[87]

There seems to be no reason to doubt the accuracy of these conclusions.   Certainly any study of immigration to Virginia in the Seventeenth century is woefully incomplete if it fails to take into consideration the very considerable proportion of free settlers. On the other hand, it is probable that a similar study of the lists for a later date would show a smaller percentage of freemen. However this may be, it is evident that by far the larger part of the newcomers at all periods must have been indentured servants intended for service in the tobacco fields. In 1638 Richard Kemp wrote Secretary Windebanke that "of hundreds which are yearly transported, scarce any but are brought in as merchandise to make sale of."[88]

Yet it must not be forgotten that any immigration of poor freemen, however small, would have a very marked influence upon the formation of the small farmer class. Of the host of servants a certain proportion only, a proportion probably less than fifty per cent, could hope even in the most favorable times to become freeholders. If they survived the hardships and dangers of the service with their masters, it still remained for them to acquire property and win for themselves a place in the life of the colony. And to accomplish this they must display determination, intelligence, industry and thrift, qualities by no means universal among the classes in England from which the servants were chiefly drawn. But for the free immigrant there need be no period of probation. He might at once purchase his farm, erect his home, secure all necessary tools and put out his crop of tobacco. And whereas the servant usually found it possible to maintain a family only after many years of hard work, perhaps not at all, the free settler often married before leaving England and brought his wife and children with him.

In conclusion it may be said that in the first fifty years of the colony's existence conditions were very favorable for the graduation of the servant into the class of small freeholders, that the records amply prove that many succeeded in doing so, but that at this period a fair proportion of free immigrants also came to the colony. Before the expiration of the Commonwealth period was formed from these two sources, perhaps in not unequal proportions, a vigorous, intelligent, independent yeomanry, comprising fully 90 percent of all the landowners.

CHAPTER V

The Restoration Period

The people of Virginia hailed the Restoration with unaffected joy. Not only did they anticipate that the termination of the long period of civil war and unrest in England would react favorably upon their own prosperity, but they felt that Sir William Berkeley's well known loyalty and his action in proclaiming Charles II immediately after the execution of his father, might assure them the King's especial favor now that he at last had come into undisputed possession of his throne. They were doomed to bitter disappointment, however, for the Restoration brought them only hardship and suffering, discontent and rebellion.

No sooner had the royal Government been safely installed than it set to work to perfect and to enforce the colonial policy which in principle had been accepted from the first. The ties which united the colonies with the mother country were strengthened, those which gave them a common interest with foreign nations in so far as possible were snapped. The British empire was to become a unit, closely knit by economic bonds and presenting to all other nations a hostile front. With this in view Parliament passed a series of Navigation Acts, under which the trade of the colonies was regulated for many years to come.

It is necessary for us to enquire, therefore, into the effects of these laws upon the tobacco trade, for tobacco, as we have seen, was the key to the prosperity of the colony, and favorable economic conditions alone could make it possible for the newcomer to establish himself as a member of the Virginia yeomanry. If the strict enforcement of the Navigation Acts should bring low prices for tobacco and wipe out the margin of profit for the man who tilled the soil with his own hands, not only would the small planter class not expand, but might actually decline in numbers.

There were three main features of the colonial legislation of Parliament during this period, all of them interrelated and all tending toward the one great object of keeping the English plantations for the English. It was provided that the chief colonial products such as tobacco and sugar should be sent only to England or to English colonies, that the colonies should with few exceptions import goods only from British territory, that all products taken to or from any colony should be conveyed only in English vessels manned by crews composed mainly of Englishmen.

In committing itself to this policy the royal Government felt that the plantations would play a useful and necessary part in the great system which was planned, and in so doing would find prosperity. It had been the hope of the English people that their colonies would produce the articles which were so badly needed by the mother country to revive her waning industry and permit a greater measure of economic independence. Although more than half a century had passed since the first foothold had been gained upon the American continent, this expectation was as far from realization as ever. The colonies, from Massachusetts to Barbados were producing, not the articles which England especially needed, but those for which they had the greatest natural aptitude, especially tobacco and sugar. And these staples they sent, not to England alone, but to various foreign countries as well.

In short the vision of a closely knit, self-sustaining empire, the vision which had been in men's minds for many decades before the founding of Jamestown, seemed to have proved

delusive. The colonies were developing interests and commercial connections hostile to those of the mother country,
were nourishing the manufactures and shipping of foreign nations almost as much as those of England. And this the Government at London would not tolerate. The colonial trade
with strangers must come to an end. If Virginia and Maryland produced more tobacco than the English market could
absorb, they could find ready relief by turning their energies
into other channels. Let them furnish the old country with
pig iron or potash or silk or ship-stores and they would find
ready and eager purchasers. So reasoned the English, and as
their views were backed by the mandates of Crown and Parliament, the colonists were forced to submit. If they could fit
themselves into the system prescribed for them, all would be
well and good; if they found this impossible, they would have
to suffer without hope of redress.

And suffer Virginia did for a full quarter of a century. The
tobacco of the Chesapeake bay colonies had long since reached
the point where it required a world market. If confined to
England alone, only a fraction of the output could be consumed and disaster was certain. It was well enough for the
Government to restrict the importation of Spanish leaf and
to prohibit the planting of tobacco in England, these regulations could do no more than give the colonists undisputed
possession of the home market, and the home market was not
enough. This point seems to have been ignored by those
writers who have contended that the strict enforcement of the
British colonial system in itself entailed no hardship upon the
tobacco colonies.

"It is obvious that any criticism of England's regulation of
the colonial tobacco trade, which is based on a laissez-faire
social philosophy," says George Lewis Beer, in *The Old Colonial System,* "is equally applicable to the arrangement by

means of which the tobacco planter secured exlusive privileges in the home market."[1]   Yet it is certain that the tobacco growers of England could never have competed with Maryland and Virginia had there been free trade.   The prohibition of planting in the old country was necessary only because of the tariff, varying from 200 per cent in 1660 to 600 per cent in 1705, upon the colonial product.   And though the exclusion of Spanish tobacco was a more real benefit, for the Spaniard produced varieties unknown in Virginia, there is exaggeration here also.   This is clearly shown by the fact that at the end of the Seventeenth century England was sending millions of pounds of her colonial tobacco to Spain itself.[2]   The leaf was brought from Virginia and Maryland, forced to pay a duty of about fifty per cent, and re-exported to the Spanish ports, where it found a ready sale.   Had there been free exchange of commodities, the English colonies would have sold to Spain more tobacco than the Spanish colonies to England.

In truth the loss of the foreign market was a terrible disaster.   In framing the Navigation Acts it was not the intention of the Government to stop entirely the flow of tobacco to the continent of Europe, but to divert it from the old channels and make it pass through England.   It was therefore provided that in case the leaf was shipped out again to foreign ports, all the duties, except one half of the Old Subsidy, should be withdrawn.[7]   The remaining half penny, however, amounted to forty or fifty per cent of the original cost of the goods, and proved at first an almost insuperable barrier to the European trade.   Moreover, the shortage of ships which resulted from the exclusion of the Dutch merchants, the expense of putting in at the English ports, the long and troublesome procedure of reshipping, all tended to discourage the merchants and hamper re-exportation.

We may take for granted also that the resentment of Holland at the Navigation Acts, which struck a telling blow at her maritime prestige, played an important part in blocking foreign trade. The Dutch had been the chief European distributors of the Virginia and Maryland tobacco, and if they refused to take it, now that it could be secured only in England, it would pile up uselessly in the London warehouses. They understood well enough that the half penny a pound duty was a tribute levied upon them by their most dangerous rival. It is not surprising that instead of bowing to the new restrictions, they sought to free their trade entirely from dependence on British tobacco, by fostering the cultivation of the plant in their own country.

The colonists found an able defender in the merchant John Bland. In a Remonstrance addressed to the King this man set forth with remarkable clearness the evils which would result from the Navigation Acts, and pleaded for their repeal. The Hollander was already beginning to plant tobacco, he said, and would soon be able to supply all his needs at home. "Will he, after accustomed to the tobacco of his own growth," he asked, "ever regard that which is in Virginia? Will he ever afterwards be induced to fetch it thence, when he finds his profit nigher at home? Will he ever buy that of us, when by passing so many hands, and so much charge contracted thereon, is made so dear, that he can have it cheaper in his own territories? (Surely no.) Therefore it clearly appears, that being so, of necessity we must lose that Trade and Commerce."

"If the Hollanders must not trade to Virginia, how shall the Planters dispose of their Tobacco? The English will not buy it, for what the Hollander carried thence was a sort of tobacco not desired by any other people, nor used by us in England but merely to transport for Holland. Will it not then perish on the Planters hands? . . . Can it be believed that from England more ships will be sent than are able to bring thence what tobacco England will spent? If they do bring more, must they not lose thereby both stock and Block, principle and charges? The tobacco will not vend in England, the Hollanders will not fetch it from England; what must become thereof? . . . Is not this a destruction to the commerce? For if men lose their Estates, certainly trade cannot be encreased."[8]

The enforcement of the trade laws was indirectly the cause of still another misfortune to the colonies, for the two wars with Holland which grew out of it reacted disastrously upon their trade. In fact, on each occasion the small stream of tobacco which had trickled over the dam of restrictions into foreign countries was for a time almost entirely cut off. Not only did the tobacco exports to Holland itself come to an end, but the Dutch war vessels played havoc with the trade between England and other countries and even between England and her colonies.

The loss of their foreign exports was calamitous to the planters. Had the demand for tobacco been more elastic, the consequences might not have been so fatal, for declining prices would have stimulated consumption and made it possible for England to absorb most of the output. But the duty kept up the price and the result was a ruinous glut in the English market. Tobacco sufficient for a continent poured into the kingdom, where since the normal outlet was blocked by the half penny a pound on re-exported leaf, it piled up uselessly.

The effect upon prices was immediate. The planters were forced to take for their crops half of what they had formerly received and had reason for rejoicing if they could dispose of it at all. In 1662 Governor Berkeley and other leading citizens stated that the price of tobacco had fallen so low that it would not "bear the charge of freight and customs, answer the adventure, give encouragement to the traders and sub-

sistence to the inhabitants."[9]   In 1666 Secretary Thomas
Ludwell told Lord Arlington that tobacco was "worth nothing."[10]   Later in the same year the planters complained that
the price was so low that they were not able to live by it.[11]
"For the merchants, knowing both our necessities and the un-
consumable quantities of tobacco we had by us," they said,
"gave us not the twentieth part of what they sold it for in
England."[12]   Tobacco had so glutted the markets, it was declared, and brought the planter so small a return, that he could
"live but poorly upon it."   In fact, the merchants in 1666
had left the greater part of the two preceding crops upon their
hands.[13]

"Twelve hundred pounds of tobacco is the medium of men's
crops," wrote Secretary Ludwell to Lord John Berkeley in
1667, "and half a penny per pound is certainly the full medium
of the price given for it, which is fifty shillings out of which
when the taxes . . . shall be deducted, is very little to a poor
man who hath perhaps a wife and children to cloath and other
necessities to buy.   Truly so much too little that I can at-
tribute it to nothing but the great mercy of God . . . that
keeps them from mutiny and confusion."[14]   The following
year he wrote in similar vein.   The market was glutted; a
third of the planters' tobacco was left on their hands; the rest
sold for nothing.[15]

The Governor and Council declared that the merchant "al-
lows not much above a farthing a pound for that which the
planter brings to his door.   And if there shall be any amongst
us who shall be able to ship his tobacco on his own account,
it will be at such a rate as the tobacco will never repay him,
since they are inforced to pay from £12 to £17 per ton freight,
which usually was but at seven pounds."[16]   "A large part of
the people are so desperately poor," wrote Berkeley in 1673,
"that they may reasonably be expected upon any small ad-

vantage of the enemy to revolt to them in hopes of bettering their condition by sharing the plunder of the colony with them."[17] That matters had not changed in 1681 is attested by the statement of the Council that the impossibility of disposing of their tobacco without a heavy loss overwhelmed both Virginia and Maryland, and brought upon them a "vast poverty and infinite necessity."[18] "The low price of tobacco staggers the imagination," Lord Culpeper wrote to Secretary Coventry, "and the continuance of it will be the speedy and fatal ruin of this noble Colony."[19]

These distressing conditions bore with telling weight upon the small planters. The margin of profit which formerly had made it possible for the freedman to advance rapidly was now wiped out entirely and the poor man found it impossible to keep out of debt. In 1668 Secretary Ludwell declared that no one could longer hope to better himself by planting tobacco.[20] Eight years later Nathaniel Bacon, in justifying his rebellion declared that the small farmers were deeply in debt and that it was "not in the power of labor or industry" to extricate them.[21] "The poverty of Virginia is such," said a certain John Good in 1676, "that the major part of the inhabitants can scarce supply their wants from hand to mouth, and many there are besides can hardly shift without supply one year."[22] In 1673 the Governor and Council reported that of the planters, "at least one third are single persons (whose labor will hardly maintain them) or men much in debt," who might reasonably be expected to revolt to the Dutch upon any small advantage gained by them.[23] In 1680 they again reported that "the indigency of the Inhabitants is such that they are in noe manner capacitated to support themselves."[24] Three years later they wrote that "the people of Virginia are generally, some few excepted, extremely poor, not being able to provide against the pressing necessities of their families."[25]

Despite this repeated and explicit testimony of the misery and poverty of the colony during this period, which resulted from the stagnation of the tobacco market after the passage of the Navigation Acts, the surprising statement is made by Mr. George Lewis Beer, in *The Old Colonial System,* that England's trade restrictions had nothing to do with Bacon's Rebellion. "It has been at various times contended," he says, "that the uprising was, in part at least, one against the laws of trade and navigation. If there had existed in Virginia any widespread and well defined feeling of antagonism to these laws, it would unquestionably have found expression in the county grievances. Most of these reports were drawn up in a number of articles, and in all there were nearly two hundred of such separate subdivisions, yet only three of this number refer in any way to these statutes. There is no valid reason for assuming that the commercial system played any part whatsoever, or was in any degree, an issue, in the upheaval of 1676."[26]

If by this statement it is meant that Bacon and his men did not rebel in order to force the repeal of the Navigation Acts, or even that they did not have the acts in mind at the time, there are many students of Virginia history who will agree with it. But if Mr. Beer means that these laws, with their baleful effect upon the prosperity of Virginia, did not produce the conditions fundamental to the rising, he is certainly wrong. The evidence is overwhelming.

Surely no one will deny that misery, poverty and nakedness are breeders of sedition. Had it not been for the Navigation Acts there would not have been so many desperate persons in Virginia ready at any excuse to fly in the face of the Government. Bacon's men were just the type of miserably poor freemen that Berkeley several years before had feared would rebel. He himself, in his proclamation of Feb. 10, 1677, spoke of them as "men of mean and desperate fortunes."[27] William Sherwood called the rebels rude and indigent persons, alluding to them as "tag, rag and bobtayle."[28] Over and over again they are described as the multitude, the rabble, the skum.

Exception must be taken also to the statement that had there existed in Virginia any well-defined feeling of antagonism to the Navigation Acts it would have found expression in the county grievances. It should be remembered that these reports had been called for by the commissioners sent over by Charles II to investigate the troubles. The men who drew them up occupied the position of defeated rebels, and the grievances were primarily a list of excuses for their treason. They all stood trembling for their property, if they had any, and for their miserable lives. The memory of the fate of Drummond and Bland and Arnold and many others of their fellow rebels was fresh in their minds. It is not reasonable to suppose that they would tell the King that they had risen in arms against his authority in order to secure the overthrow of laws which his Majesty considered of such vital importance, laws which concerned intimately the royal revenue. Such a declaration would not have seconded successfully their plea for mercy. This is made amply clear by the reception accorded one of the few complaints which did actually touch the Navigation Acts. The commissioners report it to the King as "an extravagant request for liberty to transport their tobacco to any of his Majesty's plantations without paying the imposts, payable by act of Parliament, etc. This head is wholly mutinous—to desire a thing contrary to his Majesty's royal pleasure and benefit and also against an act of Parliament."[29]

Despite the obviously ruinous effects of the Navigation Acts upon Virginia, Mr. Beer makes the assertion that there was no very serious and general opposition to them in Virginia. "Apart from the criticisms of Bland and Berkeley," he says, "there was virtually no complaint against the system of trade enjoined by the Navigation Acts. While the Barbados Assembly and that colony's governors were vociferous in their protests, the Virginia legislature remained strangely mute."[30]

This silence on the part of the Virginia Assembly can by no means be interpreted as an indication that the people of the colony felt the Navigation Acts to be equitable and not injurious to their interests. It meant only that no Assembly under Sir William Berkeley would dare protest against an act which had received the royal sanction. That would have seemed the veriest treason to the fiery old loyalist. And the Assembly was entirely under Sir William's control. The members of both Houses were his creatures and his henchmen. Over and over again it is testified that the Assembly did nothing more than register his will.[31] If then it did not protest, it was because Sir William did not wish it to protest.

But this does not prove that the planters were not angered and alarmed at the stringent acts. That they considered them baleful is amply proved by their continuous complaints of the economic ruin which had overtaken the colony. The method they chose of combatting the trade laws, a method apt to be far more effective than the angry protests of the Barbados Assembly, was to send the Governor to England to use his influence at Court to have the acts modified or repealed. And Berkeley did what he could. While in England he wrote a paper called *A Discourse and View of Virginia,* which he hoped would induce the Government to change its policy in regard to the colonies. "Wee cannot but resent," he said, "that 40,000 people should be impoverished to enrich little more than 40 merchants, who being the whole buyers of our tobacco, give us what they please for it. And after it is here sell as they please, and indeed have 40,000 servants in us at cheaper rates, than other men have slaves, for they find them

meat and drink and clothes. We furnish ourselves and their
seamen with meat and drink, and all our sweat and labor as
they order us, will hardly procure us coarse clothes to keep us
from the extremities of heat and cold."[32]   That Sir William
was but the mouthpiece of the colony in this protest there can
be no doubt.

But his pleadings were in vain. England would not change
the laws which were the expression of her settled colonial
policy. The planters must adjust themselves to changed conditions no matter how bitter was the experience. Sir William was told to go home to report to the Virginians that they
need not kick against the pricks, but that England would be
most pleased could they turn from the all-absorbing culture
of tobacco to the production of the raw materials she so greatly
desired. And Berkeley did return determined to exert every
effort to lead the colonists into new prosperity by inducing
them to devote a part of their energies to basic commodities.
In fact he promised that in seven years he would flood the
British market with new Virginia goods.[33]

Although he set to work with his accustomed vigor to make
good this boast, he met with but scant success. Lack of efficient and skilled labor, high wages, and not very favorable
natural conditions, made it impossible for him to compete with
the long-established industries of Europe. After a few years
all attempts to make silk and potash and naval stores were
abandoned, and the planters continued to put their trust in
tobacco.

That Berkeley was never persuaded that the Navigation
Acts were just or beneficial is shown by his answer to the
query of the Lords of Trade in 1671, when they asked him
what impediments there were to the colony's trade. "Mighty
and destructive," he replied, "by that severe act of Parliament
which excludes us from having any commerce with any na-

tion in Europe but our own, so that we cannot add to our plantation any commodity that grows out of it . . . for it is not lawful for us to carry a pipe-staff or a bushel of corn to any place in Europe out of the King's dominions. If this were for his Majesty's service or the good of his subjects we should not repine, whatever our sufferings are for it. But on my soul it is the contrary of both."[35]

Nor is this the only direct testimony that the colonists were filled with bitterness against the Navigation Acts. In 1673, during the war with Holland, Sir John Knight declared that "the planters there do generally desire a trade with the Dutch and all other nations, and speak openly there that they are in the nature of slaves, so that the hearts of the greatest part of them are taken away from his Majesty and consequently his Majesty's best, greatest and richest plantation is in danger, with the planters' consent, to fall into the enemy's hands, if not timely prevented."[36] This is corroborated by the Council itself, in an official letter to the King. "For in this very conjuncture had the people had a distasteful Governor," they wrote, "they would have hazarded the loss of this Country, and the rather because they doe believe their Condicon would not be soe bad under the Dutch in Point of Traffique as it is under the Merchants who now use them hardly, even to extremity."[37]

It is evident, then, that throughout the entire reign of Charles II the unhappy effects of the trade restrictions made of Virginia, which formerly had been the land of opportunity for the poor man, a place of suffering, poverty and discontent. The indentured servant who came over after 1660 found conditions in the colony hardly more favorable for his advancement than in England. The price of tobacco was now so low that it was not possible for a man, by his unassisted efforts, to make a profit by its cultivation. If Thomas Ludewell is correct in estimating the return from the average crop at fifty shillings, the lot of the poor man must have been hard indeed. Hungry he need not be, for food continued to be abundant and easy to obtain, but of all that the merchants gave him in return for his tobacco—clothing, farm implements, household furnishings—he had to content himself with the scantiest supply. And only too often his pressing needs brought him into hopeless debt. As for imitating his predecessors of the earlier period in saving money, purchasing land and servants and becoming a substantial citizen, the task was well nigh impossible of accomplishment.

It would be expected, then, that even the most exhaustive investigation could reveal but a few indentured servants, coming over after 1660, who succeeded in establishing themselves in the Virginia yeomanry. And such, indeed, is the case. Fortunately we have at hand for the period in question the means of determining this matter with an exactness impossible for the first half of the century. Nicholson's rent roll of 1704 supplies a complete list, with the exception of those in the Northern Neck, of every landowner in Virginia. At the same time we have in the Land Office at Richmond, the names of many thousands of persons listed as headrights, constituting almost all the immigrants who came in during the years from 1666 to the end of the century. Thus by comparing the two lists and trying to identify on the rent roll the names found in the patents, it is possible to fix the proportion of servants who won for themselves at this time places among the landowning class.

Selecting the year 1672 as typical of the Restoration period, we find that an examination of 672 of the names which are listed as headrights, eleven only can be identified with any degree of certainty upon the rent roll. Of 1116 names examined in the years from 1671 to 1674 inclusive, only 26 are positively those of persons listed as landowners in 1704. After making due allowance for the fact that uncertainty exists in a number of other cases, and that some who prospered must have died in the intervening years, it is safe to say that not more than five or six per cent of the indentured servants of this period succeeded in establishing themselves as independent planters.

These conclusions are borne out by the slowness with which the population increased during the years following the passage of the Navigation Acts. In the Commonwealth period the colony had advanced by leaps and bounds, and the inhabitants, estimated at 15,000 in 1649,[38] were placed by Berkeley thirteen years later at 40,000.[39] Under the system which existed during these years, when the colonists enjoyed a comparatively free trade, the population had tripled. But after 1660, while the Virginia tobacco was dumped upon the restricted English market and prices fell lower and lower, no such rapid growth is noted. In 1671, nine years after his first estimate, Governor Berkeley still placed the population at 40,000.[40] And even if we accept the statement of the Virginia agents sent to England to secure a charter for the colony that in 1675 the number of inhabitants was 50,000, it is evident that some pernicious influence was at work to retard the development of England's most important American province.[41] A drop in the rate of increase from 200 per cent during the thirteen years prior to 1662, to 25 per cent in the thirteen years following, is a clear index to the startling change brought about in the colony by the British trade regulations.

These figures are the more significant in that there was no appreciable slackening of the stream of servants. It is probable that in the period from 1662 to 1675, which marked this estimated increase of 10,000 persons, fully 20,000 immigrants had come to the colony.[42] The patent rolls for 1674 alone give the names of 1931 headrights, and this year is by no means exceptional. No wonder Edward Randolph was surprised at the smallness of the population and wrote to the Board of Trade that it should be investigated why Virginia had not grown more, "considering what vast numbers of servants and others had been transported thither."[43]

But Randolph failed to realize that it is not the volume of immigration but the number of people a country will support which in the end determines the size of the population. It was not enough to pour into the colony tens of thousands of poor settlers; opportunity had also to be afforded them for earning an adequate living. And this opportunity, because of the enforcement of the Navigation Acts and the consequent ruin of trade, they did not have in Virginia. Throughout the Restoration period not more than forty or fifty thousand people could exist upon the returns from the tobacco crop, and beyond that the population could hardly rise. If more poured in, they must of necessity live in misery and rags, or migrate to other colonies where more favorable conditions existed.

We are not at present concerned with what become of this surplus population, but only with the fact that the Navigation Acts brought to a dead halt the process of moulding freedmen and other poor settlers into a prosperous yeomanry. By the year 1660 this class seems to have reached its highest development, and had a rent roll of land owners been drawn up at that date it would doubtless have shown almost as many names as that of 1704. In fact it is fortunate that in the bitter years from 1660 to 1685 it did not succumb entirely. With the price of tobacco so low that no profit was to be derived from it, with his family in rags, the small planter might well have sold his land to his more wealthy neighbor and joined the newly freed servants in moving on to western Carolina or to the northern colonies.

In fact it is an indication of the solid character of the Virginia yeomanry that it survived to enter the Eighteenth century, that under Andros and Nicholson as well as under Sir William Berkeley it was the soundest element in the life of the colony. Had it not been for the crowning misfortune of the introduction of great swarms of negro slaves, sooner or later it would have come once more into its own, would have carved out for itself a new prosperity, would have filled Virginia from the Atlantic to the Alleghanies.

CHAPTER VI

THE YEOMAN IN VIRGINIA HISTORY

PERHAPS it would have been impossible for the Virginia yeoman to survive the dark days of the Restoration period had it not been for the fact that in the matter of his food supply he was independent of England and her vexatious trade restrictions. He might be in rags, but there was no reason why he should ever feel the pangs of hunger. Seldom in any climate, in any age has food existed in such extraordinary variety and in such lavish abundance.

Almost every planter, even the poorest, was possessed of cattle. The *Perfect Discription* states that in 1649 there were in the colony "of Kine, Oxen, Bulls, Calves, twenty thousand, large and good."[1] Fifteen years later the number had increased to 100,000.[2] Many a little farmer, too poor to afford the help of a servant or a slave, had cattle more than sufficient for his every need. John Splitimber, a planter of meagre means, died in 1677 owning eight cows and one bull.[3] John Gray, whose entire personal estate was valued only at 9,340 pounds of tobacco, possessed at his death six cows, six calves, two steers and one heifer.[4] The inventory of the goods of Richard Avery, another poor planter, shows three steers, one heifer, three small cattle and one calf.[5] The yeoman not only secured from these animals a goodly supply of beef, but milk in abundance from which he made butter and cheese. The steers he used as beasts of burden.

The meat which most frequently appeared upon the table of the poor man was that of swine. The planter marked his hogs and turned them loose in the woods to feed upon roots and acorns.　On the other hand, sheep did not multiply in the colony, for the woods were not suited for their maintenance, and those areas which had been cleared of trees could more profitably be utilized for agriculture than for pasture lands. Mutton was a rare delicacy even with the well-to-do.[6]

Poultry were exceedingly numerous.　At the time of the Company it was stated that the planter who failed to breed one hundred a year was considered a poor manager. The *Perfect Discription* says that the poultry—"Hens, Turkies, Ducks, Geece"—were without number.[7]　Moreover, the wild fowls of the inland waterways were so numerous that even the least skilful of huntsmen could readily bring down enough for the needs of his family, and the mallard, the goose, the canvasback appeared regularly in season upon every table.[8]

The planter always devoted a part of his land to the production of the grain which was needed for his personal requirements. "They yearly plow and sow many hundred acres of Wheat," it was said, "as good and faire as any in the world."[9] At the same time maize grew so readily and its cultivation proved so cheap, that cornbread formed a part of the diet not only of the planters themselves, but of their servants and slaves.

From his garden, an inevitable accompaniment of every plantation, the farmer secured a large variety of vegetables— potatoes, asparagus, carrots, turnips, onions, parsnips; besides such fruits as strawberries, gooseberries, raspberries; from his orchard he had apples, pears, quinces, apricots, peaches.[10] Honey was abundant, and there were few householders who did not have hives under the eaves of their outbuildings.　One planter, a Mr. George Pelton, is said to have made a profit of £30 from his bees.[11]　There were also many wild swarms in the woods, which yielded a delicious return to the colonial bee-hunters.[12]

It is easy to understand, then, why there were no complaints of hunger even in the days when poverty was almost universal. The Virginia yeoman spread always an abundant table. "He that is lazy and will not work," said the author of *New Albion,* "needs not fear starving, but may live as an Indian, sometimes Oysters, Cockles, Wilkes, Clams, Scollons two moneths together; sometimes wilde Pease and Vetches, and Long Oates, sometimes Tuckaho, Cuttenoman ground, Nuts, Marhonions, sometimes small nuts, Filbirds, Wallnuts, Pokeberries, ten sorts of Berries, Egs of Foul, small Fish in Coves at low water will teach him to live idly." "It must needs follow then that diet cannot be scarce, since both rivers and woods afford it, and that such plenty of Cattle and Hogs are every where, which yield beef, veal, milk, butter, cheese and other made dishes, porke, bacon and pigs, and that as sweet and savoury meat as the world affords, these with the help of Orchards and Gardens, Oysters, Fish, Fowle and Venison, certainly cannot but be sufficient for a good diet and wholsom accommodation, considering how plentifully they are, and how easie with industry to be had."[13]

But the little planter, with the advent of the Navigation Acts, often suffered keenly from a lack of adequate clothing. Again and again the letters of the period state that the poor man was reduced to rags, that he could not protect his family from the winter's cold. There was some manufacture of cloth in the home, but the planter usually trusted to the foreign trader to bring him every article of clothing. He had neither the implements nor the skill to supply his own needs. During the Restoration period, and again at the time of the war of the Spanish Succession, when the price of tobacco fell so very low, many families succeeded in producing enough homespun to supply their most pressing needs.[14] But with the return of better conditions they laid aside the loom and the wheel, and resumed their purchase of English cloth.

In normal times the poor planter was comfortably clad. Edward Williams, in *Virginia Richly Valued,* advised every new immigrant to bring a monmouth cap, a waistcoat, a suit of canvas, with bands, shirts, stockings and shoes.[15] The author of *New Albion* thought that each adventurer should provide himself with canvas or linen clothes, with shoes and a hat.[16]

The houses of the small planters were small but comfortable. "Pleasant in their building," says John Hammond, "which although for most part they are but one story besides the loft, and built of wood, yet contrived so delightfully that your ordinary houses in England are not so handsome, for usually the rooms are large, daubed and whitelimed, glazed and flowered, and if not glazed windows, shutters which are made very pritty and convenient."[17] *The New Description of Virginia,* published in 1649, says: "They have Lime in abundance for their houses, store of bricks made, and House and Chimnies built of Brick, and some of Wood high and fair, covered with Shingell for Tyle."[18]

In the days of the Company most of the houses seem to have been made of logs, and Butler, in his *Virginia Unmasked,* declared that they were the "worst in the world," and that the most wretched cottages in England were superior to them.[19] But the period of which Butler wrote was exceptional, and before long the growing prosperity of the colony made possible a great improvement in the dwellings of the people. The rough log cabin gave way to the little framed cottage with chimneys at each end.

A residence erected in one of the parishes of the Eastern Shore in 1635 to serve as a parsonage may be accepted as typical of the better class of houses in Virginia at this time. It was made of wood, was forty feet wide, eighteen deep and had a chimney at each end. On either side was an additional apartment, one used as a study, the other as a buttery.[20] For the poor man this was far too pretentious, and he had to content himself with a home perhaps thirty by twenty feet, containing at times two or three apartments, at times only one.

But such as it was it gave him ample protection against the heat of summer and the cold of winter. Fuel he never lacked. When the frosts of December and January came upon him, he had only to repair to the nearest forest, axe in hand, to supply himself with wood in abundance. In this way, not only would he keep a roaring blaze in his open fireplace, but would widen the space available for the next summer's tobacco crop.

The surroundings of the planter's residence were severely plain. In the yard, which usually was uninclosed, towered a cluster of trees, a survival of the primeval forest. Nearby was the garden, with its flowers and vegetables, the dove-cote, the barn, the hen house, perhaps a milk house or even a detached kitchen. In some cases wells were sunk, but the use of natural springs was more common.[21]

Of the plantation itself, only a fraction was under cultivation at one time. Tobacco was exceedingly exhausting to the soil, but the cheapness of land led the planters to neglect the most ordinary precautions to preserve its fertility. They sowed year after year upon the same spot, until the diminishing yield warned them of approaching sterility, and then would desert it to clear a new field. This system made it necessary for them to provide for the future by securing farms far larger in extent than was dictated by their immediate requirements. They had to look forward to the day when their land would become useless, and if they were provident, would purchase ten times more than they could cultivate at any one time. Thomas Whitlock, in his will dated 1659, says: "I give to my son Thomas Whitlock the land I live on, 600 acres, when he is of the age 21, and during his minority to my wife. The land not to be further made use of or by planting or seating than the first deep branch that is commonly rid over, that my son may have some fresh land when he attains to age."[22]

One may gain an idea of the condition of the very poorest class of freemen by an examination of the inventory of the estate of Walter Dorch, drawn up in 1684. This man possessed two pairs of woollen cards, and one spinning wheel, valued at 100 pounds of tobacco, one chest at eighty pounds, four old trays at twenty pounds, two runletts at forty pounds, one pail and one skillet at sixty pounds, one bowl at two pounds, one feather bed, two pillows and three old blankets at 120 pounds of tobacco, three glass bottles at twenty pounds, one couch frame at forty pounds, one pair of pot-hooks at forty, 800 tenpenny nails at forty-five, and one old table and one sifter at twenty pounds. In all the estate was valued at 587 pounds of tobacco.[23]

John Gray, who died in 1685, left personal property worth 9,340 pounds of tobacco, consisting in part of six cows and six calves, four yearlings, two steers, one heifer, one barrel of corn, one bull, ten hogs and one horse. He had no servants and no slaves.[24] In better circumstances was Richard Avery, who seems to have been a tanner by profession. The inventory of his estate, recorded in 1686, includes one horse with bridle and saddle, a cart and a yoke of steers, eight head of cattle, 25 hogs, 118 hides, various kinds of tools, lumber to the value of 400 pounds of tobacco, four pieces of earthenware, four beds with mattresses and covers, poultry to the value of 180 pounds of tobacco, some wheat in the ground and a batch of wearing linen. The entire personal estate was valued at 14,050 pounds of tobacco. It included no servants or slaves.[25]

John Splitimber, who is entered as a headright to Thomas Harwood in 1635, is typical of the planter who rose from small beginnings to a state of comparative prosperity. This man, at his death in 1677, possessed eight cows, one bull, four year-lings, four mares, 35 hogs, two horses, two bolsters, a pillow, two blankets, a mattress, two bedsteads, two guns, fifty-six pounds of pewter, two rugs, a table, three chests, one old couch, two iron pots, two kettles, two stilyards, shovel and tongs, two smothering irons, two axes, a few carpenter's tools, a saddle and bridle, four casks, clothing to the value of 1,100 pounds of tobacco, a frying pan, a butter pat, a jar, a looking glass, two milk pans, one table cloth, nine spoons, a churn, a bible. The appraisers placed the total value at 18,277 pounds of to-bacco.[26] The inventory records no servants or slaves, but it is probable that Splitimber at times made use of indentured labor, as in November 1648 and again in 1652, we find him taking up land due for the transportation of certain persons to the colony.[27]

Of similar estate was Christopher Pearson, of York county. His personal property included bedding valued at £7, linen at 18 shillings, pewter at £1.18.0, brass at six shillings, wooden ware at £4.13.6 comprising three chairs and one table, a couch, four old chests, a cask, two ten gallon rundletts, a cheese press, a box of drawers, an old table, three pails, a spinning wheel with cards, two sifting trays, a corn barrel, three bedsteads, four sives, a funnel; iron ware valued at £2.12.0, including three pots, two pot-rocks, a pestal, a frying pan, a looking glass; three cows appraised at £6.5.0, a yearling at ten shill-ings, a colt at two pounds sterling. The entire estate was valued at £25.19.6.[28]

It must not be imagined, however, that Virginia, even in the early years of its settlement, contained no men of wealth or rank. Industry and intelligence bore their inevitable fruit in the little colony, with the result that here and there certain planters acquired an enviable pre-eminence among their fel-lows. The *New Description* mentions several such cases.

Captain Matthews "hath a fine house," it says, "and all things answerable to it; he sowes yeerly store of Hempe and Flax, and causes it to be spun; he keeps Weavers, and hath a Tan-house, causes Leather to be dressed, hath eight Shoemakers employed in their trade, hath forty Negro servants, brings them up to Trades in his house. He yeerly sowes abundance of Wheat, Barley, &c. The Wheat he selleth at four shillings the bushell; kills store of Beeves, and sells them to victuall the Ships when they come thither: hath abundance of Kine, a brave Dairy, Swine great store, and Poltery; he married a Daughter of Sir Thomas Hinton, and in a word, keeps a good house, lives bravely, and a true lover of Virginia; he is worthy of much honor."[29]

This description is interesting because it shows not only the extent of the holdings of certain planters at this early date, but that their prosperity had the same foundation as that of the more numerous class of wealthy men of the Eighteenth century. In both cases slavery and plantation manufacture would seem to have been the open sesame to success. It is notable that of the very limited number of men in Virginia prior to 1700 who stand out above their fellows in the readiness with which they acquired property, almost all gathered around them a goodly number of negroes.

Among the prominent planters of the first half of the Seventeenth century was George Menefie, famous for his orchard which abounded in apple, pear and cherry trees, and for his garden which yielded all kinds of fruits, vegetables, and flowers; Richard Bennett, a man of large property who had in one year "out of his Orchard as many Apples as he made 20 Butts of Excellent Cider"; Richard Kinsman, who for three or four years in succession secured "forty or fifty Butts of Perry made out of his Orchard, pure and good."[30]

In the second half of the century the class of the well-to-do, although somewhat more numerous, was still restricted to a small group of prominent families, many of them connected by marriage. Among the best known men are Nathaniel Bacon, Sr., Thomas Ballard, Robert Beverely, Giles Brent, Joseph Bridger, William Byrd I, John Carter, John Custis I, Dudley Digges, William Fitzhugh, Lewis Burwell, Philip Ludwell I, William Moseley, Daniel Parke, Ralph Wormeley, Benjamin Harrison, Edward Hill, Edmund Jennings and Matthew Page. But so few were their numbers that the Governors more than once complained that they could not find men for the Council of State qualified for that post by their wealth and influence.

The depository of power for the Virginia yeomanry was the House of Burgesses. This important body was elected by the votes of the freeholders, and faithfully represented their interests. Here they would bring their grievances, here express their wishes, here defend themselves against injustice, here demand the enactment of legislation favorable to their class. The hope of the people lay always in the Burgesses, Bacon the rebel tells us, "as their Trusts, and Sanctuary to fly to."[31] And though the commons usually elected to this body the leading men of each county, men of education and wealth if such were to be found, they held them to a strict accountability for their every action.[32] Many of the best known members of the Council of State served their apprenticeship in the Burgesses. But whatever the social status of the Burgess, he felt always that he was the representative of the poor planter, the defender of his interests, and seldom indeed did he betray his trust.[33] This no doubt was with him in part a matter of honor, but it also was the result of a consciousness that unless he obeyed the behests of his constituency he would be defeated if he came up for re-election.

The House of Burgesses, even in the days when the colony

was but an infant settlement stretching along the banks of the James, did not hesitate to oppose the wishes of the King himself. In 1627 Charles I sent instructions for an election of Burgesses that he might gain the assent of the planters through their representatives to an offer which he made to buy their tobacco.[34] Although the Assembly must have realized that its very existence might depend upon its compliance with the King's wishes, it refused to accept his proposal.[35] In 1634 Charles again made an offer for the tobacco, but again he encountered stubborn opposition. The Secretary of the colony forwarded a report in which he frankly told the British Government that in his opinion the matter would never go through if it depended upon the yielding of the Assembly.[36]

In 1635 the people again showed their independent spirit by ejecting Sir John Harvey from the Government and sending him back to England. It is true that the Council members took the lead in this bold step, but they would hardly have gone to such lengths had they not been supported by the mass of small planters.[37] In fact, one of the chief grievances against the Governor was his refusal to send to the King a petition of the Burgesses, which he considered offensive because they had made it "a popular business, by subscribing a multitude of hands thereto." And some days before the actual expulsion Dr. John Pott, Harvey's chief enemy, was going from plantation to plantation, inciting the people to resistance and securing their signatures to a paper demanding a redress of grievances.[38]

The attitude of the small planters during the English civil war and Commonwealth period is equally instructive. Certain writers have maintained that the people of Virginia were a unit for the King, that upon the execution of Charles I his son was proclaimed with the unanimous consent of the planters, that the colony became a refuge for English cavaliers,

that it surrendered to Parliament only when conquered by an
armed expedition and that it restored Charles II as King of
Virginia even before he had regained his power in England.

All of this is either misleading or entirely false. It is true
that the Assembly proclaimed Charles II King in 1649 and
passed laws making it high treason for any person to uphold
the legality of the dethronement and execution of his father.[39]
But this was largely the work of Sir William Berkeley and
the small group of well-to-do men who were dependent upon
him for their welfare. The very fact that it was felt necessary to threaten with dire punishment all who spread abroad
reports "tending to a change of government," shows that there
existed a fear that such a change might be effected.[40] How
many of the small planters were at heart friendly to Parliament it is impossible to say, but the number was large enough
to cause Sir William Berkeley such serious misgivings as to
his own personal safety that he obtained from the Assembly
a guard of ten men to protect him from assassination.[41]

Nor can it be said that Virginia was forced into an unwill-
ing submission to Parliament. It is true that an expedition
was sent to conquer the colony, which entered the capes, sailed
up to the forts at Jamestown and there received the formal
surrender of the colony.[42] But this surrender was forced
upon the Governor as much by the wishes of the people as by
the guns of the British fleet. In fact, the expedition had been
sent at the request of certain representatives of the Parlia-
mentary faction in Virginia, who made it clear to the Commonwealth leaders that the colony was by no means unanimous
for the King, and that it was held to its allegiance only by the
authority and firm will of the Governor.[43] That the British
Council of State expected to receive active assistance from
their friends in Virginia is evident, for they gave directions
for raising troops there and for appointing officers.[44] And

there can be no doubt that the imposing military force which had been gathered to defend Jamestown was not called into action chiefly because Berkeley became convinced that it could not be relied upon to fight against the Commonwealth soldiers.

The new regime which was introduced with the articles of surrender made of Virginia virtually a little republic.   In England the long cherished hope of the patriots for self-government was disappointed by the usurpation of Oliver Cromwell.   But the commons of Virginia reaped the reward which was denied their brothers of the old country.   For a period of eight years all power resided in the House of Burgesses.   This body, so truly representative of the small planter class, elected the Governor and specified his duties.   If his administration proved unsatisfactory they could remove him from office.   The Burgesses also chose the members of the Council.   Even the appointing of officials was largely theirs, although this function they usually felt it wise to delegate to the Governor.[45] In fact, Virginia was governed during this period, the happiest and most prosperous of its early history, by the small proprietor class which constituted the bulk of the population.

Nor is it true that the people voluntarily surrendered this power by acknowledging the authority of Charles II before the actual restoration in England.   After the death of Cromwell, when the affairs of the mother country were in chaos and no man knew which faction would secure possession of the government, the Virginia Assembly asked Sir William Berkeley to act again as their chief executive.   But it was specifically stipulated that he was to hold his authority, not from Charles, but from themselves alone.[46]   In this step the people were doubtless actuated by an apprehension that the monarchy might be restored, in which case it would be much to their advantage to have as the chief executive of the colony the former royal Governor; but they expressly stated that they held themselves in readiness to acknowledge the authority of any Government, whatever it might be, which succeeded in establishing itself in England. So far was Sir William from considering himself a royal Governor, that when the King actually regained his throne, he wrote with no little apprehension, begging forgiveness for having accepted a commission from any other source than himself.[47]

It was the small farmer class which suffered most from the despotic methods of Berkeley during the Restoration period— the corrupting of the House of Burgesses, the heavy taxes, the usurpation of power in local government, the distribution of lucrative offices—and it was this class which rose in insurrection in 1676. It is notable that in the course of Bacon's Rebellion the great mass of the people turned against the Governor, either approving passively of his expulsion, or actually aiding his enemies. When Sir William appealed for volunteers in Gloucester county while Bacon was upon the Pamunkey expedition, he could hardly muster a man.[48] And the forces which eventually he gathered around him seem to have included only a handful of leading citizens, such men as Philip Ludwell, Nathaniel Bacon, Sr., Giles Brent and Robert Beverley, together with a mass of indentured servants and others who had been forced into service. It is this which explains the apparent cowardice of the loyal forces, who almost invariably took to their heels at the first approach of the rebels, for men will not risk their lives for a cause in which their hearts are not enlisted.

And though the small farmers lost their desperate fight, though their leaders died upon the scaffold, though the oppressive Navigation Acts remained in force, though taxes were heavier than ever, though the governors continued to encroach upon their liberties, they were by no means crushed and they continued in their legislative halls the conflict that had gone against them upon the field of battle. But the political struggle too was severe. It was in the decade from 1678 to 1688 that the Stuart monarchs made their second attempt to crush Anglo-Saxon liberty, an attempt fully as dangerous for the colonies as for England. The dissolving of the three Whig Parliaments, and the acceptance of a pension from Louis XIV were followed not only by the execution of liberal leaders and the withdrawal of town charters in the mother country, but by a deliberate attempt to suppress popular government in America. It was not a mere coincidence that the attack upon the Massachusetts charter, the misrule of Nicholson in New York, the oppressions of the proprietor in Maryland and the tyranny of Culpeper and Effingham in Virginia occurred simultaneously. They were all part and parcel of the policy of Charles II and James II.

These attempts met with failure in Virginia because of the stubborn resistance they encountered from the small farmer class and their representatives in the House of Burgesses. The annulling of statutes by proclamation they denounced as illegal; they protested bitterly against the appointment of their clerk by the Governor; they fought long to retain their ancient judicial privileges; they defeated all attempts of the King and his representatives in Virginia to deprive them of the right to initiate legislation and to control taxation. And with the Glorious Revolution of 1688-89, which put an end forever to Stuart aggressions, they could feel that their efforts alone had preserved liberty in Virginia, that they might now look forward to long years of happiness and prosperity. The Virginia yeoman reckoned not with slavery, however, and slavery was to prove, in part at least, his undoing.

CHAPTER VII

WORLD TRADE

IN 1682 the depression which for nearly a quarter of a century had gripped the tobacco trade, somewhat abruptly came to an end. "Our only commodity, tobacco, having the last winter a pretty quick market, hath encouraged ye planters," wrote Secretary Spencer to the Board of Trade in May, 1683.[1] Apparently the tide had turned. From this time until the beginning of the War of the Spanish Succession more than two decades later we hear little complaint from Virginia, while there are excellent reasons to suppose that the colony was experiencing a period of growth and prosperity.

In truth the tobacco trade, upon which the planters staked their all, now expanded with startling rapidity, and each year the merchants were forced to add more bottoms to the fleet which sailed for England from the Chesapeake. During the early years of the Restoration period tobacco exports from Virginia and Maryland had made but little advance. In 1663 they amounted to 7,367,140 pounds, six years later they were 9,026,046 pounds.[2] In 1698, however, the output of Virginia and Maryland was estimated by the merchant John Linton to be from 70,000 to 80,000 hogsheads.[4] Since the hogshead usually contained from 500 to 600 pounds, these figures mean that the planters were then raising from 35,000,000 to 48,000,000 pounds of tobacco. And this conclusion is supported by the fact that the crop of 1699 is valued at £198,115, which at a penny a pound would indicate about 47,000,000 pounds.[5] In fact, the production of tobacco in the ten years from 1689 to 1699 seems to have tripled, in the years from 1669 to 1699 to have quadrupled. In 1669 the planters considered themselves fortunate if their industry yielded them a return of £30,000; at the end of the century they could count with a fair degree of certainty upon six times that amount.

For Virginia this startling development was all-important. During the darkest days of the Restoration period her share of the total returns from the tobacco crop could hardly have exceeded £10,000; in 1699 it was estimated at £100,000. Even if we accept the conservative statement that the average number of hogsheads exported from Virginia in the last decade of the century varied from 35,000 to 40,000,[6] the planters still would have received £75,000 or £80,000. From dire poverty and distress the colony, almost in the twinkling of an eye, found itself in comparative ease and plenty.

Nor is the reason difficult to discover. It had never been the intention of the British Government to destroy the foreign trade of the colonies, the Navigation Acts having been designed only to force that trade through English channels. The planters were still at liberty to send their tobacco where they would, provided it went by way of England and paid the duty of a half penny a pound. That these restrictions so nearly put an end to shipments to the continent of Europe was an unfortunate consequence which to some extent had been foreseen, but which for the time being it was impossible to avoid.

It was undoubtedly the hope of the Government that the foreign market would eventually be regained and that the colonial tobacco would flow from the colonies into England and from England to all the countries of Europe. Prior to 1660 Holland had been the distributing centre for the tobacco of Virginia and Maryland; now England insisted upon taking this rôle upon herself. But the authorities at London were hardly less concerned than the planters themselves at the difficulties encountered in effecting this change and the unfortunate glut in the home markets which followed.

None the less they persisted in the policy they had adopted, even clinging stubbornly to the half penny a pound re-export duty, and trusting that in time they could succeed in conquering for their tobacco the lost continental markets. In this they were bitterly opposed by the Dutch with whom it became necessary to fight two wars within the short space of seven years. Yet steadily, although at first slowly, they made headway. In 1681 the commissioners of the customs refused the request for a cessation of tobacco planting in the colonies, on the ground that to lessen the crop would but stimulate production in foreign countries and so restrict the sale abroad of the Virginia and Maryland leaf.[7] This argument has been denounced by some as both specious and selfish, yet it was fully justified by the situation then existing. After all, the only hope for the planters lay in conquering the European market and the way to do this was to flood England with tobacco until it overflowed all artificial barriers and poured across the Channel. And eventually this is just what happened. Since tobacco was piling up uselessly in the warehouses and much of it could not be disposed of at any price, it was inevitable that it should be dumped upon the other nations of Europe. There is in this development a close parallel with the commercial policy of Germany in the years prior to the world war, when no effort was spared to produce a margin of all kinds of wares over the home needs, which was to be exported at excessively low prices. This margin was a weapon of conquest, a means of ousting the merchants of other nations from this market or that. And when once this conquest had been effected, the price could be raised again in order to assure a profit to the German manufacturers.

It is improbable that the English economists of the Seventeenth century, like those of modern Germany, had foreseen exactly what would happen, but the results were none the less similar. When once the English leaf had secured a strong hold upon the Baltic and upon France and Spain, it was a matter of the greatest difficulty to oust it, especially as the ever increasing influx of slaves made it possible for the planters to meet the lower prices of foreign competitors and still clear a profit. Thus it was that during the years from 1680 to 1708 the Chesapeake tobacco succeeded in surmounting all the difficulties placed in its way by the Navigation Acts, the necessity of the double voyage, the re-export duty of a half penny a pound, and so gradually flooded the continental market.

It is unfortunate that figures for re-exported tobacco during the earlier years of the Restoration period are lacking. In 1688, however, it is stated that the duty of a half penny a pound was yielding the Crown an annual revenue of £15,000, which would indicate that about 7,200,000 pounds were leaving for foreign ports.[8] Ten years later, if we may believe the testimony of John Linton, exports of tobacco totalled 50,000 or 60,000 hogsheads, or from 25,000,000 to 30,000,000 pounds. Not more than a fourth of the colonial leaf, he tells us, was consumed in England itself.[9] Once more Virginia and Maryland were producing tobacco for all Europe, once more they enjoyed a world market.

This trade was extended from one end of the continent to the other. Vessels laden with American tobacco found their way not only to the ports of France and Holland and Spain, but even to the distant cities of Sweden and Russia.[10] The Baltic trade alone amounted to from 5,000 to 10,000 hogsheads, and added from £10,000 to £24,000 to the income of the planters. The chief Russian port of entry was Narva, which took annually some 500 hogsheads, but large quantities were shipped also to Riga and Raval.[11]   The northern nations bought the cheaper varieties, for no tobacco could be too strong for the hardy men of Sweden and Russia.

The trade was of great importance to England, as the leaf, after it had gone through the process of manufacture, sold for about six pence a pound, yielding to the nation in all from £60,000 to £130,000.[12]   As the English were still largely dependent upon the Baltic for potash and ship stores, this constituted a most welcome addition to the balance of trade.   To the colonies also it was vital, carrying off a large part of the annual crop, and so tending to sustain prices.

France, too, proved a good customer for English tobacco, and in the years prior to the War of the Spanish Succession took annually from 8,000 to 10,000 hogsheads, or from 4,000,-000 to 6,000,000 pounds.[13]   Micajah Perry reported to the Lords of Trade that from 6,000 to 10,000 hogsheads went to France from London alone, while a very considerable amount was sent also from other ports.[14]

Far more surprising is the fact that even Spain consumed millions of pounds of English leaf.   With her own colonies producing the best tobacco in the world and in the face of its practical exclusion from the English market, it is strange that the Government at Madrid should have permitted this commerce to continue.   The obvious course for the Spaniards under the economic theories of the day would have been to exclude English tobacco, both in order to protect their own planters and to retaliate for the restrictions upon their product. Yet it is estimated that from 6,000 to 10,000 hogsheads entered Spain each year.[15]   A pamphlet published in 1708 entitled *The Present State of Tobacco Plantations in America* stated that before the outbreak of the war then raging, France and Spain together had taken annually about 20,000 hogsheads.[16]

The Dutch, too, despite their bitter rivalry with the British, found it impossible to do without Virginia tobacco. Purchasing the finest bright Orinoco, they mixed it with leaf of their own growth in the proportion of one to four, and sold it to other European nations. In this way they sought to retain their position as a distributing center for the trade and to give employment to hundreds of poor workers. In all the Dutch seem to have purchased from England about 5,000 hogsheads a year.[17]

The enhanced importance of the tobacco trade is reflected in a steady increase of British exports to Virginia and Maryland. The planters, now that they found it possible to market their leaf, laid out the proceeds in the manufactured products of England. At the end of the Seventeenth century the two colonies were importing goods to the value of £200,000 annually. In 1698, which was an exceptionally good year, their purchases were no less than £310,133.[18]

In short the tobacco colonies had at last found their proper place in the British colonial system. Both they and the mother country, after long years of experimentation, years of misfortune and recrimination, had reached a common ground upon which to stand. Although Maryland and Virginia still fell short of the ideal set for the British colonies, although they failed to furnish the raw stuffs so urgently needed by the home industries, at least they yielded a product which added materially to shipping, weighed heavily in the balance of trade and brought a welcome revenue to the royal Exchequer.

The Crown reaped a rich return from tobacco, a return which grew not only with the expansion of the trade, but by the imposition from time to time of heavier duties. In the period from 1660 to 1685, when the tariff remained at two pence a pound, the yield must have varied from £75,000 to £100,000. If we assume that the average consumption in England was 9,000,000 pounds and the average exports 3,000,000 the total revenue would have been £81,250. In 1685, however, an additional duty of three pence a pound was placed upon tobacco upon its arrival in England, all of which was refunded when the product was re-exported. In 1688, when the tobacco consumed in England was 8,328,800 pounds, the old and new duties, amounting in all to five pence, must have yielded £173,515. When to this is added £15,000 from the half penny a pound on the 7,200,000 pounds of leaf sent abroad, the total reaches £188,515.

In 1698 still another penny a pound was added to the tax, making a grand total of six pence on colonial tobacco disposed of in England. This new duty, together with the rapid increase in the foreign trade, enriched the Exchequer by another £100,000. In 1699, if we assume that 12,000,000 pounds were consumed in England, the return would have been £300,000; while half a penny a pound on 36,000,000 pounds of re-exported leaf, would have brought the total to £375,000. That this figure was approximately correct we have evidence in the statement of the author of *The Present State of the Tobacco Plantations,* written in 1705, that the revenue yielded by the tobacco of Virginia and Maryland amounted annually to £400,000.[19] This sum constituted a very appreciable proportion of the royal income, so appreciable in fact as to make the tobacco trade a matter of vital importance in the eyes of the King's ministers. They were charged at all times to avoid any contingency which might lessen the imports and reduce the customs.

The increase in the tobacco trade stimulated industry, not only by increasing exports to Virginia and Maryland, but also by creating a new English industry. For most of the tobacco, before it was sent abroad, was subjected to a process of manufacture, by which the leaf was cut and rolled and otherwise prepared for the consumer. This industry gave employment to hundreds of poor persons in England and required a considerable outlay of capital.[20]

To British navigation the trade was vital. Each year scores of merchantmen crossed to the Chesapeake and swarmed in every river and creek, delivering their English goods to the planters and taking in return the hogsheads of tobacco. In 1690 the tobacco fleet numbered about 100 ships, aggregating 13,715 tons; in 1706 it counted no less than 300 sails.[21] Nor must it be forgotten that re-exported tobacco also added many a goodly merchantman to the navy and gave employment to many a seaman. Altogether Virginia and Maryland constituted an invaluable asset, an asset which ranked in importance secondly only to the sugar plantations.

It would naturally be supposed that the fortunate turn of events which restored to the tobacco colonies their European market would have reacted favorably upon the small planters of Virginia, not only insuring plenty to those already established, but adding new recruits from the ranks of the indentured servants; that the process of making prosperous freemen from the poor immigrants who flocked to the colony, the process interrupted by the passage of the Navigation Acts, would have been resumed now that these laws no longer prevented the flow of tobacco into the continental countries.

Such was not the case, however. A comparison of the lists of immigrants with the rent roll of 1704 shows that but an insignificant proportion of the newcomers succeeded in establishing themselves as landowners. In four lists examined for the year 1689, comprising 332 names, but seven persons can be positively identified upon the rent roll. In 1690, eight lists of 933 names, reveal but twenty-eight persons who were landowners in 1704. Of 274 immigrants listed in 1691, six only appear on the Roll. In 1695, seven lists comprising 711 names, show but ten who possessed farms nine years later. Of 74 headrights appearing in 1696, but two are listed on the roll; of 119 in 1697 only nine; of 169 in 1698 one only; of 454 in 1699, only seven; of 223 in 1700 but six.[22] All in all not more than five per cent. of the newcomers during this period prospered and became independent planters. Apparently, then, the restored prosperity of the colony was not shared by the poorer classes, the increased market for tobacco did not better materially the chances of the incoming flood of indentured servants.

The explanation of this state of affairs is found in the fact that tobacco, despite its widened market, experienced no very pronounced rise in price. The average return to the planters during the good years seems to have been one penny a pound.[23] This, it is true, constituted an advance over the worst days of the Restoration period, but it was far from approaching the prices of the Civil war and Commonwealth periods. For the poor freedman, it was not sufficient to provide for his support and at the same time make it possible to accumulate a working capital. He could not, as he had done a half century earlier, lay aside enough to purchase a farm, stock it with cattle, hogs and poultry, perhaps even secure a servant or two. Now, although no longer reduced to misery and rags as in the years from 1660 to 1682, he could consider himself fortunate if his labor sufficed to provide wholesome food and warm clothing. How, it may be asked, could Virginia and Maryland produce the vast crops now required by the foreign trade, if the price was still so low? Prior to and just after Bacon's Rebellion the planters repeatedly asserted that their labors only served to bring them into debt, that to produce an extensive crop was the surest way for one to ruin himself. Why was it that twenty years later, although prices were still far below the old level, they could flood the markets of the world?

The answer can be summed up in one word—slavery. The first cargo of negroes arrived in the colony in 1619 upon a Dutch privateer. Presumably they were landed at Jamestown, and sold there to the planters.[24] The vessel which won fame for itself by this ill-starred action, was sailing under letters of marque from the Prince of Orange and had been scouring the seas in search of Spanish prizes. Although the Dutch master could have had no information that slaves were wanted in the colony, he seems to have taken it for granted that he would not be forbidden to dispose of his human freight.

The introduction of this handful of negroes—there were butt wenty in all—was not the real beginning of the slave system in the colonies. For many years the institution which was to play so sinister a part in American history did not flourish, and the slaves grew in numbers but slowly. In the Muster Roll of Settlers in Virginia, taken in 1624, there were listed only 22 negroes.[25] Sixteen years later the black population probably did not exceed 150.[26] In 1649, when Virginia was growing rapidly and the whites numbered 15,000, there were but 300 negroes in the colony.[27] A sporadic importation of slaves continued during the Commonwealth period, but still the number was insignificant, still the bulk of the labor in the tobacco fields was done by indentured servants and poor freeholders.

In 1670 Governor Berkeley reported to the Board of Trade that out of a total population of 40,000, but five per cent were slaves.[28] Eleven years later the number of blacks was estimated at 3,000.[29] In 1635 twenty-six negroes were brought in, the largest purchaser being Charles Harmar.[30] In 1636 the importations were but seven, in 1637 they were 28, in 1638 thirty, in 1639 forty-six, in 1642 seven only, in 1643 eighteen, in 1649 seventeen.[31]   But with the passage of the years somewhat larger cargoes began to arrive.   In 1662 Richard Lee claimed among his headrights no less than 80 negroes, in 1665 the Scarboroughs imported thirty-nine.   In 1670, however, Berkeley declared that "not above two or three ships of Negroes" had arrived in the province in the previous seven years.[32]

It is evident, then, that during the larger part of the Seventeenth century slavery played but an unimportant rôle in the economic and social life of the colony.   The planters were exceedingly anxious to make use of slave labor, which they considered the foundation of the prosperity of their rivals of the Spanish tobacco colonies, but slave labor was most difficult to obtain.   The trade had for many years been chiefly in the hands of the Dutch, and these enterprising navigators sold most of their negroes to the Spanish plantations.   Ever since the days of Henry VIII the English had made efforts to secure a share of this profitable traffic, but with very meagre success.[33]

The Dutch had established trading stations along the African coast, guarded by forts and war vessels.   Any attempts of outsiders to intrude upon the commerce was regarded by them as an act of open aggression to be resisted by force of arms. To enter the trade with any hope of success it became necessary for the English to organize a company rich enough to furnish armed protection to their merchantmen.   But no such organization could be established during the Civil War and Commonwealth periods, and it was not until 1660 that the African Company, under the leadership of the Duke of York entered the field.[34]

This was but the beginning of the struggle, however.   The Dutch resisted strenuously, stirring up the native chieftians against the English, seizing their vessels and breaking up their stations. Not until two wars had been fought was England able to wring from the stubborn Netherlanders an acknowledgment of her right to a share in the trade. Even then the Virginians were not adequately supplied, for the sugar islands were clamoring for slaves, and as they occupied so important a place in the colonial system they were the first to be served. Throughout the last quarter of the Seventeenth century negroes in fairly large numbers began to arrive in the Chesapeake, but it was only in the years from 1700 to 1720 that they actually accomplished the overthrow of the old system of labor and laid the foundations of a new social structure. Throughout the Seventeenth century the economic system of the tobacco colonies depended upon the labor of the poor white man, whether free or under terms of indenture; in the Eighteenth century it rested chiefly upon the black shoulders of the African slave.

There could be no manner of doubt as to the desirability of the slaves from an economic standpoint, apparently the only standpoint that received serious consideration. The indentured servant could be held usually for but a few years. Hardly had he reached his greatest usefulness for his master than he demanded his freedom. Thus for the man of large means to keep his fields always in cultivation it was necessary constantly to renew his supply of laborers. If he required twenty hands, he must import each year some five or six servants, or run the risk of finding himself running behind. But the slave served for life. The planter who had purchased a full supply of negroes could feel that his labor problems were settled once and for all. Not only could he hold the slaves themselves for life, but their children also became his property and took their places in the tobacco fields as soon as they approached maturity.

Thus in the end the slave was far cheaper. The price of a servant depended largely upon the cost of his passage across the ocean. We find that William Matthews, having three years and nine months to serve, was rated in the inventory of his master, John Thomas, at £12.[35] A servant of Robert Leightenhouse, having two years to serve, was put at £9;[36] while on the other hand we find another listed in the estate of Colonel Francis Epes, also having two years to serve, at only £5.[37] A white lad under indenture for seven years to Mr. Ralph Graves was valued at £10.[38] On the whole it would seem that the price of a sturdy man servant varied from £2 to £4 for each year of his service. On the other hand a vigorous slave could be had at from £18 to £30. Assuming that he gave his master twenty-five years of service, the cost for each year would be but one pound sterling. There could be no doubt, then, that in the mere matter of cost he was much cheaper than the indentured white man.

It is true that the negro was none too efficient as a laborer. Born in savagery, unacquainted with the English tongue, knowing little of agriculture, it was a matter of some difficulty for him to accustom himself to his task in the tobacco fields. Yet when his lesson had been learned, when a few years of experience had taught him what his master expected him to do, the slave showed himself quite adequate to the requirements of the one staple crop. The culture of tobacco is not essentially difficult, especially when pursued in the unscientific manner of the colonial period. It required many, but not skilled hands. The slave, untutored and unintelligent, proved inadequate to the industrial needs of the northern colonies. The niceties of shipbuilding were beyond his capacities, he was not needed as a fisherman, he was not a good sailor, he was useless in the system of intensive agriculture in vogue north of Maryland. But in the tobacco field he would do. He could not at first tend so many plants as his white rival, he could not produce tobacco of such fine quality, but what he lacked in efficiency he more than made up for in cheapness.

The African seems to have withstood remarkably well the diseases indigenous to eastern Virginia. There are occasional reports of epidemics among the slaves, but usually they were fairly immune both to malaria and dysentery. A census taken in 1714, when there were perhaps 15,000 negroes in the colony, records burials for sixty-two slaves only.[39] The births of slaves for the same year totalled 253.[40] These figures indicate not only the excellent physical condition in which these black workers were kept by their masters, but the rapidity with which they were multiplying. The low death rate is in part explained by the fact that only strong men and women were transported to the colonies, but it is none the less clearly indicative of the ease with which the African accustomed himself to the climate of tidewater Virginia.

As a rule the negro was more docile than the white servant, especially if the latter happened to be from the ruder elements of English society. He was not so apt to resist his master or to run away to the mountains. Yet plots among the blacks were not unknown. In 1710 a conspiracy was discovered among the slaves of Surry and James City counties which was to have been put into execution on Easter day. The negroes planned to rise simultaneously, destroy any who stood in their way, and make good their escape out of the colony. Among the chief conspirators were Jamy, belonging to Mr. John Broadnax, Mr. Samuel Thompson's Peter, Tom and Cato of Mr. William Edwards, Great Jack and Little Jack of Mr. John Edwards, and Will belonging to Mr. Henry Hart. "Two or three of these were tried this general court," wrote Colonel Jennings, "found guilty and will be executed. And I hope their fate will strike such a terror in the other Negroes as will keep them from forming such designs for the future."[41] The lesson did not prove lasting, however, for in 1730 a number of slaves from Norfolk and Princess Anne counties assembled while the whites were at church, and chose officers to command them in a bold stroke for freedom. As in the previous attempt they were discovered, many arrested and several of the ringleaders executed.[42]

Neither the merchants nor the planters seem to have been conscious of any wrong in the seizure and sale of negroes. They regarded the native Africans as hardly human, mere savages that were no more deserving of consideration than oxen or horses. And as it was right and proper to hitch the ox or the horse to the plow, so it was equally legitimate to put the negro to work in the fields of sugar cane or tobacco. Whatever hardships he had to endure upon the voyage to America or by reason of his enforced labor, they considered amply compensated by his conversion to Christianity.

It is true that the colony of Virginia early in the Eighteenth century imposed a heavy duty upon the importation of slaves, but it did so neither from any consciousness of wrong in slavery itself or a perception of the social problems which were to grow out of it. At the time the price of tobacco was declining rapidly and many planters were losing money. Feeling that their misfortunes arose from overproduction, which in turn was the result of the recent purchases of negroes, the colonial legislators decided to check the trade. "The great number of negroes imported here and solely employed in making tobacco," wrote Governor Spotswood in 1711, "hath produced for some years past an increase in tobacco far disproportionate to the consumption of it . . . and consequently lowered the price of it."[43] "The people of Virginia will not now be so fond of purchasing negroes as of late," declared President Jennings of the Virginia Council in 1708, "being sensibly convinced of their error, which has in a manner ruined the credit of the country."[44]

During the years from 1680 to 1700 slaves arrived in the colony in increasing numbers. In 1681 William Fitzhugh, in a letter to Ralph Wormeley, refers to the fact that several slave ships were expected that year in the York river.[45] At this period, for the first time in Virginia history, we find negroes in large numbers entered as headrights upon the patent rolls. In 1693 Captain John Storey received a grant of land for the importation of 79 negroes, in 1694 Robert Beverley brought in seventy, in 1695 William Randolph twenty-five.[46] Before the end of the century it is probable that the slaves in Virginia numbered nearly 6,000, and had already become more important to the economic life of the colony than the indentured servants.[47]

The chief purchasers at this time were men of large estates. The advantages of slave labor were manifest to planters of the type of William Byrd or William Fitzhugh, men who had built up fortunes by their business ability. It is but natural that they should have turned early from the indentured servant to stock their plantations with the cheaper and more remunerative African workers.

As the English secured a stronger hold upon the African trade slaves arrived in ever increasing numbers. During the years from 1699 to 1708 no less than 6,843 came in, a number perhaps exceeding the entire importations of the Seventeenth century.[48] In the summer of 1705 alone 1,800 negroes arrived.[49] With what rapidity the black man was taking the place of the indentured servant and the poor freeman as the chief laborer of the colony is shown by the fact that in 1708, in a total tithable list of 30,000, no less than 12,000 were slaves. President Jennings at the same time reported that the number of servants was inconsiderable.[50] "Before the year 1680 what negroes came to Virginia were usually from Barbadoes," Jennings told the Board of Trade in 1708. "Between 1680 and 1698 the negro trade become more frequent, tho not in any proportion to what it hath been of late, during which the African Company have sent several ships and others by their licence having bought their slaves of the Company brought them here for sale, among which lately Alderman Jeffreys and Sir Jeffry Jeffreys were principally concerned."[51]

The wars of Charles XII, however, which proved disastrous to the Baltic trade, and the War of the Spanish Succession which cut off exports of tobacco to France and Spain, caused a serious decline in prices and made it impossible for the planters to continue the large purchases of slaves. This fact, together with the duty which had been imposed with the express purpose of keeping them out, reduced the importations to a minimum during the years from 1710 to 1718.[52] But with the reopening of the tobacco market and the return of prosperity to Virginia, the black stream set in again with redoubled force. In 1730, out of a total population of 114,000, no less than 30,000 were negroes.[53] In other words the slaves, who in 1670 had constituted but five per cent of the people, now comprised twenty-six per cent. Slavery, from being an insignificant factor in the economic life of the colony, had become the very foundation upon which it was established.

As we have seen it was not slavery but the protracted accumulation of surplus stocks of tobacco in England which had broken the long continued deadlock of the tobacco trade during the Restoration period and caused the overflow into continental markets. That the labor of blacks at first played no essential part in the movement is evident from the fact that in 1682 when it first became pronounced, the slave population of Virginia and Maryland was still insignificant. But that the trade not only continued after the glut in England had been cleared up, but increased with startling rapidity, was unquestionably the result of more universal use of negroes in the years immediately preceding the War of the Spanish Succession. Slavery so cheapened the cost of production that it was now quite possible for those who used them to pay the half penny a pound duty on reëxported tobacco in England, and still undersell all rivals in the European market. Before many years had passed the tobacco trade, with all that it meant both to England and to the colonies, rested almost entirely upon the labor of the savage black man so recently brought from the African wilds.

That this fact was fully understood at the time is attested by various persons interested in the colony and the trade. In 1728 Francis Fane, in protesting against the imposition of a new tax in Virginia on the importation of slaves declared "that Laying a Duty on Negroes can only tend to make them scarcer and dearer, the two things that for the good of our Trade and for the Benefit of Virginia ought chiefly to be guarded against, since it is well known that the cheepness of Virginia tobacco in European Marketts is the true Cause of the great Consumption thereof in Europe, and one would have therefore Expected rather to have seen an Act allowing a premium on the Importation of Negroes to have Encouraged the bringing them in, than an Act laying so large a Duty to discourage their Importation."[54] Similarly Colonel Spencer wrote to the Board of Trade. "The low price of tobacco requires it should be made as cheap as possible. The Blacks can make it cheaper than Whites, so I conceive it is for his Majesty's interest full as much as the Country's or rather much more, to have Blacks as cheap as possible in Virginia."[55]

It is evident, then, that the opening of the European market and the vast expansion of the tobacco trade, while bringing prosperity to the larger planters, was no great boon to the man who tilled his fields with his own hands. It assured him a ready sale for his crop, it is true, but at prices so low as to leave him a very narrow margin of profit. The new era which was opening, the so-called golden era of Virginia history, was not for him. Virginia in the Eighteenth century was to be the land of the slave holder, not of the little planter.

CHAPTER VIII

BENEATH THE BLACK TIDE

THE importation of slaves in large numbers reacted almost immediately upon the migration of whites to Virginia. As we have seen, the stream of indentured servants that poured across the Atlantic remained remarkably constant throughout almost all of the Seventeenth century. The larger planters were always in need of laborers, and they looked to the surplus population of England to supply them. But with the coming of the blacks all was changed. The Virginians saw in the slave ships which now so frequently entered their rivers the solution of all their problems. And so the influx of white men and women from the mother country dwindled and almost died out, while in its place came a still greater stream from the coast of Africa.

At the time of Bacon's Rebellion the annual importation of servants was between 1,500 and 2,000. The headrights for 1674 show 1931 names.[1] Seven years later the whites were still arriving in large numbers, the rolls for 1682 having 1,565 names. As the century drew to a close, however, the effect of the slave trade upon white immigration is reflected in the dwindling number of headrights. The change that was taking place is illustrated by a patent of 13,500 acres to Ralph Wormleley for the transportation of 249 persons, 149 of whom were white and 100 black.[2] Yet so late as 1704 the servants were still coming in appreciable numbers. In 1708 however, the number of servants at work in the colony had dwindled away almost entirely.[3] In 1715 the names of white persons listed as headrights was but ninety-one; in 1718 but 101.[4] In other

words, the first great migration of Englishmen to continental
America, a migration extending over a century and comprising
from 100,000 to 150,000 men, women and children, had practically come to an end.

English statesmen at the time looked upon this event as an
unalloyed blessing. The day had passed when they felt that
there existed a surplus of labor at home and that the country
was in need of blood letting. The proper policy was to keep
Englishmen in England, to devote their energies to local industries and so strengthen the economic and military sinews
of the nation. And if unemployment existed, it was the correct policy to bring work to the idle rather than send the idle
out of the country in quest of work.[5] And the colonies were
to be utilized, no longer as outlets for the population, but as a
means to the upbuilding of local industry. They were to
supply a market for English goods, keep employed English
mariners and furnish the tobacco and sugar which when re-
exported weighed so heavily in the balance of trade. And
since these great staple crops could be produced by the work
of slaves, it was thought highly advantageous for all concerned
that the negro should replace the white servant in both the
tobacco and the sugar fields. The planters would profit by the
lowered cost of production, English industry would gain by
the increased volume of traffic, the Crown revenues would be
enhanced and English laborers would be kept at home.[6]

Apparently the deeper significance of this great movement
was entirely lost upon the British economists and ministers.
They had no conception of the advantage of having their
colonies inhabited by one race alone and that race their own.
From the first their vision was too restricted to embrace
the idea of a new and greater Britain in its fullest sense.
They could not bring themselves to look upon the soil of
Virginia and Maryland as a part of the soil of an extended

England, upon the Virginians and Marylanders as Englishmen, enjoying privileges equal to their own. They could not realize the strength that would come from such an empire as this, the mighty future it would insure to the Anglo-Saxon race.

Their conception was different. The British empire must consist of two distinct parts—mother country and colonies. And in any clash of interest between the two, the former must prevail. It was not their intent that the colonies should be purposely sacrificed, that they should be made to pay tribute to a tyrannical parent. In fact, they earnestly desired that the plantations should prosper, for when they languished English industry suffered. But in their eyes the colonies existed primarily for the benefit of England. England had given them birth, had defended them, had nurtured them; she was amply justified, therefore, in subordinating them to her own industrial needs.

Thus they viewed the substitution of the importation of slaves to the tobacco colonies for the importation of white men purely from an English, not an Anglo-Saxon, point of view. Had it been a question of bringing thousands of negroes to England itself to drive the white laborers from the fields, they would have interposed an emphatic veto. But with the structure of colonial life they were not greatly concerned. In 1693, when James Blair secured from the King and Queen a gift for his new college at Williamsburg, Attorney-General Seymour objected vigorously, stating that there was not the least occasion for such an institution in Virginia. Blair reminded him that the chief purpose of the college was to educate young men for the ministry and begged him to consider that the people of the colony had souls to be saved as well as the people of England. "Souls! Damn your souls," snapped the Attorney-General, "make tobacco."[7] It would be unfair to say that the British Government took just the same view of the colonists as did Seymour, but there can be no doubt that their chief concern in the plantations was centered upon the size of their exports to England and of their purchases of English goods. And as the slaves could make more tobacco than the indentured servants, it became the settled policy of the Crown to encourage the African trade in every possible way.

The influx of slaves not only put almost a complete end to the importation of white servants, but it reacted disastrously upon the Virginia yeomanry. In this respect we find a close parallel with the experience of ancient Rome with slave labor. In the third and second centuries before Christ the glory of the republic lay in its peasantry. The self-reliant, sturdy, liberty-loving yeoman formed the backbone of the conquering legion and added to the life of the republic that rugged strength that made it so irresistible. "To say that a citizen is a good farmer is to reach the extreme limit of praise," said Cato. Some of the ablest of the early Roman generals were recruited from the small farmer class. Fabius Maximus, the Dictator, in need of money, sent his son to Rome to sell his sole possession, a little farm of seven jugera. Regulus, while in Africa, asked that he be recalled from his command because the hired man he had left to cultivate his fields had fled with all his farm implements, and he feared his wife and children would starve.[8]

This vigorous peasantry was destroyed by the importation of hordes of slaves and the purchase of cheap foreign grain. So long as the wars of Rome were limited to Italy the number of slaves was comparatively small, but as her armies swept over the Mediterranean countries one after another and even subdued the wild Gauls and Britains, an unending stream of captives poured into the city and filled to overflowing the slave markets. Cicero, during his short campaign against the

Parthians wrote to Atticus that the sale of his prisoners had netted no less than 12,000,000 sestercias. In Epirus 100,000 men were captured; 60,000 Cimbries and 100,000 Germans graced the triumph of Marius; Caesar is said to have taken in Gaul another 100,000 prisoners. Soon the slave became the cheapest of commodities, and he who possessed even the most extensive lands could readily supply himself with the labor requisite for their cultivation.

Thus thrown into competition with slave labor the peasant proprietor found it impossible to sustain himself. The grain which he produced with his own hands had to compete in the same market with that made by slaves. It must, therefore, sell for the same price, a price so low that it did not suffice to feed and clothe him and his family. So he was forced to give up his little estate, an estate perhaps handed down to him by generations of farmers, and migrate to the city of Rome, to swell the idle and plebeian population. And once there he demanded bread, a demand which the authorities dared not refuse. So the public treasury laid out the funds for the purchase of wheat from all parts of the world, from Spain, from Africa, from Sicily, wheat which was given away or sold for a song. This in turn reacted unfavorably upon the peasants who still clung to the soil in a desperate effort to' wring from it a bare subsistence, and accelerated the movement to the city.

Thus Italy was transformed from the land of the little farmer into the land of big estates cultivated by slaves. A sad development surely, a development which had much to do with the decay and final overthrow of the mighty structure of the Roman Empire. In former times, Titus Livius tells us, "there was a multitude of free men in this country where today we can hardly find a handful of soldiers, and which would be a wilderness were it not for our slaves." "The plough is everywhere bereft of honor," wrote Virgil, while Lucian bewailed the departed peasants whose places were taken by fettered slaves.[9]

The importation of slaves to Virginia had somewhat similar results. While not destroying entirely the little farmer class, it exerted a baleful influence upon it, driving many families out of the colony, making the rich man richer, reducing the poor man to dire poverty. Against this unfortunate development the Virginia yeoman was helpless. Instinctively he must have felt that the slave was his enemy, and the hatred and rivalry which even today exists between the negro and the lowest class of whites, the so-called "poor white trash," dates back to the Seventeenth century.

The emigration of poor persons, usually servants just freed, from Virginia to neighboring colonies was well under way even at the time of Bacon's Rebellion. In 1677 complaint was made of "the inconvenience which arose from the neighborhood of Maryland and North Carolina," in that Virginia was daily deprived of its inhabitants by the removal of poor men hither. Runaway servants were welcomed in both places, it was asserted, while the debtor was accorded protection against prosecution.[10] This early emigration was caused, of course, not by the importation of slaves, for that movement had not yet assumed important proportions, but by the evil consequences of the Navigation Acts. The Virginia yeoman moved on to other colonies because he found it impossible to maintain himself at the current price of tobacco.

The continuance of the movement, for it persisted for a full half century, must be ascribed to the competition of negro labor. Like the Roman peasant, the Virginia yeoman, to an extent at least, found it impossible to maintain himself in the face of slave competition. The servant, upon the expiration of his term, no longer staked off his little farm and settled down to a life of usefulness and industry. The poor planter who had not yet fully established himself, sold or deserted his fields and moved away in search of better opportunities and higher returns.

This migration was not the first of its kind in the English colonies, for the movement of Massachusetts congregations into the valley of the Connecticut antedated it by several decades. Yet it furnishes an interesting illustration of the lack of permanency in American life, of the facility with which populations urged on by economic pressure of one kind or another change localities. The great movement westward over the Appalachian range which followed the War of 1812, the pilgrimages of homesteaders to the northwest and the Pacific coast, find their precedent in the exodus of these poor families from the tobacco fields of Virginia.

In the last decade of the Seventeenth century the migration assumed such large proportions that the Board of Trade became alarmed and directed Francis Nicholson to enquire into its cause in order that steps might be taken to stop it. The emigrant stream that directed itself northward did not halt in eastern Maryland, for conditions there differed little from those in Virginia itself. The settlers went on to the unoccupied lands in the western part of the colony, or made their way into Delaware or Pennsylvania. "The reason why inhabitants leave this province," wrote Nicholson, while Governor of Maryland, "is, I think, the encouragement which they receive from the Carolinas, the Jerseys, and above all from Pennsylvania, which is so nigh that it is easy to remove thither. There handicraft tradesmen have encouragement when they endeavor to set up woolen manufactures."[11]

Although this explanation does not go to the root of the matter, it was in part correct. The northern colonies held out far greater opportunities for the poor man than the slave choked fields of tidewater Maryland and Virginia. The industries of Pennsylvania and Delaware and the Jerseys demanded a certain degree of skill and yielded in return a very fair living. In other words, the poor settlers in Virginia, finding that tobacco culture was now based upon the cheap labor of African slaves, moved away to other localities where intelligence still brought an adequate reward.

The Maryland House of Delegates, when asked to give their opinion in this matter, thought that it was a desire to escape the payment of debts which made some of the "meaner inhabitants" seek shelter in Delaware Bay and the Carolinas. They came nearer the real cause when they added that the low price paid by the merchants for tobacco obliged many to leave.[12] Nicholson was not satisfied with this answer. "They will not directly own," he wrote, "that setting up manufactures and handicraft-trades in Pennsylvania, the large tracts of land held by some persons here and the encouragement given to illegal traders are the causes that make people leave this province. They would have it that they wish to avoid the persecution of their creditors, which causes them to shelter themselves among the inhabitants of the Lower Counties of Delaware Bay and of Carolina. The low price of tobacco has obliged many of the planters to try their fortune elsewhere, and the currency of money in Pennsylvania, which here is not, draws them to that province from this."[13]

In Virginia the difficulty of securing desirable land because of the large tracts patented by rich planters was usually assigned as the reason for the migration of poor families. This view of the matter was taken by Edward Randolph, the man who had won the undying hatred of the people of Massachusetts by his attempts to enforce the Navigation Acts there and by his attacks upon their charter. In 1696 Randolph did Virginia the honor of a visit, and although encountering there none of the opposition which had so angered him in New England, he sent to the Board of Trade a memorial concerning the colony, criticising the government severely. It should be inquired into, he said, how it comes to pass that the colony (the first English settlement on the continent of America, begun above 80 years ago) is not better inhabited, considering what vast numbers of servants and others have yearly been transported thither. . . . The chief and only reason is the Inhabitants and Planters have been and at this time are discouraged and hindered from planting tobacco in that colony, and servants are not so willing to go there as formerly, because the members of the Council and others, who make an interest in the Government, have from time to time procured grants of very large Tracts of land, so that there has not for many years been any waste land to be taken up by those who bring with them servants, or by such Servants, who have served their time faithfully with their Masters, but it is taken up and ingrossed beforehand, whereby they are forced to hyer and pay a yearly rent for some of those Lands, or go to the utmost bounds of the Colony for Land, exposed to danger and often times proves the Occasion of Warr with the Indians."[14]

For their large holdings the wealthy men paid not one penny of quit rents, Randolph said, and failed to comply with the regulations for seating new lands. The law demanded that upon receipt of a patent one must build a house upon the ground, improve and plant the soil and keep a good stock of cattle or hogs. But in their frontier holdings the wealthy men merely erected a little bark hut and turned two or three hogs into the woods by it. Or else they would clear one acre of land and plant a little Indian corn for one year, trusting that this evasion would square them with the letter of the law. By such means, Randolph adds, vast tracts were held, all of which had been procured on easy terms and much by means of false certificates of rights. "Which drives away the inhabitants and servants, brought up only to planting, to seek their fortunes in Carolina or other places."[15]

Randolph suggested that the evil might be remedied by requiring a strict survey of lands in every county, by demanding all arrears of quit rents, by giving strict orders that in the future no grant should exceed 500 acres. These measures, he believed, would cause 100,000 acres to revert to the Crown, and "invite home those who for want of Land left Virginia." It would encourage other persons to come from neighboring colonies to take up holdings and "mightily increase the number of Planters." This would augment the production of tobacco by many thousands of hogsheads, stimulate trade and industry in England, and aid his Majesty's revenue.

The Board of Trade was deeply impressed. They wrote to Governor Andros explaining to him the substance of Randolph's report and asking what steps should be taken to remedy the evils he had pointed out. "But this seeming to us a matter of very great consequence," they added, "we have not been willing to meddle in it without your advice, which we now desire you to give fully and plainly." But Andros knew full well that it was no easy matter to make the large landowners disgorge. The thing had been attempted by Nicholson several years earlier, when suit was instituted against Colonel Lawrence Smith for arrears of quit rents upon tracts of land which had never been under cultivation.[16] But before the case came to trial Nicholson had been recalled and it was afterward compounded for a nominal sum. The proceedings had caused great resentment among the powerful clique which centered around the Council of State, and Andros was reluctant to reopen the matter. He knew of no frauds in granting patents of land, he wrote the Board, and could suggest no remedy for what was past, "being a matter of Property." He agreed, however, that to limit the size of future patents would tend to "the more regular planting and thicker seating of the frontier lands."[17]

Consequently when Francis Nicholson was commissioned as Governor in 1698, he received strict instructions to advise with the Council and the Assembly upon this matter and to report back to the Board.[18] That nothing was accomplished, however, may clearly be inferred from a letter of a certain George Larkin written December 22, 1701. "There is no encouragement for anyone to come to the Plantation," he declared, "most of the land lying at all convenient being taken up. Some have 20,000, 30,000 or 40,000 acres, the greater part of which is unimployed."[19] Two years later Nicholson himself wrote that certain recent grants were for ten or twenty thousand acres each, so that privileged persons had engrossed all the good land in those parts, by which means they kept others from settling it or else made them pay for it.[20]

Despite all the concern which this matter created, it is doubtful whether it was to any appreciable extent responsible for the continued emigration of poor families. The mere granting of patents for large tracts of land could not of itself fix the economic structure of the colony, could not, if all other conditions were favorable, prevent the establishment of small freeholds. Rather than have their fields lie idle while the poor men who should have been cultivating them trooped out of the colony, the rich would gladly have sold them in small parcels at nominal prices. In the first half century after the settlement at Jamestown, as we have seen, such a breakup of extensive holdings into little farms actually occurred. Had similar conditions prevailed in the later period a like development would have followed. But in 1630 or 1650, when slaves were seldom employed and when tobacco was high, the poor

man's toil yielded a return so large that he could well afford
to purchase a little farm and make himself independent.   In
1680 or 1700, in the face of the competition of slave labor,
he was almost helpless.   Even had he found a bit of unoccupied
ground to which he could secure a title, he could not make it
yield enough to sustain him and his family.[21]

In 1728 Governor Gooch wrote the Board of Trade that the
former belief that large holdings of frontier land had been an
impediment to settlement was entirely erroneous.   It was his
opinion, in fact, that extensive grants made it to the interest
of the owners to bring in settlers and so populate the country.
In confirmation of this he pointed to the fact that Spotsylvania
country, where many large patents had been issued, had filled
up more rapidly than Brunswick, where they had been restricted in size.[22]

In the first decade of the new century the emigration out
of the tobacco colonies continued without abatement.   With
another disastrous decline in the price of tobacco following the
outbreak of the wars of Charles XII and Louis XIV, so many
families moved over the border that the Board of Trade, once
more becoming seriously alarmed, questioned the Council as
to the causes of the evil and what steps should be taken to
remedy it.   In their reply the Councillors repeated the old
arguments, declaring that the lack of land in Virginia and
the immunity of debtors from prosecution in the proprietory
colonies were responsible for the movement.   But they touched
the heart of the matter in their further statement that the great
stream of negroes that was pouring into the colony had so increased the size of the tobacco crop that prices had declined
and the poor found it difficult to subsist.   Not only "servants
just free go to North Carolina," they wrote, "but old planters
whose farms are worn out."[23]

A year later President Jennings stated that the migration

was continuing and that during the summer of 1709 "many entire families" had moved out of the colony.[24] In fact, although but few indentured servants arrived from England after the first decade of the century, poor whites were still departing for the north or for western Carolina so late as 1730. William Byrd II tells us that in 1728, when he was running the dividing line between Virginia and North Carolina, he was entertained by a man who "was lately removed, Bag and Baggage from Maryland, thro a strong Antipathy he had to work and paying his Debts." Indeed he thought it a "thorough Aversion to Labor" which made "People file off to North Carolina."[25]

It is impossible to estimate the numbers involved in this movement, but they must have run into the thousands. For a full half century a large proportion of the white immigrants to Virginia seem to have remained there for a comparatively short time only, then to pass on to other settlements. And the migration to Virginia during these years we know to have comprised not less than thirty or thirty-five thousand persons. In fact, it would seem that this movement out of the older colony must have been a very important factor in the peopling of its neighbors, not only western Carolina and western Maryland, but Delaware and Pennsylvania.

Though many thus fled before the stream of negroes which poured in from Africa, others remained behind to fight for their little plantations. Yet they waged a losing battle. Those who found it possible to purchase slaves, even one or two, could ride upon the black tide, but the others slowly sank beneath it.

During the first half of the Eighteenth century the poor whites sought to offset the cheapness of slave made tobacco by producing themselves only the highest grades. The traders who dealt in the finest Orinoco, which brought the best prices, found it not upon the plantations of the wealthy, but of those who tended their plants with their own hands. "I must beg you to remember that the common people make the best," wrote Governor Gooch to the Lords of Trade in 1731.[26]

In fact, the wealthy planter, with his newly acquired gangs of slaves, found it difficult at this time to produce any save the lower grades of tobacco. The African was yet too savage, too untutored in the ways of civilization to be utilized for anything like intensive cultivation. "Though they may plant more in quantity," wrote Gooch, "yet it frequently proves very mean stuff, different from the Tobacco produced from well improved and well tended Grounds." "Yet the rich Man's trash will always damp the Market," he adds, "and spoil the poor Man's good Tobacco which has been carefully managed."[27] Thus the small farmer made one last desperate effort to save himself by pitting his superior intelligence against the cheapness of slave labor.

But his case was hopeless. As slavery became more and more fixed upon the colony, the negro gradually increased in efficiency. He learned to speak his master's language, brokenly of course, but well enough for all practical purposes. He was placed under the tutelage of overseers, who taught him the details of his work and saw that he did it. He became a civilized being, thoroughly drilled in the one task required of him, the task of producing tobacco. Thus the rich planter soon found it possible to cultivate successfully the higher grades, and so to drive from his last rampart the white freeholder whose crop was tended by himself alone.

Placed at so great a disadvantage, the poor man, at all times in very difficult circumstances, found it almost impossible to exist whenever conditions in Europe sent the price of tobacco down. In the years from 1706 to 1714, when the tobacco trade was interrupted by the wars of Charles XII in the Baltic region and the protracted struggle known as the War of the Spanish Succession, he was reduced to the utmost extremities.

Virginia and Maryland were learning that a prosperity founded upon one crop which commanded a world market was in unsettled times subject to serious setbacks. It was a long cry from the James and the Potomac to the Baltic ports, yet the welfare of the Virginia and Maryland planters was in no small degree dependent upon the maintenance of peaceful conditions in Poland and Sweden and Russia. A war which seriously curtailed the exportation of English leaf to the northern countries would inevitably react on the price and so bring misfortune to the colonial planters. When called before the Board of Trade to testify as to the decay of the tobacco trade, the manufacturer John Linton declared that the Baltic countries, which formerly had purchased thousands of hogsheads a year, now took comparatively few. "The Russian trade is ruined," he said.[28]

The war against France and Spain, coming at this unfortunate juncture, still further restricted the market, sent prices down to new depths and filled to overflowing the planters' cup of misfortune. "The war has stopped the trade with Spain, France, Flanders and part of the Baltic," Colonel Quary reported in a memorial to the Board of Trade, "which took off yearly 20,000 hogsheads of tobacco. Now our best foreign market is Holland."[29] The pamphlet entitled *The Present State of the Tobacco Plantations in America* stated, in 1708, that France and Spain alone had imported 20,000 hogsheads, but that both were now otherwise supplied. "The troubles in Sweden, Poland, Russia, etc., have prevented the usual exportation of great quantities to those ports. Virginia and Maryland have severely felt the loss of such exportation, having so far reduced the planters that for several years past the whole product of their tobacco would hardly clothe the servants that made it."[30]

Their misfortunes were accentuated by the fact that the Dutch took advantage of the European upheavals to gain control of a part of the tobacco trade. Upon the outbreak of the war with Louis XIV, England prohibited the exportation of tobacco either to France or to Spain, but Holland, despite her participation in the struggle, apparently took no such action. On the contrary she strained every nerve to entrench herself in the markets of her ally before peace should once more open the flood gates to Virginia and Maryland tobacco. With this in view the acreage in Holland devoted to the cultivation of the leaf was rapidly extended. "The Dutch are improving and increasing their tobacco plantations," wrote John Linton in 1706. "In 1701 they produced only 18,000 hogsheads. Last year it was 33,500 hogsheads." Plantations at Nimwegen, Rhenen, Amersfoort and Nijkerk turned out 13,400,000 pounds, while great quantities were raised on the Main, in Higher Germany and in Prussia.[31]

The Dutch mixed their own leaf with that of Virginia and Maryland in the proportion of four to one, subjected it to a process of manufacture and sent it out to all the European markets.[32] In 1707 a letter to John Linton stated that they had from thirty to forty houses for "making up tobacco in rolls," employing 4,000 men, besides great numbers of women and girls. Their Baltic exports were estimated at 12,350,000 pounds; 2,500,000 pounds to Norway, 1,500,000 to Jutland and Denmark, 4,000,000 to Sweden, 2,350,000 to Lapland, 2,000,000 to Danzig and Königsberg.[33]

With the continuation of the war on the continent Dutch competition became stronger and stronger. In 1714, when peace was at last in prospect, they seemed thoroughly entrenched in many of the markets formerly supplied by the English. "The planting of tobacco in Holland, Germany, Etc.," it was reported to the Board of Trade, "is increased to above four times what it was 20 years ago, and amounts now to as much as is made in both Virginia and Maryland." The tobacco trade, which had formerly produced some £250,000 in the balance of trade, had declined to about half that figure, exports of manufactured goods to the Chesapeake were rapidly dwindling, the number of ships engaged in carrying tobacco was greatly reduced, the merchants were impoverished, the planters were ruined.[34]

"It is hardly possible to imagine a more miserable spectacle than the poorer sort of inhabitants in this colony," the Council wrote in 1713, "whose labour in tobacco has not for several years afforded them clothing to shelter them from the violent colds as well as heats to both which this climate is subject in the several seasons. The importation of British and other European commodities by the merchants, whereby the planters were formerly well supplied with clothing, is now in a manner wholly left off and the small supplies still ventured sold at such prodigeous rates as they please. Many families formerly well clothed and their houses well furnished are now reduced to rags and all the visible marks of poverty."[35]

This unfortunate period was but temporary. With the conclusion of peace English tobacco was dumped upon the European market at a figure so low as to defy competition. And when once the hogsheads began to move, the reaction on Virginia and Maryland was rapid and pronounced. Soon prices rose again to the old levels, and the colony entered upon a period, for the larger planters at least, of unprecedented prosperity.[36] But the eight years of hardship and poverty made a lasting imprint upon the poorest class of whites. Coming as they did upon the heels of the first great wave of negro immigration, they accelerated the movement of the disrupting forces already at work. It was not by accident that the largest migration of whites to other settlements occurred just at this time and that the inquiries as to its cause are most frequent. The little planter class never fully recovered from the blow dealt it by the temporary loss of the larger part of the European tobacco trade.

The small freeholders who possessed neither servants nor slaves did not disappear entirely, but they gradually declined in numbers and sank into abject poverty. During the period of Spotswood's administration they still constituted a large part of the population. The tax list for 1716 in Lancaster, one of the older counties, shows that of 314 persons listed as tithables, 202 paid for themselves only[37] Making ample deductions for persons not owning land it would appear that more than half the planters at this date still tilled their fields only with their own labor. At the time of the American Revolution, however, the situation had changed materially, and a decided dwindling of the poor farmer class is noticeable. In Gloucester county the tax lists for 1782-83 show 490 white families, of which 320 were in possession of slaves. Of the 170 heads of families who possessed no negroes, since no doubt some were overseers, some artisans, some professional men, it is probable that not more than eighty or ninety were proprietors.[38] In Spotsylvania county similar conditions are noted. Of 704 tithable whites listed in 1783 all save 199 possessed slaves.[39] In Dinwiddie county, in the year 1782, of 843 tithable whites, 210 only were not slave holders.[40] Apparently the Virginia yeoman, the sturdy, independent farmer of the Seventeenth century, who tilled his little holding with his own hands, had become an insignificant factor in the life of the colony. The glorious promises which the country had held out to him in the first fifty years of its existence had been belied. The Virginia which had formerly been so largely the land of the little farmer, had become the land of masters and slaves. For aught else there was no room.

Before the end of the Eighteenth century the condition of the poorest class had become pitiable. The French philosopher Chastellux who spent much time in Virginia during the American Revolution testifies to their extreme misery. "It is there that I saw poor persons for the first time since crossing the ocean," he says. "In truth, near these rich plantations, in which the negro alone is unhappy, are often found miserable huts inhabited by whites whose wan faces and ragged garments give testimony to their poverty."[41]

Philip Fithian, in his *Journal,* describes the habits of this class and is vigorous in his condemnation of the brutal fights which were so common among them. "In my opinion animals which seek after and relish such odius and filthy amusements are not of the human species," he says, "they are destitute of the remotest pretension of humanity."[42] Even the negroes of the wealthy regarded these persons with contempt, a contempt which they were at no pains to conceal.

The traveller Smyth thought them "kind, hospitable and generous," but illiberal, noisy and rude," and much "addicted to inebriety and averse to labor." This class, he says, "who ever compose the bulk of mankind, are in Virginia more few in numbers, in proportion to the rest of the inhabitants, than perhaps in any other country in the universe."[43]

But it must not be imagined that slavery drove out or ruined the entire class of small farmers, leaving Virginia alone to the wealthy. In fact, most of those who were firmly established remained, finding their salvation in themselves purchasing slaves. Few indeed had been able to avail themselves of the labor of indentured servants; the cost of transportation was too heavy, the term too short, the chances of sickness or desertion too great. But with the influx of thousands of negroes, the more enterprising and industrious of the poor planters quite frequently made purchases. Although the initial outlay was greater, they could secure credit by pledging their farms and their crops, and in the end the investment usually paid handsome dividends and many who could not raise the money to buy a full grown negro, often found it possible to secure a child, which in time would become a valuable asset.

This movement may readily be traced by an examination of the tax lists and county records of the Eighteenth century. In Lancaster even so early as 1716 we find that the bulk of the slaves were in the hands, not of wealthy proprietors, but of comparatively poor persons. Of the 314 taxpayers listed, 113 paid for themselves alone, 94 for two only, 37 for three, 22 for four, thirteen for five, while thirty-five paid for more than five. As there were but few servants in the colony at this time it may be taken for granted that the larger part of the tithables paid for by others were negro slaves. It would seem, then, that of some 200 slave owners in this country, about 165 possessed from one to four negroes only. There were but four persons listed as having more than twenty slaves, William Ball with 22, Madam Fox with 23, William Fox with 25 and Robert Carter with 126.[44]

Nor did the class of little slave holders melt away as time passed. In fact they continued to constitute the bulk of the white population of Virginia for a century and a half, from the beginning of the Eighteenth century until the conquest of the State by Federal troops in 1865. Thus we find that of 633 slave owners in Dinwiddie county in 1782, 95 had one only, 66 had two, 71 three, 45 four, 50 five, making an aggregate of 327, or more than half of all the slave holders, who possessed from one to five negroes.[45] In Spotsylvania there were, in 1783, 505 slave owners, of whom 78 possessed one each, 54 two, 44 three, 41 four, and 30 five each. Thus 247, or nearly 49 per cent of the slave holders, had from one to five slaves only. One hundred and sixteen, or 23 per cent, had from six to ten inclusive.[46]   The Gloucester lists for 1783 show similar conditions.   There were in this country 320 slave holders, having 3,314 negroes, an average of about 10⅓ for each owner.   Fifty had one each, 41 had two each, 9 had three, 30 had four and twenty-six had five.   Thus 156, or about half of all the owners, had from one to five slaves.[47]   In Princess Anne county, of a total of 388 slave owners, 100 had one each, 56 had two each and forty-five had three each.[48]

Records of transfers of land tend to substantiate this testimony, by showing that the average holdings at all times in the Eighteenth century were comparatively small.   In the years from 1722 to 1729 Spotsylvania was a new county, just opened to settlers, and a large part of its area had been granted in large tracts to wealthy patentees.   Yet the deed book for these years shows that it was actually settled, not by these men themselves, but by a large number of poor planters.   Of the 197 transfers of land recorded, 44 were for 100 acres or less and 110 for 300 acres or less.   The average deed was for 487 acres.   As some of the transfers were obviously made for speculative purposes and not with the intent of putting the land under cultivation, even this figure is misleading.   The average farm during the period was probably not in excess of 400 acres.   One of the most extensive dealers in land in Spotsylvania was Larkin Chew who secured a patent for a large tract and later broke it up into many small holdings which were sold to new settlers.[49]

This substitution of the small slave holder for the man who used only his own labor in the cultivation of his land unquestionably saved the class of small proprietors from destruction. Without it all would have been compelled to give up their holdings in order to seek their fortunes elsewhere, or sink to the condition of "poor white trash."   Yet the movement was in many ways unfortunate.   It made the poor man less industrious and thrifty. Formerly he had known that he could win nothing except by the sweat of his brow, but now he was inclined to let the negro do the work. Slavery cast a stigma upon labor which proved almost as harmful to the poor white man as did negro competition. Work in the tobacco fields was recognized as distinctly the task of an inferior race, a task not in keeping with the dignity of freemen.

Jefferson states that few indeed of the slave owners were ever seen to work. "For in a warm climate," he adds, "no man will labour for himself who can make another labour for him."[50] Chastellux noted the same tendency, declaring "that the indolence and dissipation of the middling and lower classes of white inhabitants of Virginia is such as to give pain to every reflecting mind."[51]

Slavery developed in the small farmers a spirit of pride and haughtiness that was unknown to them in the Seventeenth century. Every man, no matter how poor, was surrounded by those to whom he felt himself superior, and this gave him a certain self-esteem. Smyth spoke of the middle class as generous, friendly and hospitable in the extreme, but possessing a rudeness and haughtiness which was the result of their "general intercourse with slaves."[52] Beverley described them as haughty and jealous of their liberties, and so impatient of restraint that they could hardly bear the thought of being controlled by any superior power. Hugh Jones, Anbury, Fithian and other Eighteenth century writers all confirm this testimony.

Despite the persistence of the small slave holder it is obvious that there were certain forces at work tending to increase the number of well-to-do and wealthy planters. Now that the labor problem, which in the Seventeenth century had proved so perplexing, had finally been solved, there was no limit to the riches that might be acquired by business acumen, industry and good management. And as in the modern industrial world the large corporation has many advantages over the smaller firms, so in colonial Virginia the most economical way of producing tobacco was upon the large plantations.

The wealthy man had the advantage of buying and selling in bulk, he enjoyed excellent credit and could thus often afford to withhold his crop from the market when prices were momentarily unfavorable, he could secure the best agricultural instruments. Most important of all, however, was the fact that he could utilize the resources of his plantation for the production of crude manufactured supplies, thus to a certain extent freeing himself from dependence upon Birtish imports and keeping his slaves at work during all seasons of the year. Before the Eighteenth century had reached its fifth decade every large plantation had become to a remarkable degree self-sustaining. Each numbered among its working force various kinds of mechanics—coopers, blacksmiths, tanners, carpenters, shoemakers, distillers. These men could be set to work whenever the claims of the tobacco crop upon their time were not imperative producing many of the coarser articles required upon the plantation, articles which the poor farmer had to import from England. For this work white men were at first almost universally made use of, but in time their places were taken by slaves. "Several of them are taught to be sawyers, carpenters, smiths, coopers, &c.," says the historian Hugh Jones, "though for the most part they be none of the aptest or nicest."[53]

The carpenter was kept busy constructing barns and servants' quarters, or repairing stables, fences, gates and wagons. The blacksmith was called upon to shoe horses, to keep in order ploughs, hinges, sickles, saws, perhaps even to forge outright such rough iron ware as nails, chains and hoes. The cooper made casks in which to ship the tobacco crop, barrels for flour and vats for brandy and cider. The tanner prepared leather for the plantation and the cobbler fashioned it into shoes for the slaves. Sometimes there were spinners, weavers and knitters who made coarse cloth both for clothing and for bedding. The distiller every season made an abundant supply of cider, as well as apple, peach and persimmon brandy.

And the plantation itself provided the materials for this varied manufacture. The woods of pine, chestnut and oak yielded timber for houses and fuel for the smithy. The herd of cattle supplied hides for the tanner. The cloth makers got cotton, flax and hemp from the planter's own fields, and wool from his sheep. His orchard furnished apples, grapes, peaches in quantities ample for all the needs of the distiller. In other words, the large planter could utilize advantageously the resources at hand in a manner impossible for his neighbor who could boast of but a small farm and half a score of slaves.[54]

It was inevitable, then, that the widespread use of slave labor would result in the gradual multiplication of well-to-do and wealthy men. In the Seventeenth century not one planter in fifty could be classed as a man of wealth, and even so late as 1704 the number of the well-to-do was very narrowly limited. In a report to the Lords of Trade written in that year Colonel Quary stated that upon each of the four great rivers of Virginia there resided from "ten to thirty men who by trade and industry had gotten very competent estates."[55] Fifty years later the number had multiplied several times over.

Thus in Gloucester county in 1783, of 320 slave holders no less than 57 had sixteen or more. Of these one possessed 162, one 138, one 93, one 86, one 63, one 58, two 57, one 56, one 43 and one 40.[56] In Spotsylvania, of 505 owners, 76 had sixteen or more. Of these Mann Page, Esq., had 157, Mrs. Mary Daingerfield had 71, William Daingerfield 61, Alexander

Spotswood 60, William Jackson 49, George Stubblefield 42, Frances Marewither 40, William Jones 39.[57]

The Dinwiddie tax lists for 1783 show that of 633 slave holders, no less than 60 had twenty-one or more negroes. Among the more important of these were Robert Turnbull with 81, Colonel John Banister with 88, Colonel William Diggs with 72, John Jones with 69, Mrs. Mary Bolling with 51, Robert Walker with 52, Winfield Mason with 40, John Burwell with 42, Gray Briggs with 43, William Yates with 55, Richard Taliaferro with 43, Major Thomas Scott with 57, Francis Muir with 47.[58] The wealth of the larger planters is also shown by the large number of coaches recorded in these lists, which including phaetons, chariots and chairs, aggregated 180 wheels.

Thus it was that the doors of opportunity opened wide to the enterprising and industrious of the middle class, and many availed themselves of it to acquire both wealth and influence. Smyth tells us that at the close of the colonial period there were many planters whose fortunes were "superior to some of the first rank," but whose families were "not so ancient nor respectable."[59] It was the observation of Anbury that gentlemen of good estates were more numerous in Virginia than in any other province of America.[60]

In fact the Eighteenth century was the golden age of the Virginia slave holders. It was then that they built the handsome homes once so numerous in the older counties, many of which still remain as interesting monuments of former days; it was then that they surrounded themselves with graceful furniture and costly silverware, in large part imported from Great Britain; it was then that they collected paintings and filled their libraries with the works of standard writers; it was then that they purchased coaches and berlins; it was then that men and women alike wore rich and expensive clothing.

This movement tended to widen the influence of the aristocracy and at the same time to eliminate any sharp line of demarkation between it and the small slave holders. There was now only a gradual descent from the wealthiest to the poor man who had but one slave. The Spotsylvania tax lists for 1783 show 247 slaveholders owning from one to five negroes, 116 owning from six to ten inclusive, 66 owning from eleven to fifteen inclusive, and seventy-six owning more than fifteen.[61] In Gloucester 156 had from one to five slaves, 66 from five to ten inclusive, 41 from eleven to fifteen inclusive, and fifty-seven over fifteen. Thus in a very true sense the old servant holding aristocracy had given way to a vastly larger slave holding aristocracy.

It is this fact which explains the decline in power and influence of the Council in Virginia, which was so notable in the Eighteenth century. This body had formerly been representative of a small clique of families so distinct from the other planters and possessed of such power in the government as to rival the nobility of England itself. Now, however, as this distinction disappeared, the Council sank in prestige because it represented nothing, while the House of Burgesses became the mouthpiece of the entire slave holding class, and thus the real power in the colonial Government.

Historians have often expressed surprise at the small number of Tories in Virginia during the American Revolution. The aristocratic type of society would naturally lead one to suppose that a large proportion of the leading families would have remained loyal to the Crown. Yet with very few exceptions all supported the cause of freedom and independence, even though conscious of the fact that by so doing they were jeopardizing not only the tobacco trade which was the basis of their wealth, but the remnants of their social and political privileges in the colony. When the British Ministry tried to wring from the hands of the Assembly the all-important control over taxation which all knew to be the very foundation of colonial self-government, every planter, the largest as well as the smallest, felt himself aggrieved, for this body was the depository of his power and the guardian of his interests. A hundred years before, when the commons rose against the oppression and tyranny of the Government, the wealthy men rallied to the support of Sir William Berkeley and remained loyal to him throughout all his troubles. In 1775 there was no such division of the people; the planters were almost a unit in the defense of rights which all held in common.

It is obvious, then, that slavery worked a profound revolution in the social, economic and political life of the colony. It practically destroyed the Virginia yeomanry, the class of small planters who used neither negroes nor servants in the cultivation of their fields, the class which produced the bulk of the tobacco during the Seventeenth century and constituted the chief strength of the colony. Some it drove into exile, either to the remote frontiers or to other colonies; some it reduced to extreme poverty; some it caused to purchase slaves and so at one step to enter the exclusive class of those who had others to labor for them. Thus it transformed Virginia from a land of hardworking, independent peasants, to a land of slaves and slave holders. The small freeholder was not destroyed, as was his prototype of ancient Rome, but he was subjected to a change which was by no means fortunate or wholesome. The wealthy class, which had formerly consisted of a narrow clique closely knit together by family ties, was transformed into a numerous body, while all sharp line of demarkation between it and the poorer slave holders was wiped out. In short, the Virginia of the Eighteenth century, the

Virginia of Gooch and Dinwiddie and Washington and Jefferson, was fundamentally different from the Virginia of the Seventeenth century, the Virginia of Sir William Berkeley and Nathaniel Bacon. Slavery had wrought within the borders of the Old Dominion a profound and far reaching revolution.

NOTES TO CHAPTER I

[1] Peter Force, Tracts and Other Papers, Vol. III, A True Declaration, p. 25.

[2] Purchas, Vol. XVIII, pp. 437-438.

[3] Peter Force, Tracts and Other Papers, Vol. III, A True Declaration, p. 23.

[4] Alexander Brown, The Genesis of the United States, Vol. I, p. 37.

[5] Peter Force, Tracts and Other Papers, Vol. I, Nova Brittania, pp. 21-22.

[6] Hakluyt, Discourse, pp. 89-90.

[7] Hakluyt, Discourse, p. 105.

[8] Hakluyt, Discourse, p. 31.

[9] Hakluyt, Discourse, pp. 14-15.

[10] Alexander Brown, The First Republic in America, p. 49.

[11] Alexander Brown, The Genesis of the United States, Vol. I, p. 349; Peter Force, Tracts and Other Papers, Vol. I, Nova Brittania, pp. 16-17.

[12] Alexander Brown, The Genesis of the United States, Vol. I, p. 239.

[13] Alexander Brown, The Genesis of the United States, Vol. I, p. 202.

[14] P. A. Bruce, Economic History of Virginia, Vol. II, p. 445.

[15] Neill, The Virginia Company of London, p. 338.

[16] Randolph Manuscript, p. 212.

[17] P. A. Bruce, Economic History of Virginia, Vol. II, p. 440; Alexander Brown, The Genesis of the United States, Vol. I, p. 239.

[18] P. A. Bruce, Economic History of Virginia, Vol. II, p. 441.

[19] P. A. Bruce, Economic History of Virginia, Vol. II, p. 443.

NOTES TO CHAPTER II

[1] P. A. Bruce, Economic History of Virginia, Vol. I, p. 161; Alexander Brown, The First Republic in America, p. 232.

[2] William Strachey, Historie of Travaile into Virginia Britannia, p. 121; P. A. Bruce, Economic History of Virginia, Vol. I, p. 162.

[3] Ralph Hamor, True Discourse, pp. 24, 34.

[4] G. L. Beer, The Origins of the British Colonial System, p. 79.

[5] Edward Arber, The Works of Captain John Smith, p. 535.

[6] Alexander Brown, The First Republic in America, p. 268.

[7] G. L. Beer, The Origins of the British Colonial System, p. 87.

[8] G. L. Beer, The Origins of the British Colonial System, p. 81.

[9] Alexander Brown, The First Republic in America, p. 268.

[10] Virginia Magazine of History and Biography, Vol. IX, pp. 40-41.

[11] Virginia Magazine of History and Biography, Vol. IX, pp. 176-177.

[12] P. A. Bruce, Economic History of Virginia, Vol. II, p. 416.

[13] Alexander Brown, The Genesis of the United States, Vol. I, pp. 355-356.

[14] The lack of towns in Virginia was a source of great regret to the English Government, and more than once attempts were made to create them by artificial means.

[15] Even at the end of the Seventeenth century the average price for land in the older counties was about thirty pounds of tobacco an acre.

[16] P. A. Bruce, Economic History of Virginia, Vol. I, p. 578; Vol. II, p. 48.

[17] It was Chanco, an Indian boy living with a Mr. Pace, who revealed the plot to massacre the whites in 1622, and so saved the colony from destruction. Edward Arber, The Works of Captain John Smith, p. 578.

[18] P. A. Bruce, The Economic History of Virginia, Vol. II, p. 70.

[19] For a full discussion of this matter see p. —.

[20] Hakluyt, Vol. VII, p. 286.

[21] P. A. Bruce, Economic History of Virginia, Vol. I, p. 582.

[22] Abstracts of Proceedings of Virginia Company of London, Vol. I, pp. 28, 172; Edward Arber, The Works of Captain John Smith, p. 609.

[23] Hening, Statutes at Large, Vol. II, p. 510.

[24] P. A. Bruce, Economic History of Virginia, Vol. I, p. 603.

[25] P. A. Bruce, Economic History of Virginia, Vol. I, p. 605.

[26] Virginia Land Patents, Vol. V, Register of Land Office, Virginia State Capitol.

[27] Hening, Statutes at Large, Vol. II, p. 510.

[28] P. A. Bruce, Economic History of Virginia, Vol. I, p. 611.

[29] British Public Record Office, CO1-26-77, Berkeley to the Board of Trade.

[30] Peter Force, Tracts and Other Papers, Vol. III, Orders and Constitutions, 1619, 1620, p. 22.

[31] Virginia Land Patents, Register of Land Office, Virginia State Capitol.

[32] Calendar of State Papers, Colonial Series, 1574-1660, p. 208.

[33] Princeton Transcripts, Virginia Land Patents, Princeton University Library.

[34] Virginia Land Patents, Register of Land Office, Virginia State Capitol.

NOTES TO CHAPTER III

[1] L. G. Tyler, Narratives of Early Virginia, pp. 21-22.

[2] Abstracts of Proceedings of Virginia Company of London, Vol. II, p. 171.

[3] British Public Record Office, CO1-26-77, Berkeley to Board of Trade.

[4] Hening, Statutes at Large, Vol. I, p. 257.

[5] Hening, Statutes at Large, Vol. I, p. 411.

[6] Hening, Statutes at Large, Vol. I, p. 539.

[7] British Public Record Office, CO1-26-77, Berkeley to Board of Trade.

[8] Virginia Land Patents, Register of Land Office, Virginia State Capitol.

[9] P. A. Bruce, Economic History of Virginia, Vol. I, p. 595.

[10] J. C. Hotten, Original Lists of Emigrants to America (1600-1700).

[11] Peter Force, Tracts and Other Papers, Vol. II, New Description of Virginia, p. 3.

[12] British Public Record Office, CO1-26-77, Berkeley to Board of Trade.

[13] British Public Record Office, CO5-1359, p. 119, Colonial Entry Book, Governor Andros to the Lords of Trade.

[14] E. D. Neill, Virginia Vetusta, p. 123.

[15] Hugh Jones, Present State of Virginia, p. 61.

[16] Surry County Records, 1684-1686, Virginia State Library.

[17] York County Records, 1696-1701, Virginia State Library.

[18] Rappahannock County Deeds, 1680-1688, Virginia State Library.

[19] Essex County, Orders, Deeds, Etc., 1692-1695, Virginia State Library.

[20] J. C. Hotten, Original Lists of Emigrants to America, pp. 266-275.

[21] P. A. Bruce, Economic History of Virginia, Vol. I, pp. 529-532.

[22] Virginia Land Patents, Register of Land Office, Virginia State Capitol.

[23] Virginia Magazine of History and Biography, Vol. I, p. 30.

[24] Virginia Magazine of History and Biography, Vol. XII, p. 387.

[25] Virginia Land Patents, Register of Land Office, Virginia State Capitol.

[26] Virginia Land Patents, Register of Land Office, Virginia State Capitol.

[27] Essex County, Orders, Deeds, Etc., 1692-1695, Virginia State Library.

[28] Surry County Records, 1645-1672, p. 17.

[29] Essex County, Orders, Deeds, Etc., 1692-1695, p. 348, Virginia State Library.

[30] Virginia Land Patents, Register of Land Office, Virginia State Capitol, Vol. V.

[31] Essex County, Orders, Deeds, Etc., 1692-1695, pp. 199, 202, 205, 209, 216, 348, 394, 407, 413, Virginia State Library.

[32] H. R. McIlwaine, Journals of the House of Burgesses, 1686, p. 37.

[33] British Public Record Office, CO5-1359, pp. 91-92, Colonial Entry Book.

[34] British Public Record Office, CO5-1306, Document 116, Correspondence of the Board of Trade.

[35] British Public Record Office, CO5-1355, p. 361, Colonial Entry Book.

[36] British Public Record Office, CO5-1359, pp. 91-92, Colonial Entry Book.

[37] British Public Record Office, CO5-1405, p. 460, Council Minutes, 1680-1695.

[38] British Public Record Office, CO5-1405, pp. 544-545, Council Minutes, 1680-1695.

[39] British Public Record Office, CO5-1359, p. 345, Colonial Entry Book, 1696-1700.

[40] British Public Record Office, CO5-1339, Document 33V. Correspondence of the Board of Trade.

[41] British Public Record Office, CO5-1314, Document 63VIII, Correspondence of the Board of Trade. A copy of this interest-

ing document is published as an appendix to this volume.

[42] See appendix.

[43] See appendix.

[44] Of this land 15 acres belonged to Thomas Jefferson, probably the grandfather of President Jefferson.

[45] In the opening years of the Eighteenth century the increased importation of slaves brought about an immediate decline in the migration of whites to Virginia from England.

[46] Hening, Statutes at Large, Vol. II, p. 480. The laws governing the tithables were altered slightly from time to time.

[47] Surry County, Wills, Deeds, Etc., 1671-1684, pp. 134-138, Virginia State Library.

[48] Surry County, Wills, Deeds, Etc., 1671-1684, pp. 134-138, Virginia State Library.

[49] Surry County, Deeds, Wills, Etc., 1684-1686, pp. 59-63, Virginia State Library.

[50] Virginia Magazine of History and Biography, Vol. I, pp. 364-373.

[51] Prince George county was formed out of Charles City in 1703.

[52] Surry County, Wills, Deeds, Etc., 1671-1684; Surry County, Deeds, Wills, Etc., 1684-1686, Virginia State Library.

[53] Elizabeth City County Records, 1684-1699, Virginia State Library.

NOTES TO CHAPTER IV

[1] William and Mary Quarterly, Vol. VIII, p. 273.

[2] William and Mary Quarterly, Vol. VIII, p. 273.

[3] P. A. Bruce, Economic History of Virginia, Vol. II, p. 42.

[4] Robert Beverley, History of Virginia, p. 221.

[5] Peter Force, Tracts and Other Papers, Vol. III, Leah and Rachel, p. 11.

[6] William and Mary Quarterly, Vol. XXVI, p. 31.

[7] Peter Force, Tracts and Other Papers, Vol. III, Leah and Rachel, p. 11.

[8] In fact, it was stated by John Hammond in 1656 that many servants acquired considerable property even before the expiration of their indentures. "Those servants that will be industrious may in their time of service gain a competent estate before their Freedomes," he says, "which is usually done by many, and they gaine esteeme and assistance that appear so industrious:

There is no master almost but will allow his Servant a parcell
of clear ground to plant some tobacco in for himselfe, which he
may husband at those many idle times he hath allowed him and
not prejudice, but rejoyce his Master to see it, which in time of
Shipping he may lay out for commodities, and in Summer sell
them again with advantage, and get a Sow-Pig or two, which any
body almost will give him, and his Master suffer him to keep
them with his own, which will be no charge to his Master, and
with one year's increase of them may purchase a Cow calf or two,
and by that time he is for himself; he may have Cattle, Hogs and
Tobacco of his own, and come to live gallantly; but this must be
gained (as I said) by Industry and affability, not by sloth nor
churlish behaviour." Peter Force, Tracts and Other Papers,
Vol. III, Leah and Rachel, p. 14.

[9] Virginia Magazine of History and Biography, Vol. IV, p.
157.

[10] Virginia Magazine of History and Biography, Vol. VII, p.
262.

[11] Virginia Magazine of History and Biography, Vol. VII,
p. 261.

[12] R. L. Beer, Origins of the British Colonial System, p. 154.

[13] Virginia Magazine of History and Biography, Vol. VIII, p.
160.

[14] Virginia Magazine of History and Biography, Vol. XIII, p.
381.

[15] Peter Force, Tracts and Other Papers, Vol. II, New Description of Virginia, pp. 4-6.

[16] British Public Record Office, CO1-21, Secretary Ludwell to
Lord John Berkeley.

[17] Alexander Brown, The First Republic in America, p. 268.

[18] Virginia Magazine of History and Biography, Vol. VII, p.
267, King Charles I to the Governor and Council of Virginia.

[19] Virginia Magazine of History and Biography, Vol. I, p. 293.

[20] Virginia Magazine of History and Biography, Vol. VI, p. 376.

[21] Virginia Magazine of History and Biography, Vol. II, p. 53.

[22] Virginia Magazine of History and Biography, Vol. II, p. 394.

[23] Virginia Magazine of History and Biography, Vol. VI, p. 260.

[24] Virginia Magazine of History and Biography, Vol. VII, p.
382.

[25] Virginia Magazine of History and Biography, Vol. VIII,
p. 149.

[26] Governor Yeardley's Instructions of 1626 contain the statement that "tobacco falleth every day more and more to a baser price."

[27] Virginia Magazine of History and Biography, Vol. VII, p. 376.

[28] Virginia Magazine of History and Biography, Vol. VIII, p. 159.

[29] Virginia Magazine of History and Biography, Vol. IX, p. 177.

[30] Virginia Magazine of History and Biography, Vol. X, p. 425.

[31] G. L. Beer, Origins of the British Colonial System, p. 159.

[32] Peter Force, Tracts and Other Papers, Vol. II, New Description of Virginia, p. 4.

[33] Virginia Magazine of History and Biography, Vol. VIII, p. 150.

[34] Virginia Magazine of History and Biography, Vol. II, p. 288. In Feb. 1627, orders were issued once more that all colonial tobacco, whether of Virginia or of the West Indies, should be shipped only to London. Calendar of State Papers, 1574-1660, p. 84.

[35] Virginia Magazine of History and Biography, Vol. VIII, pp. 149, 155.

[36] British Public Record Office, CO1-12, Petition of Jan. 2, 1655.

[37] P. A. Bruce, Economic History of Virginia, Vol. I, pp. 349-356.

[38] G. L. Beer, Origins of the British Colonial System, pp. 203-204.

[39] G. L. Beer, Origins of the British Colonial System, p. 216.

[40] The author of A New Description of Virginia, published in 1649, states that "in Tobacco they can make L20 sterling a man, at 3d a pound per annum." Peter Force, Tracts and Other Papers, Vol. II, New Description of Virginia, p. 6.

[41] Virginia Magazine of History and Biography, Vol. VII, p. 382.

[42] Virginia Magazine of History and Biography, Vol. VIII, p. 149, Vol. II, p. 53, Vol. VII, p. 259.

[43] Virginia Magazine of History and Biography, Vol. VII, p. 260.

[44] Virginia Magazine of History and Biography, Vol. VIII, p. 158.

[45] Abstracts of Proceedings of Virginia Company of London, Vol. I, pp. 41-42.

[46] J. C. Hotten, Original Lists of Emigrants to America, pp. 201-265.

[47] Colonial Virginia Register, pp. 54-55.

[48] Peter Force, Tracts and Other Papers, Vol. III, p. 16.

[49] Colonial Virginia Register, pp. 68-69.

[50] Virginia Land Patents, Register of Land Office, Virginia State Capitol.

[51] Virginia Magazine of History and Biography, Vol. II, p. 420.

[52] Virginia Magazine of History and Biography, Vol. II, p. 421; Vol. IV, p. 75.

[53] Virginia Magazine of History and Biography, Vol. I, p. 77.

[54] W. A. Crozier, Virginia County Records, Vol. VI, pp. 15-18.

[55] W. A. Crozier, Virginia County Records, Vol. VI, p. 56.

[56] Virginia Land Patents, Register of Land Office, Virginia State Capitol.

[57] William and Mary Quarterly, Vol. XI, p. 271.

[58] William and Mary Quarterly, Vol. XI, p. 276.

[59] William and Mary Quarterly, Vol. XI, pp. 271-276.

[60] Virginia Colonial Register, pp. 64, 68, 70.

[61] William and Mary Quarterly, Vol. IX, p. 72.

[62] Virginia Land Patents, Vol. V, p. 224, Register of Land Office, Virginia State Capitol.

[63] W. A. Crozier, Virginia County Records, New Series Vol. I, p. 4.

[64] W. A. Crozier, Virginia County Records, Vol. VI, pp. 83, 84, 125, 126.

[65] W. A. Crozier, Virginia County Records, Vol. VII, p. 5.

[66] W. A. Crozier, Virginia County Records, Vol. VI, p. 78.

[67] W. A. Crozier, Virginia County Records, Vol. VI, pp. 77, 191, 281.

[68] W. A. Crozier, Virginia County Records, Vol. VI, p. 122.

[69] W. A. Crozier, Virginia County Records, Vol. VI, p. 192.

[70] W. A. Crozier, Virginia County Records, Vol. VI, p. 76.

[71] William and Mary Quarterly, Vol. IX, p. 144.

[72] William and Mary Quarterly, Vol. IX, p. 144.

[73] William and Mary Quarterly, Vol. XI, p. 276.

[74] Virginia Land Patents, Vol. III, Register of Land Office, Virginia State Capitol. The name is here spelled John Blackborne.

[75] Virginia Land Patents, Vol. III, Register of Land Office,

Virginia State Capitol. On the lists the name is spelled William Butcher.

[76] J. C. Wise, The Early History of the Eastern Shore of Virginia, pp. 135-137.

[77] Virginia Land Patents, Vol. IV, Register of Land Office, Virginia State Capitol.

[78] J. C. Wise, The Early History of the Eastern Shore of Virginia, p. 95.

[79] G. C. Greer, Early Virginia Immigrants, p. 68.

[80] J. C. Wise, The Early History of the Eastern Shore of Virginia, p. 376.

[81] Virginia Magazine of History and Biography, Vol. V, p. 101.

[82] W. A. Crozier, Virginia County Records, Vol. VII, p. 177.

[83] Virginia Magazine of History and Biography, Vol. VI, p. 92.

[84] Virginia Magazine of History and Biography, Vol. VI, p. 298.

[85] In 1656 John Hammond declared that though it cost six pounds sterling to go to Virginia, those who decided to make the venture could be sure that their money was well spent. He advised "any that goes over free, but in a mean condition, to hire himself for reasonable wages of Tobacco and Provision, the first year," for by that means he could live free of disbursement, and "have something to help him the next year." Peter Force, Tracts and Other Papers, Vol. III, Leah and Rachel, p. 14.

[86] Virginia Magazine of History and Biography, Vol. VIII, p. 441.

[87] Virginia Magazine of History and Biography, Vol. IX, p. 27.

[88] Virginia Magazine of History and Biography, Vol. X, p. 271.

NOTES TO CHAPTER V

[1] G. L. Beer, The Old Colonial System, Vol. II, p. 109.

[2] British Public Record Office, CO5-1315, Document 26, Correspondence of the Board of Trade.

[3] P. A. Bruce, Economic History of Virginia, Vol. I, p. 401.

[4] R. L. Beer, The Old Colonial System, Vol. I, p. 160.

[5] British Public Record Office, CO5-1316, Perry and Hyde to the Lords of Trade, Correspondence of the Board of Trade.

[6] British Public Record Office, CO5-1316, The Present State of the Tobacco Plantations in America, Correspondence of the Board of Trade.

[7] British Public Record Office, CO5-1316, Correspondence of the Board of Trade; Statutes of the Realm, Vol. IX, p. 917.

[8] Virginia Magazine of History and Biography, Vol. I, pp. 141-155.

[9] British Public Record Office, CO1-16, Petition of Berkeley and Others, Aug. 26, 1662.

[10] British Public Record Office, CO1-20, Thomas Ludwell to Secretary Arlington, May 1, 1666.

[11] British Public Record Office, CO1-20, Sir William Berkeley and others to Secretary Arlington, July 13, 1666.

[12] British Public Record Office, CO1-20, Sir William Berkeley and others to Secretary Arlington, July 13, 1666.

[13] British Public Record Office, CO1-21, Thomas Ludwell to Lord Arlington, Feb. 12, 1667.

[14] British Public Record Office, CO1-21, Thomas Ludwell to Lord John Berkeley.

[15] British Public Record Office, CO1-23, p. 19, Ludwell to Lord Arlington.

[16] British Public Record Office, CO1-21, Governor and Council to the King.

[17] British Public Record Office, CO1-30, p. 51, Petition of the Governor and Council.

[18] British Public Record Office, CO5-1356, p. 408, Report of the Council to the King.

[19] British Public Record Office, CO5-1355, p. 385, Colonial Entry Book.

[20] British Public Record Office, CO1-23, p. 19, Ludwell to Lord Arlington, July 20, 1665.

[21] British Public Record Office, CO5-1371, p. 246, Colonial Entry Book.

[22] British Public Record Office, CO5-1371, pp. 232-240, Dialogue Between John Good and Nathaniel Bacon, Colonial Entry Book, 1677.

[23] British Public Record Office, CO1-30, p. 51, Petition of the Governor and Council to the King, July 1673.

[24] British Public Record Office, CO5-1355, p. 410, Colonial Entry Book.

[25] British Public Record Office, CO5-1356, p. 179, Colonial Entry Book.

[26] G. L. Beer, The Old Colonial System, Vol. II, p. 147.

[27] British Public Record Office, CO5-1371, p. 276, Colonial Entry Book.

[28] British Public Record Office, CO5-1371, p. 276, Colonial Entry Book.

[29] This view of the matter has the support of the dean of **Virginia** historians, Dr. Philip Alexander Bruce. Dr. Bruce writes: "No less an authority than Robert Beverley, the historian, states that the Navigation Acts had a sensible influence in precipitating Bacon's Rebellion. In the early life of this writer he must have been closely associated with hundreds of people who had been through the uprising, and knew much, by direct observation, of the currents that governed it. The elder Beverley was thoroughly informed and thus, in his own home, the son had the best of opportunities of learning the truth. Beverley himself declared that the Acts were causing discontent among the people, long before the Rebellion actually occurred, and so did John Bland in his memorable petition. There is no doubt that the Acts, by keeping alive a sense of friction, left the people in just the state of mind to seize with eagerness on the more palpable wrongs which were specifically brought forward as the justification for resistance. It was really the groundwork of the movement, though if it had been the only cause, might not have precipitated open resistance to the Government.

[30] G. L. Beer, The Old Colonial System, Vol. II, p. 115.

[31] Secretary Thomas Ludwell in a long report to the British Government spoke of the Virginia Government as Berkeley's own, "Which I so term," he explains, "because he is the sole author of the most substantial parts of it, either for Lawes or other inferior institutions." British Public Record Office, CO1-20.

[32] British Museum, Egerton Manuscript, 2395, f. 356b.

[33] British Public Record Office, CO1-19, Berkeley to Lord Arlington, Aug. 1, 1665.

[34] P. A. Bruce, Economic History of Virginia, Vol. I, pp. 399-400.

[35] British Public Record Office, CO1-26-77, Berkeley to the Board of Trade.

[36] British Public Record Office, CO1-30-78, Memorial of John Knight, Oct. 29, 1673.

[37] British Public Record Office, CO1-30-71, Council of Virginia to the King, 1673.

[38] Peter Force, Tracts and Other Papers, Vol. II, New Description of Virginia, pp. 1-16.

[39] British Museum, Egerton Manuscript, 2395, f. 356b, A Discourse and View of Virginia.

[40] British Public Record Office, CO1-26-77, Berkeley to the Board of Trade.

[41] British Public Record Office, CO1-34-95, Petition of Francis Moryson, Thomas Ludwell and Robert Smith.

[42] Virginia Land Patents, Register of Land Office, Virginia State Capitol.

[43] British Public Record Office, CO5-1359, pp. 20, 21, 22, Colonial Entry Book.

NOTES TO CHAPTER VI

[1] Peter Force, Tracts and Other Papers, Vol. II, New Description of Virginia, p. 3.

[2] British Public Record Office, CO1-30, pp. 17, 51.

[3] Surry County Wills, Deeds, Etc. 1671-1624, Virginia State Library.

[4] Surry County Wills, Deeds, Etc. 1684-1686, pp. 34-35, Virginia State Library.

[5] Surry County Wills, Deeds, Etc. 1684-1686, pp. 86-87, Virginia State Library.

[6] P. A. Bruce, Economic History of Virginia, Vol. II, p. 199.

[7] Peter Force, Tracts and Other Papers, Vol. II, New Description of Virginia, p. 3.

[8] P. A. Bruce, Economic History of Virginia, Vol. II, p. 200.

[9] Peter Force, Tracts and Other Papers, Vol. II, New Description of Virginia, p. 3.

[10] Peter Force, Tracts and Other Papers, Vol. II, New Description of Virginia, p. 18.

[11] Peter Force, Tracts and Other Papers, Vol. II, New Description of Virginia, p. 15.

[12] P. A. Bruce, Economic History of Virginia, Vol. II, p. 201.

[13] Peter Force, Tracts and Other Papers, Vol. III, Leah and Rachel, p. 13.

[14] British Public Record Office, CO5-1316, Statement of Mr. Perry and Captain Hyde, Correspondence of the Board of Trade.

[15] Peter Force, Tracts and Other Papers, Vol. III, Virginia Richly Valued, p. 10.

[16] Peter Force, Tracts and Other Papers, Vol. II, New Albion, p. 32.

[17] Peter Force, Tracts and Other Papers, Vol. III, Leah and Rachel, p. 18.

[18] Peter Force, Tracts and Other Papers, Vol. II, New Description of Virginia, p. 7.

[19] Abstracts of Proceedings of the Virginia Company of London, Vol. II, p. 171.

[20] P. A. Bruce, Economic History of Virginia, Vol. II, p. 153.

[21] P. A. Bruce, Economic History of Virginia, Vol. II, pp. 160-161.

[22] Virginia Magazine of History and Biography, Vol. V, p. 285.

[23] Surry County Wills, Deeds, Etc. 1684-1686, p. 7, Virginia State Library.

[24] Surry County Wills, Deeds, Etc. 1684-1686, pp. 34-35, Virginia State Library.

[25] Surry County Wills, Deeds, Etc. 1684-1686, pp. 86-87, Virginia State Library.

[26] Surry County Wills, Deeds, Etc. 1671-1684, Virginia State Library.

[27] John Splitimber paid for himself alone in the tithable lists of 1675.

[28] York County Records, 1694-1702, Virginia State Library.

[29] Peter Force, Tracts and Other Papers, Vol. II, New Description of Virginia, p. 15.

[30] Peter Force, Tracts and Other Papers, Vol. II, New Description of Virginia, p. 14.

[31] British Public Record Office, CO5-1371, p. 241.

[32] "I would have all men consider how meanly we are provided of men of learning, ability and courage, nay indeed of honesty, to stand up in the people's behalf and oppose the oppressing party," said Nathaniel Bacon in 1676. British Public Record Office, CO5-1371, p. 246.

[33] The most notable case of betrayal is that of Isaac Allerton, who sold himself to the Governor for the promise of a seat in the Council of State. British Public Record Office, CO5-1356, pp. 125-126, Colonial Entry Book.

[34] British Public Record Office, CO1-4.

[35] P. A. Bruce, Economic History of Virginia, Vol. I, pp. 287-288.

[36] Virginia Magazine of History and Biography, Vol. X, p. 271.

[37] British Public Record Office, CO1-8, p. 48.

[38] British Public Record Office, CO1-8.

[39] Hening, Statutes at Large, Vol. I, pp. 360-361.

[40] Hening, Statutes at Large, Vol. I, p. 361.

[41] Hening, Statutes at Large, Vol. I, p. 355.

[42] Hening, Statutes at Large, Vol. I, p. 363.

[43] Sixth Report of Royal Commission on Historical Manuscripts, Part I, Instructions to Sir George Ayscue, Sept. 26, 1651.

[44] The commissioners were Capt. Robert Dennis, Richard Ben-

nett, Thomas Stegge and Captain William Claiborne, all of whom
with the exception of Dennis were Virginians.

[45] Hening, Statutes at Large, Vol. I, pp. 371, 373.

[46] Southern Literary Messanger, Jan. 1845; Charles Campbell,
History of Virginia, p. 74.

[47] Southern Literary Messanger, Jan. 1845.

[48] British Public Record Office, CO5-1371, p. 387, Colonial
Entry Book.

NOTES TO CHAPTER VII

[1] British Public Record Office, CO5-1356, p. 104, Colonial Entry Book.

[2] G. L. Beer, The Old Colonial System, Vol. I, p. 40.

[3] British Public Record Office, CO5-1305, Document 23, Correspondence of the Board of Trade.

[4] British Public Record Office, CO5-1345, Document 16, Correspondence of the Secretary of State.

[5] G. L. Beer, The Old Colonial System, Vol. I, p. 42.

[6] Calendar of State Papers, Colonial Series, 1702.

[7] British Public Record Office, CO5-1355, pp. 381-385, Colonial
Entry Book.

[8] G. L. Beer, The Old Colonial System, Vol. I, p. 168.

[9] British Public Record Office, CO5-1315, Document 16, Correspondence of the Board of Trade.

[10] British Public Record Office, CO5-1315, Document 91.

[11] British Public Record Office, CO5-1345, Document 16, John
Linton to the Board of Trade, Correspondence of the Secretary
of State.

[12] British Public Record Office, CO5-1315, Report of John Linton on the Tobacco Trade, Correspondence of the Board of
Trade.

[13] British Public Record Office, CO5-1345, Document 16, Correspondence of the Secretary of State.

[14] British Public Record Office, CO5-1315, Document 26, Correspondence of the Board of Trade.

[15] British Public Record Office, CO5-1315, Document 26, Correspondence of the Board of Trade.

[16] British Public Record Office, CO5-1316, Correspondence of
the Board of Trade.

[17] British Public Record Office, CO5-1340, Document 91, Col.
Quary's Memorial.

[18] R. L. Beer, The Old Colonial System, Vol. I, p. 42.

[19] British Public Record Office, CO5-1316, Correspondence of the Board of Trade; CO5-1360, p. 233, Governor Nicholson to the Lords of Trade.

[20] British Public Record Office, CO5-1315, Document 91, Col. Quary's Memorial.

[21] British Public Record Office, CO5-1315, Correspondence of the Board of Trade, Letter of Col. Quary Sept. I, 1706.

[22] Princeton Transcripts, Virginia Land Patents, Princeton University Library.

[23] Britain Public Record Office, CO5-1359, pp. 107-108, Colonial Entry Book. In 1699 Gov. Nicholson stated that Orinoco was bringing 20 shillings the hundredweight and Sweetscented 25 shillings and up, which he considered an unusually good return. British Public Record Office, CO5-1359, p. 322.

[24] P. A. Bruce, Economic History of Virginia, Vol. II, p. 66.

[25] J. C. Hotten, Original Lists of Emigrants to America, pp. 202-265.

[26] P. A. Bruce, Economic History of Virginia, Vol. II, p. 89.

[27] Peter Force, Tracts and Other Papers, Vol. II, New Description of Virginia, p. 3.

[28] British Public Record Office, CO1-26-77, Berkeley to the Board of Trade.

[29] British Public Record Office, CO5-1355, p. 345, Lord Culpeper's account of his compliance with the King's instructions, Dec. 1681.

[30] P. A. Bruce, Economic History of Virginia, Vol. II, p. 75.

[31] P. A. Bruce, Economic History of Virginia, Vol. II, p. 75.

[32] British Public Record Office, CO1-26-77, Berkeley to the Board of Trade.

[33] G. L. Beer, The Old Colonial System, Vol. I, p. 323.

[34] G. L. Beer, The Old Colonial System, Vol. I, pp. 324-325.

[35] York County Records, 1664-1672, Virginia State Library.

[36] York County Records, 1694-1702, Virginia State Library.

[37] Henrico Records, 1677-1692, Virginia State Library.

[38] York County Records, 1694-1697, Virginia State Library.

[39] British Public Record Office, CO5-1317, Correspondence of the Board of Trade.

[40] British Public Record Office, CO5-1317, Correspondence of the Board of Trade.

[41] British Public Record Office, CO5-1406, Minutes of the

Council March 21, 1710, CO5-1363, pp. 189-191, Colonial Entry Book.

[42] British Public Record Office, CO5-1322, Governor Gooch to the Lords of Trade, Sept. 14, 1730; Feb. 12, 1731.

[43] British Public Record Office, CO5-1363, pp. 317-324, Colonial Entry Book.

[44] British Public Record Office, CO5-1362, pp. 369-373, Colonial Entry Book.

[45] P. A. Bruce, Economic History of Virginia, Vol. II, p. 83.

[46] Princeton Transcripts, Virginia Land Patents, Princeton University Library.

[47] P. A. Bruce, Economic History of Virginia, Vol. II, p. 108.

[48] British Public Record Office, CO5-1316, Correspondence of the Board of Trade.

[49] British Public Record Office, CO5-1314, Document 66, Governor Nott to the Board of Trade.

[50] British Public Record Office, CO5-1362, pp. 365-367, Colonial Entry Book.

[51] British Public Record Office, CO5-1362, pp. 365-367, Colonial Entry Book.

[52] During these years the planters were too impoverished to purchase slaves. The decline in the tobacco trade produced a feeling among the people that the colony had been overstocked with blacks.

[53] British Public Record Office, CO5-1322, Correspondence of the Board of Trade, Report of Governor Gooch.

[54] British Public Record Office, CO5-1322, Francis Fane to the Lords of Trade, Dec. 10, 1728.

[55] British Public Record Office, CO5-1356, p. 139, Colonial Entry Book.

NOTES TO CHAPTER VIII

[1] Princeton Transcripts, Virginia Land Patents, Princeton University Library.

[2] Princeton Transcripts, Virginia Land Patents, Princeton University Library.

[3] British Public Record Office, CO5-1362, pp. 365-367, Colonial Entry Book.

[4] Virginia Land Patents, Register of Land Office, Virginia State Capitol.

[5] G. L. Beer, The Old Colonial System, Vol. I, p. 28.

[6] G. L. Beer, The Old Colonial System, Vol. I, pp. 320-321.

[7] Jared Sparks, The Works of Benjamin Franklin, Vol. X, iii.

[8] Maurice Vanlaer, La Fin d'un Peuple, pp. 38-39.

[9] Maurice Vanlaer, La Fin d'un Peuple, pp. 112-117.

[10] British Public Record Office, CO1-39-38.

[11] Calendar of State Papers, Colonial Series, 1696-1697, p. 420.

[12] Calendar of State Papers, Colonial Series, 1696-1697, p. 500.

[13] Calendar of State Papers, Colonial Series, 1696-1697, p. 546.

[14] British Public Record Office, CO5-1359, pp. 20, 21, 22.

[15] British Public Record Office, CO5-1359, pp. 20, 21, 22.

[16] British Public Record Office, CO5-1359, p. 23, Colonial Entry Book.

[17] British Public Record Office, CO5-1359, p. 113, Andros to the Lords of Trade, July 1, 1697.

[18] British Public Record Office, CO5-1359, pp. 266-303, Colonial Entry Book.

[19] British Public Record Office, CO5-1312, p. 409A, Correspondence of the Board of Trade.

[20] British Public Record Office, CO5-1360, p. 441, Colonial Entry Book.

[21] Rent Roll of 1704, p. 46.

[22] British Public Record Office, CO5-1321, Correspondence of the Board of Trade, Gooch to the Lords of Trade, Nov. 6, 1728.

[23] British Public Record Office, CO5-1362, pp. 374-382, Colonial Entry Book.

[24] British Public Record Office, CO5-1364, p. 27, Colonial Entry Book.

[25] J. S. Bassett, Writings of William Byrd, p. 31.

[26] British Public Record Office, CO5-1322, Gooch to the Lords of Trade, Feb. 27, 1731.

[27] British Public Record Office, CO5-1321, Gooch to the Lords of Trade, Aug. 9, 1728.

[28] British Public Record Office, CO5-1315, Document 16, Correspondence of the Board of Trade.

[29] British Public Record Office, CO5-1315, Document 91, Correspondence of the Board of Trade.

[30] British Public Record Office, CO5-1316, Correspondence of the Board of Trade.

[31] British Public Record Office, CO5-1315, Document 16.

[32] British Public Record Office, CO5-1315, Document 91, Correspondence of the Board of Trade.

[33] British Public Record Office, CO5-1315, Correspondence of the Board of Trade.

[34] British Public Record Office, CO5-1316, Account of the tobacco trade by Perry and Hyde, June 2, 1714.

[35] British Public Record Office, CO5-1316, Petition of the Council, Correspondence of the Board of Trade.

[36] British Public Record Office, CO5-1318, Address of King and Queen county inhabitants to Spotswood; address of Westmoreland inhabitants; letter of Spotswood to Lords of Trade, Dec. 22, 1718.

[37] William and Mary Quarterly, Vol. XXI, pp. 106-122.

[38] Virginia Magazine of History and Biography, Vol. XII, pp. 414-416.

[39] Virginia Magazine of History and Biography, Vol. IV, pp. 297-299.

[40] William and Mary Quarterly, Vol. XXVI, pp. 97-106, 196-201, 250-258.

[41] Chastellux, Travels in North America, p. 291.

[42] Philip Fithian, Journal and Letters, p. 243.

[43] Smyth, A Tour of the United States, Vol. I, p. 58.

[44] William and Mary Quarterly, Vol. XXI, pp. 106-122.

[45] William and Mary Quarterly, Vol. XXVI, pp. 97-106, 196-201, 250-258.

[46] Virginia Magazine of History and Biography, Vol. IV, pp. 297-299.

[47] Virginia Magazine of History and Biography, Vol. XII, p. 415.

[48] Lower Norfolk County Antiquary, Vol. IV, p. 144.

[49] W. A. Crozier, Virginia County Records, Vol. I, pp. 88-110.

[50] Thomas Jefferson, Notes on Virginia, Edition of 1801, p. 321.

[51] Chastellux, Travels in North America, p. 292 note.

[52] Smyth, A Tour of the United States, Vol. I, p. 66.

[53] Hugh Jones, History of Virginia, p. 36.

[54] Rowland, Life of George Mason, Vol. I, pp. 101, 102; Philip Fithian, Journal and Letters, pp. 67, 104, 130, 130, 138, 217, 259; P. A. Bruce, Economic History of Virginia, Vol. II, pp. 411, 418.

[55] British Public Record Office, CO5-1314, Document 63IV.

[56] Virginia Magazine of History and Biography, Vol. XII, p. 415.

[57] Virginia Magazine of History and Biography, Vol. IV, pp. 292-299.

[58] William and Mary Quarterly, Vol. XXVI, pp. 97-106, 196-201, 250-258.

[59] Smyth, A Tour of the United States, p. 67.

[60] Anbury, Travels Through America, Vol. II, p. 330.

[61] Virginia Magazine of History and Biography, Vol. XII, p. 415.

APPENDIX

RENT ROLL OF VIRGINIA

1704-1705

A True and Perfect Rent Roll of all the Lands held of her Maj^{tie} in Henrico County, Aprill 1705

A

Andrews Thomas	396
Ascoutch Mary	633
Archer Jno	335
Adkins Jno	125
Archer Geo	1738
Aldy John	162
Akins James Senr	200
Asbrook Peter Senr	200
Akins James Junr	218
Allin Widd^o	99
	4106

B

Byrd Esqr	19500
Bolling Robt	500
Bolling John	831
Bevill John	495
Branch X^{to}	646
Blackman Wm	175
Bridgwater Sam	280
Bowman John Junr	300
Bowman Edwd	300
Branch Benj	550
Brown Martha	893
Bullington Benj	100
Bowman Lew	65
Bullington	144
Bevell Essex	200
Baugh John	448
Baugh James	458
Burton Isaac	100
Bottom John	100
Bayley Abr	542
Brooks Jane belonging to Wm Walker New Kent..	550
Braseal Henry	200
Brazeal Henry Junr	300

Burton Robt	1350
Burgony John	100
Branch James	555
Burrows Wm. Wm. Blackwell New Kent	63
Branch Thomas	540
Bailey Thomas	251
Branch Matthew	947
Burton Wm	294
Bullington Robt	100
Broadnax Jno Jr	725
Beverley Robt	988
	33590

C

Cheatham Tho	300
Cox Batt	100
Cox John	150
Cox George	200
Chamberlaine Maj. Tho	1000
Childers Abr. Senr	368
Cannon John	108
Cox Wm	300
Childers Ab^r Junr	100
Clark Wm	333
Clark John	300
Cox Rich^d	300
Cardwell Tho	350
Crozdall Roger	200
Cock Wm	1535
Cock Richd Senr	2180
Childers Philip Senr	50
Childers Philip	300
Childers Tho	300
Carter Theod	75
Cock Capt Thomas	2976½
Couzins Charles	362
Clerk Alonson	604

Cock James 1506
Curd Edwd 600
Cock Rich^d 476
Cock Jno 98

15171½

D

Dixon Nicholas 150
Dodson Wm 100
Douglas Charles 63

313

E

Edwd Tho 676
Entroughty Derby 200
Ealam Robt 400
Ellis John 217
East Tho Sen 475
East Tho 554
East Edwd 150
Epes Capt Fra^s 2145
Evans Charles 225
Ealam Martin 130
Epes Isham, Epes Fra. Jun^t
each 444½ acres 889

6061

F

Field Peter Major 2185
Farrar Capt Wm 700
Farrar Tho 1444
Farrar Jno 600
Fowler Godfrey 250
Ferguson Robert 230
Ferris Wm 50
Franklin James Sen 250
Franklin James Jun 786
Ferris Richd Sen 550
Farmer Henry 100
Forrest James 138
Forrest John 150
Fetherstone Henry 700
Farloe John Sen 100
Farloe John Jun 551
Faile John 240

9024

G

Gilley Grewin Arrian 2528
Gee Henry 435
Good John Sen 600

Garthwaite Saml 50
Garthwaite Ephriam 163
Granger John 472
Gill John 235
Good Saml 588
Gower James Grigs Land.. 500

5571

H

Hill James 795
Holmes Rich 100
Harris Thomas 357
Harris Tim^o 250
Hill Rosam^d 1633
Hobby Lawrence 500
Hatcher John 215
Haskins Edward 225
Hatcher Edward Sen 150
Hunt Geo 200
Hughs Edward 100
Hancock Samuel 100
Holmes Thomas 50
Hambleton James 100
Hutchins Nich^o 240
Hatcher Benj Sen 250
Hatcher Wm Jun 50
Hobson Wm 150
Hatcher Wm Sen 208
Hatcher Henry 650
Hancock Robert 860
Harris Mary 94
Hall Edward 184
Herbert Mrs 1360
Hudson Robert 281

9242

J

Jones Hugh 934
Jefferson Thomas 492
Jones Philip 1153
Jorden Henry 100
Jamson John 225
Jackson Ralph 250

3154

K

Kennon Elizabeth 1900
Knibb Samuel 209
Knibb Solomon 833
Kendall Richard 400

3342

L

Liptroil Edward	150
Lewis Wm	350
Lester Darens	100
Ladd Wm	70
Ligon Elizabeth Widdow ⎰	
Ligon Mary Widdow ⎱	1341
Laforce Reu	100
Lochett James	50
Lownd Henry	516
Lockitt Benj	104
Ligon Richard	1028
Ligon Hugh	150
	——
	3959

M

Mann Robert	100
Matthews Edward	330
Moseby Edward	150
Moseby Arthur	450
	——
	1030

N

Nunnally Richard	70

O

Osbourn Thomas	288
Owen Thomas	68
	——
	356

P

Perkinson John	622
Perrin Ann	500
Pleasants John	9669
Parker Wm	100
Parker Nich Sen	500
Pledge Jno	100
Powell Robert	150
Peice John	130
Pleasants Jos	1709
Porter Wm	305
Peirce Wm	175
Peirce Francis	312
Paine Thomas	300
Portlock Elizabeth	1000
Pero Henry	350
Pattram Ira	778
Pride Wm Sen	1280
Pollard Thomas Sen	130

Perkinson Seth	50
Pinkitt Wm	192
Pinkitt Thomas	300
Pattison Joseph	500
Porter John	100
Pollard Thomas Jun	235
Pollard Henry	235
Pinkitt John .....'........	215
	———
	19937

R

Robertson Geo	1445
Ragsdaile Godfrey	450
Rawlett Peter	164
Russell Charles	200
Rowlett Wm	200
Rowen Francis	148
Robertson John	415
Rouch Rachell	300
Robertson Thomas	200
Russell John	93
Royall Joseph	783
Redford John	775
Randolph Col Wm includ-	
ing 1185 acres swamp ...	9465
	———
	14648

S

Steward Jno Jun	902
Scott Walter	550
Soane Capt Wm	3841
Stanley Edward	300
Snuggs Charles	400
Sewell Wm	59
Smith Humphrey	40
Sharp Robert	500
Stovoll Barth°	100
Skerin Widdow	75
Steward Daniell	270
Smith Obadiah	200
Stowers Widdow	200
Sarrazin Stephen	120
	——
	7557

T

Tancocks Orphans	1230
Trent Henry	224
Turpin Thomas	491
Turpin Philip	444
Turpin Thomas	100

Turner Henry	200
Taylor Thomas	475
Tanner Edward	217
Traylor Edward	100
Totty Thomas	260
Traylor Wm	730
	4471

V

Veden Henry	100

W

Woodson John	4060
Williams Robert	300
Woodson Robert Jun	1157
Ward Richard	300
Watson John Sen	1603
Walthall Wm	500
Walthall Henry	832
Whitby Wm	215
Watkins Henry Sen	100
Webb John	100
Watkins Thomas	200
Woodson Rich	180
Woodson Widdow	650
Williamson Thomas	1077
Webb Giles	7260
Wood Thomas	50
Watkins Wm	120
Watkins Jos	120
Watkins Edward	120
Ward Seth	700
Wood Moses	100
Wilkinson Jos	75½
Wilkinson John	130
Worsham John	1104
Womack Abr	560
Willson Jno Sen	1686
Willson Jno Jun	100
Walthall Richard	500
Wortham Geo	400
Wortham Charles	90
Womack Wm	100
	24489½

W	24489½
V	100
T	4471

S	7557
R	14648
P	19937
O	396
N	70
M	1030
L	3959
K	3342
J	3154
H	9242
G	5571
F	9024
E	6061
D	313
C	15171½
B	33590
A	4106
	165814

Out of which must be deducted these several quantities of land following Viz:

Tancocks Orphans Land	1230
Allens Orphans Land	99
	1329

An account of Land that hath been concealed

John Steward Jun	2
Thomas Jefferson	15
Thomas Turpin	10
Henry Gee	10
Stephen Sarrzen	10
Mr. Lownd	1
James Atkin Sen	32
Matthew Branch	10
James Franklin	360
James Hill	50
Rosemond Hill	33
John Bullington	44
Benjamin Lockett	4
John Russell	23
Charles Douglas	13
Col Randolph Carless Land	1049
	1669

The Quit Rent being 162719 acres.

A Rent Roll of all the Lands held in the County of Prince George for the Year 1704

A

Thomas Anderson	450
Wm Aldridge	160
Mr. Charles Anderson	505
Richard Adkinson	200
Thomas Adams	250
Matthem Anderson	349
Henry Ally	390
Wm Anderson	235
Jno Anderson	228
Henry Anderson	250
Robert Abernathy	100
Jno Avery	100
	3217

B

Richard Bland	1000
Robert Birchett	375
Arthur Biggins	200
James Benford	461
Jno Barloe	50
Charles Bartholomew	600
Philip Burlowe	350
Nicholas Brewer	100
Jno Bishop Sen	100
Jno Bishop Jun	100
Isaac Baites	360
Thomas Busby Capt	300
Thomas Busby	200
Wm Batt	750
Coll Byrd Esq	100
Edward Birchett	886
Coll Bolling	3402
Edmund Browder	100
Matus Brittler	510
Jno Butler	1385
Andrew Beck	300
Henry Batt	790
Wm Butler	283
Thomas Blitchodin	284
	12986

C

Thomas Curiton	150
Henry Chammins	300
Capt Clements	1920
Wm. Claunton	100
Robert Catte	100

Bartho Crowder	75
Thomas Clay	70
Jno Coleman	200
George Crook	489
Francis Coleman	150
Jno Clay	350
Wm Coleman Jun	100
George Croohet	30
James Cocke	750
Robert Carlill	100
Jno Clerk	83
Richarl Claunton	100
Stephen Cock for	
Jones Orphans	2405
	7622

D

Thomas Daniell	150
Roger Drayton	270
Joseph Daniell	50
Jno Doby	500
George Dowing	100
Wm Davis	100
Jno Duglas	300
Richard Darding	500
Christopher Davis	50
Thomas Dunkin	136
	2156

E

Robert Ellis	50
Jno Epes Sen	530
Wm Epes Sen	750
Jno Epes	300
Wm Epes	633½
Edward Epes	500
Littlebury Epes	833½
Benj Evans	700
Thomas Edwards	250
Dan Epes	200
Jno Evans	800
Jno. Ellis Jun	400
John Ellis Sen	400
Mary Evans	400
Peter Evans	270
Capt Francis Epes	226
	7243

F

Jno Freeman	300
Wm Frost	50
Jno Fountaine	350
Robert Fellows	418
Elizabeth Flood	100
Benj Foster	923
Jno Field	100
	2241

G

Jno Green	125
Richard Gord	100
David Goodgamd	479
James Greithian	363
Major Goodrich	900
Thomas Goodwin	150
Hubert Gibson	250
Richard Griffith	335
James Griffin	100
Charles Gee	484
Charles Gillam	200
Hugh Goelightly	500
Lewis Green	149
Wm Grigg	200
John Gillam	1000
John Goelightly	100
	5435

H

Coll Hill	1000
Daniell Hickdon	280
Robert Harthorn	243
Jno Hamlin	1484½
Coll Harrison Esq	150
Ralph Hill	175
Wm Harrison	1930
Wm Heath	320
Edward Holloway	100
Robert Hobbs	100
Jno Hobbs Sen	250
Edward Holloway Sen	620
Jno Hobbs	100
James Harrison	200
Gilbert Haye	200
Richard Hudson	75
Gabriell Harrison	150
Robert Hix	1000
Joseph Holycross	84
Charles Howell	125
Sam Harwell	125

Isaac Hall	450
Jno Howell	183
Thomas Howell	25
Mrs. Herbert	3925
Jno Hixs	216
Richard Hamlin	240
Thomas Harnison	1077
Elizabeth Hamlin	250
Wm Hulme	100
Jeffrey Hawkes	125
Adam Heath	300
Jno Hill	160
Jno Hardiman	872
Justance Hall	614
	17366

J

Wm Jones Jun	230
Wm Jones Sen	600
Henry Jones	200
Robert Jones	241
Edmund Irby	800
Nich. Jarrett	700
James Jackson	80
Adam Ivie	200
Thomas Jackson	60
James Jones Sen	1100
Henry Ivye	450
Peter Jones	621
Ricard Jones	600
Ralph Jacskon	110
Joshua Irby	200
John Jones	350
	6542

K

Richard Kirkland	300
John King	50
Henry King	650
Arthur Kavanah	60
Ensobius King	100
	1160

L

John Livesley	300
Samuel Lewey	100
Jno Lumbady	400
Jno Leeneir	100
Mrs Low	70
Sam Lewey for Netherland Orphans	498

Thomas Lewis Sen	200
Hugh Liegh	762
Francis Leadbeatter	100
Jno Leadbeatter	400
Wm Low	1584
	3114

M

Wm Madox	190
Robert Munford	339
James Mingo Sen	500
Matt Marks	1500
Samuell Moody	328
Francis Mallory	100
Daniell Mallone	100
Jno Mayes	365
Richard More	472
Henry Mitchell Sen	100
Jno Mitchell	170
Wm Mayes	763
Edward Murrell	100
Thomas Mitchell Jun	100
Peter Mitchell	305
Henry Mitchell Jun	200
Francis Maberry	347
James Matthews	100
Jno Martin	200
	6839

N

Richard Newman	120
Walter Nannaley	299
	419

O

Nicholas Overburry	809
Jno Owen	25
	834

P

George Pasmore	330
Francis Poythwes Sen	1283
Joseph Pattison	200
George Pail	246
Nathaniel Phillips	150
Jno Price	50
Wm Peoples	150
Elizabeth Peoples	235
Joseph Perry	275

Richard Pigeon	524
Thomas Potts	200
Joseph Pritchett	50
Jno Petterson	373
George Pace	1000
Ephram Parkam	300
Thomas Poythres	616
Dand Peoples	60
Grace Perry	100
Jno Poythres Jun	916
Jno Petterson	420
Mr Micajah Perry	600
	9203

R

Jno Roberts	316
Nath. Robinson	100
Roger Reace Jun	100
Henry Read	75
Roger Reace Sen	100
Wm Reanes	250
Frances Raye	300
Jno Reeks	50
Wm Rachell	100
Timothy Reading Sen	460
Jno Riners	200
Edward Richardson	300
Coll Randolph	226
	2677

S

Matthew Smart	100
Wm Standback	150
Thomas Symmons	566
James Salmen	477
Wm Savage	150
Wm Sandborne	40
Jno Scott	300
Martin Shieffield	150
James Smith	67
John Stroud	60
Richard Seeking	100
Wm Sexton	50
James Leveaker	710
Chichester Sturdivant	214
Daniell Sturdivant	850
Richard Smith	550
Jno Spaine	118
Matthew Sturdivant	150
Capt Stith	470½
	8272½

T

Major Henry Tooker for the Merchants in London ...	4600
George Tilliman	446
Jno Tilliman	530
Wm Tomlinson	400
Adam Tapley	977
Capt Jno Taylor	1700
Mich. Taburd	150
Majr Tooker	181
Robert Tooker	400
Robert Tester	170
Joseph Tooker	200
Wm Tempel	100
Jno Thornhill	350
Jno Taylor	100
Nath. Tatham Jun	200
Samuel Tatham Sen	100
Samuel Tatham Jun	195
Henry Talley	639
Richard Turberfield	140
Francis Tucker	100
Nath. Tatham Sen	501
Jno Thrower	250
Thomas Thrower	150
James Taylor	306
Sanders Tapley	300
Thomas Tapley	300
James Thweat Sen	715
James Thweat Jun	100
Elizabeth Tucker	212
Thomas Taylor	400
Edward Thrower	150
	14462

V

Jno Vaughan	169
Samuel Vaugham	169
Nath. Vrooin	150
Daniell Vaughan	169
James Vaughan	169
Richard Vaughan	309
Wm Vaughan	309
Thomas Vinson	550
Nicholas Vaughan	169
	2163

W

John Woodlife Sen	644
Wm Wallis	200
Jno Wickett	250
Capt. James Wynn	860
Jno Woodlife Jun	750
Jno Winningham Jun	200
Richard Wallpoole	625
Jno Womack	550
Capt Thomas Wynn	400
Jno Wall	233
Thomas Winningham	100
Elizabeth Woodlife	844
Richard Worthern	1600
Richard Winkles	450
Capt Nicholas Wyatt	700
Antho Wyatt	250
Valentine Wiliamson	250
Hurldy Wick	600
Wm Wilkins	900
Francis Wilkins	150
Robert Winkfield	107
Jarvis Winkfield	100
Henry Wall	275
Jno Wilkins	150
James Williams	1436
George Williams	216
Jno White	150
Edward Winningham	100
Samuel Woodward	600
	13684

Y

Dannell Young	283
John Young	200
	583

A	3217
B	12986
C	7622
D	2156
E	7243
F	2241
G	5435
H	17366½
J	6542
K	1160
L	5114
M	6839
N	419
O	834
P	9203
R	2677
S	8272

T	....	14462
V	....	2163
W	....	13684
Y	....	583

127218½

Deduct the new discovered
Land 10000

Accounted for 117218½

Orphans Land which is refulld
paying Quit Rents for viz:
Mr. John Bannister Orphans
per Stephen Cock 1970
Capt Henry Batesorph and
their Mother Mrs Mary
Bates 1200

Capt Henry Randolph Or-
phans per Capt Giles
Webb 129
Morris Halliham Orphans
ped Robert Rivers 200
Crockson Land formerly
& who it belongs to now I
cannot find 750

4245

117218½ acres at 24 lb tob° per
100 is ....28132 lb tobacco
at 5s per lb is...... 70 6 6
Sallary 10 per cent.... 7 0 10½

63 5 7½

per William Epes Sheriff

Rent Roll of all the Lands held of her Maj^tie In Surry County Anno Domini 1704

A

Allin Arthur Major	6780
Andrews Bartho	375
Avery Jno	150
Atkins Thomas	80
Averett Jno	120
Atkinson Richard	100
Andrews Thomas	190
Andrews Robert	130
Andrews David	225

8150

B

Baker Henry Coll	850
Bruton James	500
Bennett James	200
Bland Sarah	1455
Browne Jno	600
Benbridge George	200
Bighton Richard	590
John Bell	180
Berham Robert	650
Blake Wm	200
Browne Edward	200
Bincham Jno	100
Bennett Richard	200
Baker Sarah	50
Briggs Sarah	300
Baxter Joell	100

Briggs Samuel	300
Blico Christopher	50
Brigs Charles	331
Brigs Henry	100
Bentley	180
Blackbun Wm	150
Blunt Thomas	1355
Bookey, Edward	180
Browne Wm Coll	2510
Browne Wm Capt	398
Bineham James	157
Bullock Mary	100
Barker Jno	1160
Bagley Peter	100
Barker Jery	420
Bunell Hezichiah	150
Bougher Phill	100
Baile Jno	250
Bagley Edward	350

14716

C

Chapman Benjamin	500
Cockin Wm	100
Cocker Jno	900
Crafort Robert	1000
Crafort Carter	100
Chambers Wm	50
Clark Jno	100

Cook Elizabeth	200
Carriell Thomas	100
Clements Jno	387
Clarke Jno	100
Cook Elizabeth	200
Carriell Thomas	100
Clements Jno	387
Clark Robert	400
Checett James	50
Cotten Walter	257
Cotten Thomas	257
Collier Jno	350
Collier Joseph	40
Cock Wm	630
Cock Walter	875
Cooper James	100
Cleaments Francis	600
Collier Thomas	550
Candenscaine Obedience	200
	7746

D

Dicks James	400
Davis Arthur	460
Drew Thomas	800
Drew Edward	600
Delk Roger	790
David Arthur	50
Dean Richard	100
Davis Nath.	157
	3357

E

Edward Wm Mr.	2755
Evans Antho	100
Edward John	470
Ellitt Wm	250
Edmund Howell	300
Ellis James	180
Edmund Wm	100
Ellis Edward	30
Ellis James	170
Ezell Geirge	150
Ellis Jere	50
Evans Abrah.	150
	4705

F

Flake Robert	200
Foster Anne	200

Ford George	100
Flood Walter	820
Flood Thomas	150
Ford Elias	200
Flemin Lawrence	360
Foster Christo	500
Foster Wm	100
Ferieby Benj	170
	2800

G

Gray Wm Capt	1750
Gray Wm Jun	1050
Grines Austis	100
Gwalney Wm	400
Gray Jno	200
Gwalney Wm	225
Goodman Wm	200
Gillham Hinche	658
Griffin John	200
Gully Richard	50
Gray Wm	100
Green Edward	200
Green Richard	260
	5393

H

Harrison Benj Coll	2750
Harrison Nath. Capt	2177
Hunt Wm	4042
Holt Elizabeth	1450
Holt John	150
Holt Thomas Capt	538
Holt Wm	630
Harris Wm	150
Hart Henry	725
Humfort Hugh	150
Hancock John	60
Hart Robert	600
Humphrey Evan	70
Hollyman Mary	290
Harde Thomas	900
Hill Robert	200
Holloman Richard	480
Hargrove Bryan	100
Humfort Wm	50
Hill Lyon	300
Holloman Thomas	450
Heath Adam	200
Harrison Daniell	70
Ham Richard	75
Heart Thomas	750

Hyerd Thomas 50
Hunt Wm 696
Horne Richard 100
Hollingsworth Henry 60
Howell Wm 50

18413

J

Jackman Jos John Mr. 2980
Jones James 1000
Jarrell Thomas 115
Jarrett Charles 615
Judkins Samuell 100
Judkins Wm 100
Jurdan George 620
Jarrett Fardo 630
Johnson Wm 360
Johnson John 350
Jurdan Richard 350

7220

K

Kigan Mary 200
Killingworth Wm 60
Knott Wm 300

560

L

Ludwell Philip Coll 1100
Lancaster Robert 100
Lacey Mary 100
Lang Mary 77
Lane Thomas 200
Lane Thomas Jun 200
Laughter Jno 300
Laneere George 300
Lasley Patrick 520
Lucas Wm 315

3212

M

Matthew Edmund 50
Merriell George 250
Moorland Edward 225
Mason Elizabeth 300
Mallory Francis 147
Merrett Matt. 60
Middleton Thomas 100

Moss Wm 100
Moreing John 695
Mierick Owen 250

2177

N

Newton Wm 225
Newton Robert 250
Newitt Wm 330
Norwood Richard 80
Nicholl George 150
Nichols Robert 230
Noeway Barefoot 150
Norwood George 330

1745

P

Park Mary 100
Pittman Thomas Jun 100
Phillips, John 270
Price John 340
Pettoway Elizabeth 650
Pulystone Jno 1400
Parker Richard 269
Phelps Humphrey 100
Pully Wm 300
Procter Joshua 660
Persons John 830
Phillips Wm 300
Pettfort Jno 200
Pettfort Wm 50

5569

R

Randolph Wm Coll 1655
Ruffice Elizabeth 3001
Reynolds Robert 150
Richardson Joseph 300
Reynolds Elizabeth 150
Reagon Frances 200
Roads Wm 150
Rolling George 106
Road Wm 450
Rose Richard 100
Raehell George 70
Rowling Jno 476
Rohings Wm 596
Roger Wm 450

7854

S

Scat Joseph	295
Sims George	200
Secoms Nicholas	800
Savage Charles	358
Stringfellow Richard	75
Suger Jno	250
Sewurds Anne	300
Sharp Thomas	70
Sewins Thomas	400
Steward John	200
Smith Richard	200
Savage Mary	263
Smith Thomas	750
Swann Wm	1800
Shrowsbury Joseph	260
Shrowsbury Francis	820
Savage Henry	200
Short Wm	400
Scarbro Edw	150
Scagin Jno	100
Simmons Jno	1300
Shrowsbury Thomas	566
Stockly Richard	100
Smith Thomas	380
	10237

T

Thompson Samuell	3104
Tooker Henry Major	700
Taylor Ethelred	538
Thorp Joseph	250
Tyous Thomas	400
Taylor Richard	77
	5069

V

Vincent Mary	187

W

Wright Thomas	100
Williams Charles	100
Wall Joseph	150
Williams Wm	300
Ward Thomas	100
Wall Joseph Jun	150
Warren Allen	300
Warren Thomas	1040
Watkins Richard	1345
Williams Roger	150

Webb Robert	340
Wattkins John	1160
Warren Robert	150
Welch Henry	100
Warrick John	80
Wilkinson Matthew	200
Wiggins Thomas	300
Waple Jno	300
Witherington Nicholas	100
Will Roger	78
White Charles	136
	6679

Y

Young John	300

A	8150
B	14716
C	7746
D	3357
E	4705
F	2800
G	5393
H	18413
J	7220
K	560
L	3212
M	2177
N	1745
P	5569
R	7854
S	10237
T	5069
V	187
W	6679
Y	300
	116089

New Land allowed per order	3841
	112248

Aprill 19th 1705

Errors excepted per
Jos Jno. Jackman Sheriff.

Persons denying payment for Lands held in this County (viz) Capt Tho Holt as belonging to Mr. Tho Benules Orphans 950
Mrs. Mary White 200

1150

Lands held by persons living out of the Country

Capt Jno Taylor	850
Mrs. Sarah Low	500
Mr. Jno Hamlin	100
Capt Thomas Harrison	530
	1150
	——
	3130

Bartho Clement one tract of Land he living in England the quantity unknowne

Jno Davis one Tract Living in Isle of Wight

Geo & River Jorden one Tract & denys to pay Qt Rents for it & no persons living thereon, there is one Bray Living in Warwick has a small tract Land

A List of her Maj^{tys} Q^t Rents For the Isle Wighte County in the Year 1704

Jno Atkins	200	Matt. Jorden	1950
James Atkinson	400	Thomas Newman	360
Wm Exam	1440	George Readich	790
Wm Brown	150	Francis Lee	100
Francis Exam	200	Ph. Pardoe	100
Richard Bennett	70	Jno Parsons	155
James Briggs	100	George Moore	400
Ph. Bratley	200	Jno Mangann	100
Abr. Drawler	200	Robert Mongo	400
Jno Branch	45	Henry Martin	200
Francis Branch	50	Jno Murray	650
Edward Brantley	175	Francis Rayner	80
John Brantley	364	Jno Richardson	150
Edward Boykin	1100	James Sampson	1200
George Barloe	80	Jno Stevenson	150
Jno Geoge	200	Thomas Sherrer	200
Thomas Carter	700	Jno Sherrer	200
Reubin Cooke	250	Wm Thomas	250
Jno Clarke	850	Thomas Tooke	1228
Thomas Cook	300	Thomas Throp	350
Wm Clark	600	Baleaby Terrell	100
Edward Champion	600	Peter Vasser	230
Jno Dowles	150	Jno Williams	600
Peter Deberry	100	George Williamson	2735
Thomas Davis	100	Fra. Williamson	2035
Jno Davis	250	Thomas Wood	50
Peter Hayes	600	James Lupe	45
Christo. Hollyman	400	Elizabeth Reynolds	100
Richard Hardy	700	Jno Sojourner	240
Thomas Holyman	150	Robert Hoge	60
Jno Harris	365	Andrew Woodley	770
Silvester Hill	925	Arthur Allen	1800
Roger Hodge	300	Henry Baker	750
Arthur Jones	900	Rubin Prochter	250
Edward Jones	250	Thomas Howell	100
Richard Jones	250	Nath Whitby	170
Jno Johnson	890	Jane Atkins	600
Roger Ingram	300	Jno Mongo	100

Natt Ridley	200	Thomas Jorden	207
Jno Bell	200	Jno King	300
Wm West	250	Wm Wilkinson	200
Charles Goodrich	80	Thomas Grace	160
Jno Britt	350	Wm West	50
Jno Barnes	200	Jno Penny	300
Henry Goldham	1000	Robert Richards	100
Jno Waltham	450	Thomas Northworthy	600
Charles Edwards	400	Fra Parker	210
Wm Exam	150	Widdo Long	104
Major Lewis Burwell	7000	Trustram Northworthy	1000
Henry Applewaite	1500	George Green	250
Thomas Pitt	300	Jno Druer	100
Jno Pitt	3400	Philip Peerce	500
Mary Benn	675	Wm Best	100
Robert Clark	450	Humphrey Marshall	600
Antho Holliday	860	Thomas Brewer	200
Wm Westrah	450	Wm Smith	2100
Elizabeth Gardner	100	Samuel & Wm Bridger	12900
Jno Gardner	246	Wm Williams	100
Jno Turner	950	Richard Ratcliffe	380
Antho Foulgham	100	Joshua Jordan	150
Anne Williams	150	Daniall Sandbourne	180
Edward Harris	240	Nicholas Houghan	780
Jno Cotton	200	Mary Marshall	200
Thomas Joyner	1400	Joseph Godwin	250
Jno Lawrence	400	Joseph Bridger	580
Thomas Mandue	200	Henry Pitt	700
Wm Mayo	300	James Baron	300
Jno Garcand	100	Arthur Smith	3607
James Bryan	1200	Robert Broch	400
Wm Keate	200	Wm Godwin	400
Jno Browne	100	Hugh Bracey	1000
Francis Sanders	100	Henry Turner	350
John Rogers	200	Thomas Wootten	963
Hodges Councie	420	Richard Reynolds Esq	853
Hardy Councie	900	Richard Reynolds	746
Jno Councie	760	Jno Parnell	400
Thomas Reeves	600	Benj Deall	467
Wm Crumpler	580	Thdo. Joyner	595
Bridgeman Joyner	1100	Jno Jordan	100
Elizabeth Swan	600	Henry Wiggs	506
Thomas Jones	700	Wm Body	1375
Arthur Whitehead	250	Arthur Purcell	750
Thomas Allen	150	Jno Porteus	100
Jerimiah Exam	300	Wm West	690
Nicholas Casey	550	Simon Everett	1100
Jno Giles	1150	Walter Waters	150
Alexander Camoll	200	John Jordan	150
Jno Rutter	300	John Nevill	433
Godfrey Hunt	600	Robert Colman	1500
Wm Trygell	100	Wm Green	150
Benj Jorden	150	Mary Cobb	150

Robert Edwards	150	Henry Pope	557
Anne Jones	100	John Williams	971
Abraham Jones	600	Henry Sanders	700
John Jones	200	Jno Selloway	900
Richard Lewis	100	Jno Bardin	100
Henry Dullard	100	Phill Rayford	650
Thomas Williams	100	Phill Pearse	500
James Mercer	100	Jno Terseley	150
Poole Hall	350	Geo Northworthy	1176
Jno Howell	100	Robert Richards	450
Thomas Lovett	100	Thomas Bevan	100
George Anderson	150	Wm Hunter	150
Daniell Nottiboy	100	Madison Street	150
Henry Wilkinson	350	Thomas Wheatley	400
Jno Watkins	200	Richard Wilkinson	150
Thomas English	100	James Bragg	500
Thomas Page	203	Jno Portous	300
Francis Davis	100	Thomas Harris	350
Richard Braswell	100	Edward Harris	100
Robert Johnson	2450	Nicholas Askew	80
Jno Minshea	300	Ambrose Hadley	100
Wm Pryan	200	Widdo Powell	480
Wm Dawes	400	Thomas Jones	100
Nicholas Tyner	300	Thomas Underwood	100
Isaac Ricks	700	Robert King	300
Robert Scott	300	Thomas Giles	880
Jno Roberts	950	Lewis Smelly	550
Wm Duck	180	Wm Smelly	280
Robert Lawrence	400	Godfrey Hunt	600
Jno Denson	200	Edmund Godwin	400
Robert Smelly	600	Wm Williams	1000
Francis Bridle	250	John Wilson	1200
Roger Fearlton	237	John Bryan	200
Thomas Bullock	100	John Askew	100
Wm. Marfry	600	Samuell Bridger	200
Thomas Powell	100	Roger Nevill	200
Widdo Glyn	390	Coll Godwin	600
Jno Pope	250	Jacob Durden	500
Thomas Gayle	200		
Wm Powell	200		138533
Richard Hutchins	300	Wm Bridger.	
Henry Boseman	100		

A Compleat List of the Rent Roll of the Land in Nansemond County In Anno 1704

John Murdaugh	300	Robert Baker	50
Jno Duke	113	Isaac Sketto	100
Thomas Duke Jun	930	Edward Sketto	200
Edward Roberts	250	Antho Gumms	50
Paul Pender	240	Francis Sketto	100
Thomas Duke	400	Wm Parker	100
James Fowler	440	Francis Parker	170

Thomas Parker	300	John Harris	600
Jno Small	100	Francis Copeland	513
Moses Hall	95	Elizabeth Price	150
Edward Beamond	550	Wm Hill	150
Richard Parker	514	Thomas Spivey	200
Capt James Jessey	550	Jno Campbell	400
Wm Sanders	200	Jno Morley	100
Jno Sanders	165	Jos Rogers	15
Thomas Mansfield	60	Jno Cole	814
Wm Woodley	350	Thomas Harrald	100
Andrew Bourne	200	Christopher Gawin Jun	20
Gilbert Owen	120	Daniell Horton	200
Wm Sanders Jun	165	Wm Bruin	300
Capt John Speir	500	Peter Eason	400
Capt James Reddick	943	Anne Pugh	2300
James Griffin	500	Benj Blanchard	130
Nicholas Stallings	965	Thomas Norfleet	500
John Stallings	250	John Odum	50
Richard Stallings	165	Thomas Gough	150
Elias Stallings Jun	250	Hugh Gough	150
Joseph Baker	740	Epapap Boyne	100
Wm Jones	500	Henry Baker	375
Robert Roundtree	245	Christopher Gwin	1010
John Roundtree	475	James Speirs	200
George Spivey	200	Epaphra Benton	250
James Spivey	600	Wm Eason	180
James Knight	300	Andrew Brown	25
Jno Gorden	330	Wm Horne	100
Edward Arnold	80	Robert Reddick	200
James Mulleny	500	Henry Hackley	210
Thomas Docton	200	Thomas Roberts	30
Wm Britt	400	Abr. Reddick	400
Nath Newby	850	Jno Parker	240
Elias Stalling	470	Richard Barefield	900
Robert Lassiter	850	John Benton	660
Patrick Wood	200	Jno Pipkin	100
Wm Thompson	133	Jos Brady	250
Jonathan Kitterell	300	Christopher Dudley	200
Adam Rabey	586	Thomas Norris	100
Jno Powell	758	Thomas Wiggins	100
John Reddick	300	Patrick Lawley	50
Henry Copeland	150	Robert Warren	100
Thomas Davis	250	Richard Odium	50
Jno Smith	100	Thomas Davis	340
Thomas Harrald	652	Thomas Barefield	100
Richard Baker	40	John Eason	150
Samuell Smith	230	Jerimiah Arlin	250
Wm Hood	200	Jno Perry	870
Thomas Roundtree	350	Jno Drury	87
Henry Hill	175	Joseph Booth	987
Jno Larkhum	500	Cresham Cofield	350
Wm Vann	100	Richard Sumner	600
Joseph Cooper	267	Edward Norfleet	200

Jno Norfleet	600	John Oxley	100
Edward Moore	250	Benj. Rogers	600
Thomas Moore	200	Robert Rogers	300
James Lawry	40	Henry Jerregan	200
James Daughtie	400	Jno Hansell	500
John Wallis	150	Henry Jenkins	400
Richard Sanders Jun	100	Capt William Hunter	800
Wm Byrd	300	Jno Moore	200
James Howard	700	Richard Moore	250
John Brinkley	430	Edward Homes	300
Robert Horning	80	Fra. Cambridge	100
Wm Speirs	200	Wm Ward	200
Sarah Exum	150	Jno Rice	140
Jno Larrence	175	Wm Battaile	800
Nicholas Perry	200	Wm Spite	500
Sampson Merridith	400	Abr. Oadham	20
Coll Thomas Milner	1484	Jacob Oadam	20
Joseph Merridith	250	Jno Lee	100
Thomas Kinder	160	Wm Macklenny	200
Henry King	300	Robert Coleman	1400
Joseph Hine	150	Jno Bryan	200
Wm King	140	Wm Daughtree	100
Julian King	700	Jno Copeland	600
Mich. King	80	Jno Butler	200
Capt Tho Godwin Jun	697	James Butler	75
Henry Lawrence	200	Thomas Roads	75
Jno King	1000	Wm Collins	1220
Richard Hyne	200	Jno Hedgpath	700
Capt Francis Milner	479	Jno Holland	700
Benj Nevill	475	Robert Carr	200
Elizabeth Marler	80	Wm Waters	600
Wm Keene	200	Robert Lawrence	400
Jno Symmons	678	Wm Bryon	350
Hen: Johnson	150	Lewis Bryon	400
Jno Darden	500	James Lawrence	100
Wm Everett	150	Wm Gatlin	100
Wm Pope	890	Joseph Gutchins	250
Joseph Worrell	270	George Lawrence	400
Thomas Jemegan Jun	135	Lewis Daughtree	100
Richard Lawerence	200	Thomas Rogers	50
Jonathan Robinson	400	Jno Rogers	200
Robert Yates	150	Henry Core	50
Thomas Odium	20	Edward Cobb	100
John Barefield	300	Richard Taylor	300
John Raules	600	Robert Brewer	200
Thomas Boyt	400	Wm Osburne	200
Thomas Vaughan	200	Thomas Biswell	400
Jno Parker	300	Jno Gatlin	200
Richard Green	200	Richard Folk	100
Elizabeth Ballard	300	Thomas Parker	100
Samuell Watson	200	Peter Parker	140
Francis Spight	400	Wm Parker	140
Joseph Ballard	200	Richard Hine Jun	200

Stephen Archer	200
Charles Roades	800
Henry Roades	100
James Collings	300
Henry Holland	400
Wm Kerle	325
Joseph Holland	100
Jno Thomas Jun	100
Jno Thomas	275
Thomas Mason	350
Edward Mason	150
Jno Sanders	150
Mich Brinkley	200
James Moore	400
Henry Blumpton	1500
Jno Symmons	100
Jeremiah Edmunds	70
John Gay	200
Philip Aylsberry	100
James Copeland	390
Jno Brothers	460
Richard Creech	200
Richard Bond	90
Thomas Handcock	30
James Knott	1050
Wm Edwards	150
Robert Elkes	175
Edward Price	140
Jane Belson	100
Wm Staples	210
Robert Mountgomery	150
John Moore	100
Capt Edmund Godwin	800
Thomas Wakefield	150
Godfrey Hunt	360
Henery Wilkinson	250
Nicholas Dixon	200
George Keeley	650
Richard Taylor	300
Anne Coefield	300
Joseph Hollyday	1000
Mr. Jno Braisseur	400
Thomas Best	160
Alexander Campbell	500
Capt Charles Drury	570
Thomas Drury	75
Luke Shea	650
John Babb	500
Abraham Edwards	400
Richard Sanders	500
Antho Wallis	80
Daniell Sullivan	100
Joseph Ellis	290

Nicholas Hunter	190
Richard Webb	200
John Hare	190
Christopher Norfleet	400
Jno Heslop	148
Francis Benton	200
Capt Wm Sumner	275
Elizabeth Syrte	100
Anne Hare	600
Jno Porter	450
Edward Welsh	100
Jno Winbourne	400
Paul Pender	200
Mich Cowling	100
John Cowling	100
Rowland Gwyn	75
Andrew Ross	150
Jno Ballard	400
Benjamin Montgomery	910
Thomas Corbell	200
Jno Yates	400
Jno White	150
George White	50
Jno Bond	150
Wm Hay	100
Henry Bowes	600
Wm Sevill	85
Jno Hambleton	200
Robert Jordan	850
James Howard	25
Ruth Coefield	110
Jno Chilcott	100
Jno Rutter	80
Thomas Rutter	75
Wm. Rutter	75
Capt Barnaby Kerney	460
Thomas Cutchins	150
Robert Lawrence	130
Samuell Cahoone	240
Jno Iles	220
Thomas Sawyer	180
Wm Outland	400
Coll George Northworthy	650
Coll Thomas Godwin	810
Caleb Taylor	200
Thomas Carnell	320
Richard Bradley	250
Jno Corbin	300
Wm Sykes	150
Major Thomas Jorden	700
Richard Lovegrove	150
Thomas Davis	144
Samuell Farmer	160

Henry Bradley	500	James Murphice	160
Jno Clarke	25	Robert Peale	275
Margarett Jorden	200	John Peters	368
Wm Elkes	100	James Peters	340
Humphrey Mires	150	John Wakefield	50
James Ward	100	Richard Wynn	890
Widdow Hudnell	45	James Lockhart	800
Wm Grandberry	300	John Keeton	2000
Israell Shepherd	200		
Benj. Small	100		117024
Anne Crandberry	75	Jno Murrow	200
Charles Roberts	50		
Richard Sclator	300		117224
Robert Murrow	320	Added to make up equll	13850
Elizabeth Peters	334	the last year list	
Thomas Jones	200	which may be supposed	131074
Elizabeth Butler	200	to be held by persons	
Coll Samuell Bridger	500	that have not made both	
Jno Lawrence	100		
Thomas Jarregan	165	Persons living out of the County	
Thomas Jarregan Jun	600	and other that will not pay or give	
Wm Drury	80	account. Viz:	
Wm Butler	120	Capt Thomas Lovett	
Henry Jenkins	860	Capt Jno Wright	
Edward Bathurst	250	Fra Parker Jun	
Thomas Houffler	200	Tho Martin	
Edward Streater	200	Jno Wright	
Wm Duffield	50	Wm Lapiter	
Charles Thomas Jun	50	Jno Lapiter	
Jno Blessington	150	Capt Luke Haffield	
Ursula Goodwin	100	Mrs Elizabeth Swann	
Thomas Acwell	440		
Wm Peale	180	Errors excepted per me	
John Lambkin	50	Henry Jenkins	

An Alphabetical List of the Quit Rents of Norfolk County 1704

Ashley Dennis	150	Bayley Walter	290
Avis Widdow	50	Bruce Jno	300
Adam Wm	100	Bishop Wm	100
Alexander John	300	Bull Henry	1500
Barington Wm	100	Bucken Wm	410
Bartee Robert	150	Babington Thomas	150
Bull Robert Sen	1050	Babington Jno	150
Blanch Wm	100	Babington Rich	50
Bond Wm	200	Burges George	200
Brown Widdow	270	Burges Robert	535
Bruce Abraham	1010	Butt Richard	1840
Brown Wm	100	Brown Edward	300
Bowers Jno	166	Bigg Thomas	100
Bolton Wm	212	Balingtine Alexander	300
Byron Roger	200	Balengtine George	510

Bull Thomas	2200
Bramble Henry	100
Blake Arthur	200
Bolton Richard	700
Branton John	330
Bacheldon Joseph	300
Bush Samuell Major	1628
Balingtine Wm	60
Bowles Henry	330
Cartwright Peter	1050
Cooper Wm	150
Cooper Jno	150
Cramore George	100
Carling Walton	50
Carling Joseph	200
Curch Richard	1050
Churey Widdow	600
Cuthrell Going	470
Crekmore Edward	800
Cartwright Widdow	800
Corprew Jno	650
Corprew Thomas	650
Crekmore Jno	750
Caswell Widdow	350
Colley Jno	100
Cottell Thomas	200
Conden Thomas	390
Conner Lewis	2200
Carney Jno	100
Carney Richard	100
Collins Wm	100
Crekmore Edmund	690
Charleton Jno	50
Cutrell Thomas	150
Chapman Richard	50
Churey Thomas	100
Churey Jno	150
Dixon Jno	300
Davis Wm Sen	250
Davis Wm	158
Dresdall Robert	318
Davis Thomas	332
Desnall Wm	100
Davis Edward	300
Dalley Henry	1524
Dalley Wm	156
Davis Thomas	340
Denby Edward	100
Daniell Hugh	100
Etherdge Thomas Cooper	75
Etherdge Thomas B R	50
Etherdge Thomas Sen	34
Etherdge Thomas Jun	33

Etherdge Edward	66
Etherdge Wm	250
Etherdge Wm Jun	80
Etherdge Marmaduke	525
Edmonds John	50
Ellis Wm	200
Etherdge Edward Cooper	200
Estwood Thomas	170
Estwood John	75
Etherdge Edward Sen	33
Edwards John	250
Etherdge Charles	75
Evans Abrigall	100
Furgison Thomas	100
Freeman Jno	190
Foreman Alexander	750
Foster Henry	1000
Ferbey Jno	500
Fulsher Jno	1396
Godfry Waren	350
Godfry John	1470
Godfry Matthew	450
Grefen Jno	200
Garen Daniell	50
Guy John	110
Gwin Wm	350
Gilhgun Ferdinando	182
Gilhgan John	200
Gresnes James	150
Gaines John	50
Guy James	100
Herbert Thomas	150
Hayes Wm	200
Harris John	110
Holyday Jno	440
Hodges Joseph	50
Hoges Thomas	407
Hoges John	520
Hollowell Jno Sen	524
Hollygood Thomas	100
Hollowell Jno	200
Holsted Henry	633
Hollowell Joseph	1280
Holsted John	350
Hues Edward	1304
Hullett Jno	300
Hodges Roger	109
Hodges Thomas	50
Hodges Richard	375
Harvey Richard	265
Handberry	300
Hollowell Elener	1550
Herbert Jno	400

Hargrave Benjamin	250	Nash Thomas	50
Hartwell Richard	150	Nicholson Henry	320
Henland Jno	800	Nash Richard	100
Ivey George	496	Nicholson Wm	300
Jackson Symon	720	Norcote Thomas	273
Ives Timothy	400	Outlaw Edward	208
Ives Timothy Jun	100	Owens Wm	650
Ives John	434	Odyam Wm	200
Johnston John	275	Pearce Wm	100
Johnston Mercey	275	Peters Widdow	698
Joles Thomas	200	Portlock	360
Joyce Jno	200	Porter Samuell	100
Jolef Jno Jun	300	Prescot Moses	1200
Jenings Henry	100	Philpot Richard	200
Jolef Jno Sen	840	Powell Richard	100
Kaine Richard	50	Powell Lemuell	246
Langley Wm	1487	Powell Wm	624
Langley Thomas	878	Perkins Wm	50
Loveney James	100	Patison Robert	350
Luelling Edward	315	Roberts Jos	100
Luelling Richard	200	Robert Samuell	800
Lovell Widdow	740	Rose Robert	385
Low Henry	191	Rose Jno	60
Lane Robert	460	Randall Giles	150
Ludgall Matthew	250	Richardson Thomas	379
Levima John	510	Spring Robert	98
Lenton Wm	150	Spivey Matt	600
Mercer Thomas	600	Smith John	127
Maning Thomas	97	Scoll Thomas	400
Maning Nicholas	260	Smith Richard	600
Mones Joseph	73	Smith John	200
Matthias Matthew	100	Silvester Richard	1280
Miller Wm	1090	John Smith Sen	1200
Miller Jno	200	Sickes Walter Sen	550
Miller Widdow	100	Sickes John	200
Murden Widdow	2000	Sugg George	408
Miller Thomas	1050	Sugg Wm	200
Maund Wm	200	Sayer Francis	600
Maning Jno Sen	300	Smith Humphrey	100
Miller Joseph	882	Standbro Jno	40
Mocey Dennis Sen & Jun	160	Standley Richard	200
Mohan James	100	Sharples Henry	100
Murfrey Alexander	800	Sugg Joseph	300
Maning Jno Jun	100	Symons Thomas	166
Moseley Widdow	300	Symon James	200
Miller Widdow Sen	200	Sparrow Wm	350
Mason Thomas	125	Tuker Wm	100
Masom Lemuell	400	Thornton Francis	200
Mason Thomas	653	Thurston Matthew	100
Mason George	300	Theobald James	140
Mockey Adam	400	Thellaball Widdow	600
Newton George	1119	Tuker Richard	100
Nicholson Jno	160	Tuker Thomas	280

Taylor Jno	100	Whedon Jno Jun	320
Taylor Richard	75	White Patrick	500
Tully Jno	165	Willis John	470
Tarte Elezar Sen	300	Weldey Dorothy	25
Taylor Andrew	222	Ward Jno	320
Tuker Jno	400	Wakfield Thomas	40
Tart Alice	300	Wilden Nath	100
Tarte Elezar Jun	595	Wooding Thomas	170
Taylor Wm	265	Wood Edward	100
Trigoney Henry	200	Watford Joseph	97
Velle Moriss	335	Wate John	400
Walice Thomas	150	Wright Wm	574
Weston Edward	100	Wright James	216
Willoughby Thomas Coll	3200	Wadborn Mich	500
Weshart John	150	Williams Jane	400
Woodly Robert	350	Webb Mary	100
Williams John	125	Worminton John	200
Wilder Mich	200	Wilden Francis	100
Watkins Thomas	190	Widdick Henry	343
Williamson Jno	750		
Whedon Jno Jun	100		113684
Willoughby Thomas Capt	660	New discovered Land	1615
Whedon Wm	200		
West John	500		112069
Watson Robert	80		

An Account of the Land belonging to such persons out of the County and also others out of the County.

Wallis Richard	250	Coll Cary	
Wallis Jno	135	Tully Robinson	
Wallis Wm	450	James Daves	
Whithurst Richard	150	Robert Berrey	95
Whithurst Wm	150	Jno Bennett	33
Wilkins Wm	200	Coll Nasareth	400
Williams John	200	Cornelius Tullery	150
Whedbey George	200		
Worden James	400		James Wilson
Wilson James Jun	200		Sherriff
Wilson Lemuell	300		
Wilson James Coll	2800		
Woodward Henry	280		

Princess Anne County Rent Roll 1704

John Carraway	180	Thomas Jolley	150
Thomas More	100	Mich Ventres	450
Henry Chapman	250	Capt Blomer Bray	270
George Poole	1085	James Mecoy	200
James Whithurst	600	Francis Bond	264
Thomas Morris	63	Edward Wood	50
Thomas Joy	600	Jno Morrah	200
Thomas Scott	100	Alexander Morrah	200
George Smith	250	Ruth Woodhouse	450
Thomas Hife	200	Horatia Woodhouse	525
Richard Smith	200	Joseph White	330
Thomas Hattersley	90	Jon Basnett	250

Owen Wilbe	100	Wm. Moore	414
Mr. Wm. Corneck	1974	Mr. Henry Woodhouse	3000
Jno Oakham	390	Tully Emperor	300
David Scott	600	Jno. Godfrey	170
Jno Keeling	2000	Wm Dyer	700
Adam Keeling	500	Edward Cooper	200
Humphrey Smith	50	Wm Ship	300
Jno Halise	130	Jno Buck	250
Capt Wm Crawford	2650	Peter Mallbourn	280
Richard Williamson	450	Benjamin Roberts	100
Edward Tranter	180	Capt Jno Gibbs	3100
Jno. Sherland	800	Sarah Sanford	1200
Robert Rany	70	Henry Harrison	300
Edward Old	450	James Lemon	1500
Coll Lemuell Mason	650	Wm Wallsworth	100
Mr. Francis Emperor	400	Wm Capps	1050
James Kemp	681	Jacob Taylor	80
Bartho: Williamson	400	Stephen Pace	50
Symon Hancock Jun	200	Adam Hayes	1360
George Batten	150	Wm Chichester	400
Matth: Brinson	250	Robert Dearemore	514
Mr. Edward Mosseley Sen..	1000	Capt. Francis Morse	1300
Wm Martin	200	Patrick Anguish	150
James Joslin	100	Thomas Brock	400
Alexander Lilburn	500	Wm Brock	100
James William	100	Jno Sullivant	200
Mr. Henry Spratt	1736	Francis Sheene	300
Symon Hancock Sen	300	Jno Acksted	400
Thomas Walk	298	Charles Hendley	100
Jno Kemp	340	Duke Hill	70
Randolph Lovett	100	Job Brooks	150
Edward Davis	200	Jno Brooks	100
Jno Sammons	150	Thomas Turton	110
Elizabeth Edwards	50	Peter Crosby	250
Mr. Benj. Burroughs	800	Jno Pisburn	314
Jno Muncreef	140	James Sherwood	200
Matt: Pallett	600	Edward Cannon	550
Mrs. Thurston	290	Richard Capps	100
Lancaster Lovett	1850	John Doley	640
Robert Cartwright	260	Matthew Mathias	80
Jno. Cartwright	100	Mr. James Peters	889
Nath: Macklakan	100	Jno Owens	190
Adam Thorowgood	700	Josvas Morris	900
Henry Walstone	800	Thomas Mason	140
Edward Land	400	Wm. Wishart	200
Thomas Hall	400	Jno Russell	300
Wm. Catherill	150	Stephen Sall	250
Doctor Browne	600	Timothy Dennis	100
John Richardson	1000	George Walker	425
Robert Richmond	1000	Wm. Ashby	100
Thomas Benson	225	Charles Griffin	216
Lewis Pervine	800	Symon Franklin	100
Edward Attwood	400	Alice Thrower	125

James Wishart	225	Giles Collier	500
Richard Draught	500	Jacob Johnson	1700
Doctor Wm. Hunter	80	Alexander Willis	150
Mr. Jon Sanders	203	Richard Bonny	2000
Wm Grinto	650	Mr. James Doage	784
Henry Fithgerreld	200	Antho: Barnes	200
Coll. H. Lawson	3100	Jno. Macklalin	120
Capt. John Thorowgood	1000	Thomas Etherington	108
Robert Thorowgood	940	Jno James	328
Henry Southern	640	Wm. Woodhouse	300
John Wharton	850	John Mayho	160
Joseph Doller	150	Joseph Perry	35
Jno Briggs	600	Thomas Perry	650
Francis Jones	100	Mr. Argoll Thorowgood	1000
Thomas Lurrey	100	Capt. Wm. Moseley	600
Thomas Walker	820	Jno Moseley	325
Steph Swaine	450	Wm. Smith	180
Edward Mulsin	100	Wm. Symmons	400
George Bullock	300	Adam Forguson	120
Jno Leggett	400	Banj. Commins	200
Mark Tully	300	Jno Elkes	500
Wm. Walstone	400	Patrick White	1250
Mark Powell	550	Richard Jones	200
Elizabeth Nicholls	500	Evan Jones	600
Hugh Hoskins	50	Mich. Jones	200
Wm. Burrough	50	Richard Wicker	300
Wm. Warren	100	Henry Snaile	250
Capt. Hugh Campble	800	Mr. Samiel Bush	550
George Worrinton	400	Mr. Tully Robinson	500
James Tully	400	Jno Briberry	50
Wm. Lovett	1300	Wm. Moseley	50
Wm. Grant	150	Capt. Christ. Merchant	400
Thomas More	100	Richard Cox	50
Richard Whithurst	350	Matt. Godfrey	150
Capt. Thomas Cocke	800	Thomas Tully	600
John Comins	175	Hector Denby	600
Thomas Griffin	200	Thomas Keeling	700
Thomas Spratt	600	Wm. More	100
Jno Russell	150	Thomas Cason	550
James Heath	550	Sarah Jackson	600
David Duncon	100	Jacob More	200
Daniell Lane	350		
George Fowler	600		98728
Jno Booth	350	Henry Spratt	

A True and Perfect Rent Roll of the Lands In Elizabeth City County
for the Year 1704

Coll. Wm. Wilson	1024	Coll. Dudley Diggs	216
Mr. Wm. Smelt	150	Samuell Pearce	100
Mr. Pasquo Curle	300	Mary Jenings	250
Mr. Nicho. Curle	950	Mark Powell	184

Wm. Davis	42	Richard Roatton	50
Jno Skinner	50	Thomas Poole	1200
Thomas Baines	50	John Wheat Land	66
Wm. Latham	90	George Bell	80
Thomas Tucker	60	Widdow Ballis	350
Matthew Smell	100	George Walker	325
Charles Cooley	200	Mr. Robert Beverley	777
Jno Chandler	150	Jno House	157
Wm. Umpleet	25	Jno Bushell Jun	150
Charles Tucker	240	Roger Masinbred	50
Thomas Allin	227	John Shepherd	210
Wm. Williams per the School	600	Wm. Minsor	150
		Edward Lattimore	190
Wm Williams per himself..	260	James Baker	225
Mrs. Bridgett Jenkins	100	Thomas Tucker	60
Christopher Davis	25	Jno. Cotton	50
Wm. Spicer	60	Mark Johnson	400
Thomas Hawkins	270	Major Wm. Armistead	460
Jno Bowles	260	Coll. Antho. Armistead	2140
Jno Theodam	100	Daniell Preeday	50
Bartho. Wetherby	300	Matthew Watts	454
Jos: White	200	Bryan Penny	50
Capt. Henry Royall	750	Giles Dupra	150
Robert Bright Sen.	100	Jno Bayley	415
Thomas Naylor	100	Mary Simmons	200
George Cooper Sen	100	Jno Parish	50
Thomas Needham	100	Antho. Griggs	50
Cha: Cooper	100	Abr: Parish	100
Wm. Dunn	100	Mark Parish	200
Charles Jenings	225	Benj. Smith	650
Samuell Davill	100	Thomas Nobling per Archer	212
Paltey Davill	100	Wm. Mallory	200
Francis Rogers	200	Widdow Croashell	100
Thomas Babb per Selden ..	300	Charles Powers	400
Richard Horsley	90	Robert Charwill per Jno Young	440
Sarah Nagleer	230		
Henry Dunn	50	Samuell Fingall	333
Peter Pearce	50	Francis Savoy	50
Moses Davis	150	Mr. Edward Mihills	600
Mich: Breltuen	100	Jane Nichols	50
Henry Robinson	200	John Francis	25
Christo. Copeland	340	James Priest	50
Thomas Faulkner	50	Simon Hollier	200
Mr. James Wallace	1300	Mr. Thomas Gebb	630
Mr. Berthram Servant	418	Mr. Richard Booker	526
Robert Taylor	50	Mr. Wm. Lowry	526
Joseph Harris	50	Mr. Merry or Mrs Dunn...	500
Wm. Robinson	50	Wm. Haslyitt	100
Wm. Boswell	220	Capt. Augustine More	285
Wm. Winter	70	John More	250
John Lowry per Selden ...	110	John Passones	780
Edward Roe	100	Rebeckha Morgan	50
Henry James	100	Thomas Roberts	250

Mr. John Turner	50
Henry Lais	50
Capt. Henry Jenkins	300

Mr. Francis Ballard per Selden	460
	29560

Henry Royall Sgeriff

A True & Perfect Rent Roll of all the Lands that is held in Warwick County 1704

Major Wm. Cary	300	Francis Jones	150
Mr. Nedler Plantacon	80	Matthew Jones	750
Rober Hubbert	101	Jno. Read	875
Wm. Harwood	625	Mr. Brewer Land	1350
Richard Glanvills Orphans.	165	Mr. Henry Cary	670
Wm. Hubbert	200	Langhorne Orphans	602
Henry Gibbs	315	Coll. Coles Orphans	1350
Wm. Hewitt	150	Peter Jones	150
James Hill	135	Samuell Crew Orphans	150
John Golden	50	Samuell Symons	173
Thomas Harwood	575	Mrs. Elizabeth Whitaker..	600
Jno. Harwood	704	Capt. Miles Cary	600
Capt. Thomas Charles	100	John Cannon	75
Hump: Harwood	400	John Linton	75
Matthew Wood	300	Richard Gough	60
Edward Joyner	60	Coll. Miles Cary	1960
Coll. Dudley Diggs	4626	Mr. Jno. Mallnote	61
Elizabeth Lucas	800	Rowlands Williams	170
John Hillard	74	Robert Chapell	150
Edward Loftes	60	James Chapell	100
Wm. Rowles Orphans	150	Edward Powers	200
Samuell Hatton	225	James White	40
Isaac Goodwin	225	Peter Sawers Orphans	95
George Robinson	70	Wm. Cotton	143
Seymon Powell	250	James Cotton	70
John Dawson	300	John Croley	100
Wades Orphans	100	Stephen Burgess	128
Henry Dawson	200	Widdow Yorgen	60
John Bowger	100	George Jackson	193
Joseph Cooper	200	Sarah Ranshaw	125
Robert Roberts	60	Richard Wootton	243
George Burton	330	Samuell Hoggard	120
Capt. Mills Wells	425	James Floyd	100
Roger Daniell Orphans	196	Fr: Rice Orphans	200
Jno Hansell	100	Mr. Math Hoggard	270
Emanuell Wells	325	Widdow Chapell	321
Elizabeth Wells Widdow ..	155	Thomas Ascow	50
Widdow Lewelling	100	Garrett Ridley	300
Wm. Wells	615	Samuell Ranshaw	238
Elias Wells	50	Charle Stuckey	86
Widdow Pierce	155	Jos Naylor	100
Thomas Haynes	850	Jos Russell	150
John Scarsbrook	850	Charles Allen	295

Wm. Newberrey	100	Wm Cook	29
John Turmer	100	Jno Tignall	392
Wm. Smith	150	Thomas Mountfort	890
Elizabeth Holt	150	Joseph Mountfort	558
James Browne	150	James Priest	50
Henry Royall	246	Abr· Cawley	80
Edward Rice	375	Wm. Jones	70
Thomas Blackistone	75	Edward Davis	200
Mark Noble	215	The County Land	150
James Reynolds	75	Denbigh per Gleab	130
John Holmes	200	Mulberry Island Gleab	50
Samuell Duberry	200	Thomas Hansford	75
Edward Powers	200	Mr. Rascows Orphans	1195
Jno Hatton Orphans	93		
Wm. Lowland	25		37685
Thomas Morey	363	Thomas Hansford never	
Wm. Bracey	150	before paid	75
Cope Doyley	500		
Nath Edwards	100		37610
Samuel Groves	490	Persons out of the County	
Croncher Orphans	50	Jno Trevillian 248	
Henry Whitaker	60	Holman Orphans .. 200	448
Woodman Land	200	Robert Hubberd Sherriff	

A Rent Roll of all the Land In York County 1704

Wm. Jackson	200	David Stoner	50
Matt: Pierce	100	Ralph Hubberd	50
Jno. Latin	150	Wm. Harrison	50
Robert Cobbs	100	Jno. Wyth	100
Francis Sharp	100	Thomas Hill	930
Geo: Baskewyle	350	Thomas Vines	200
Richard Gilford	100	Morgan Baptist	100
Jos: Frith	50	Phil. Deadman	75
Wm. Jones	70	Bazill Wagstaff	127
Nath: Crawley	384	Wm. Allen	117
Thomas Crips	750	Robert Read	750
Wm. Davis	200	Jos: Mountford	307
Lewis Barnoe	80	Roger Boult	100
Arthur Lun	50	Edward Fuller	70
Jno. Bates	669	Thomas Jefferson	100
Jno Serginton	150	Henry Duke	25
Wm. Taylor	100	Jno. Hansford	100
Richard Page	150	Robert Peters	160
Wm. Jorden	580	Jno. Morland	100
Jno. Lynes	150	Wm. Lee	350
Alex: Banyman	50	Richard Burt	200
Wm. Cobbs	50	John Eaton	170
Mary Whaley	550	Rob: Starke	250
Henry Tyler	180	Robt. Harrison	200
Richard Kendall	150	Jno. Morris	125
Wm. Hansford	300	James Bates	117
Nicholas Sebrell	150	Elizabeth Jones	94

Edward Young	100
Robert Green	200
Tho: Fear	100
Edward Thomas	223
John Loyall	100
Stephen Pond	200
Wm. Wise	850
Cornelius Shoohorn	100
Joseph White	750
Daniell Park Esq.	2750
Thomas Fear Jun	130
Orlando Jones	450
Ambrose Cobbs	163
Henry Dyer	50
Wm. Davis	100
Wm. Buckner	302½
Tho. Barber	600
Elizb. Tindall	60
Dudley Diggs	1350
Wm. Hewitt	150
Mary Collier	433
Charles Collier	684
Tho. Hansford	75
Geo. Browne	150
Wm. Gibbs	50
Wm. Pekithman	650
Jno. Smith	150
Baldwin Matthews	1300
Jno Daniell	200
Seamor Powell	130
Jno. Lewis Esq.	300
Wm. Timson	1000
Jno. Page	490
Jos. Benjafield	80
Tho. Stear	60
Stephen Fouace	565
Edmund Jenings Esq.	850
Elizb. Archer	370
Wm. Coman	50
Elizb. Hansford	100
Samll: Hill	25
Jno. Anderson	50
Tho Buck	250
Lewis Burwell	2100
Robt. Crawley	400
Robt. Hyde	200
Robt. Harrison	250
Jeffry Overstreet	50
Tho. Overstreet	50
John Myhill	52
Mary Roberts	25
Benja. Stogsdall	50
Tho Wade	375
Jos: Walker	615
Jno. Sanders	100
Mongo Inglis	400
Tho Holyday	100
Jno. Williams	100
Antho: Sebrell	50
Robt. Jones	100
James Cansebee	200
Richd. Booker	200
James Morris	100
Henry Adkinson	82
Robt. Jackson	150
Anthoney Robinson	183
Hannah Lamb	50
James Calthorp	900
Tho Boulmer	265
Peter Pasque	12
Jno. Chapman	70
Jno. Pond	112
Sarah Tomkins	250
Robt. Kirby	200
Tho. Kirby	270
Edward Curtis	200
Jno. Forgison	200
Wm. Row	902
Jno. Hunt	550
Wm. Taverner	100
Armiger Wade	424
Richard Dixon	450
Edmund Jennings Esq.	1650
Jno. Persons	300
Tho. Nutting	375
Peter Manson	150
Richard Slaughter	275
James Persons	350
Tho. Roberts	450
Jno. Toomer	335
Daniell Taylor	225
Robert Hayes	220
Henry Andros	274
Jno. Wells	750
Robert Curtis	250
Tho. Cheesman Sen.	1800
Jos Potter	25
Hen: Heywood	1300
David Holyday	600
John Northern	130
Jno. Doswell	367
Isaac Powell	100
Symon Staice	200
Jno. Drewet	200
Robert Topladie	100
Jno. Potter	93

Lewis Vernum	150	Wm. Gurrow	150
James Slaughter	250	Peter Goodwin	400
Tho: Burnham	50	Robt. Snead	50
Jno: Doswell Jun	100	Edward Cawley	150
Robert Shields	400	Wm. Gorden	150
Wm. Wilson	50	Jno. Hilsman	75
Owen Davis	247	Jno. Wright	100
Tho. Walker	100	Jno. Gibons	50
Richard Nixon	150	Elizb. Goodwin	1200
Henry Clerk	100	Samuell Cooper	150
Elias Love	25	Jno. Fips	150
Wm. Howard	100	Tho Wooton	150
Jno. Sanderver	100	Edward Moss	759
Jno. Cox	50	Rebecka Watkins	100
Tho. Gibbins	100	Wm. Whitaker	1800
Tho. Hind	100	Hampton Parish	200
Tho Cheesman Jun	600	Bruton parish Gleabe	300
Wm. Browne	200	Robt. Ivy he living in	
Jno. Rogers	650	James City County &	
Jno. Moss	150	no Tennt. on ye Land	100
Jno. Lawson	100		
Nicho. Philips	150		61132½
Wm. Sheldon	750	Added to make up the	
Jno. Wayman	100	old Roll	168
Tho Edmonds	150		
Lawrence Smith	1700		61300½
James Paulmer	150	Wm. Barbar S Y C	

The Rent Roll of the Land in James City County 1704

A

Adkinson Tho	50	Bowers Wm.	50
Adkinson Henry	250	Broadnax Wm.	1683
Armestone Joshua	50	Bayley Wm	100
Adams Anne	150	Black Geo	200
Argo James	200	Bush Jno	800
Abbitt Francis	100	Ballard Tho	100
Apercon Wm.	80	Bray David	5758
Allen Richard	540	Burton Ralph	200
		Blankitt Henry	100
	1420	Brand Richard	125
		Breeding Jno.	100
B		Bruer Thackfield	350
Baker Jno.	100	Blackley Wm	142
Bentley Jno	125	Barratt Wm.	305
Bess Edmund	75	Barron Tho	100
Burwell Lewis	1350	Blankes Henry	650
Beckitt Tho	60	Bagby Tho	180
Bray James	3500	Barnes Francis	200
Bryon Jno.	100	Brackitt Tho	150
Bingley James	100	Browne Wm.	1070
Benham Jno.	50	Buxton Samuell	300
Brown James	250	Bimms Christo.	300
		Ballard Wm.	300
			300

Boman	90
Benge Robert	60
	19123

C

Center Jno	100
Clerk Wm.	1100
Charles Phill	200
Capell Tho.	200
Cearley Wm.	450
Clerk Robert	300
Clerk Sarah	200
Cole Richard	80
Cooper Tho	60
Cook Richard	75
Cosby Charles	250
Crawley Robert	460
Cryer George	100
Cobbs Ambrose	350
Cock Jonathan	250
Cowles Thomas	675
	4850

D

Dormar Jno.	100
Drummond Wm	150
Deane Jno	150
Duckitt Abraham	290
Danzee Jno Jacob Coignan	4111
Deane Tho	80
Deane Wm	100
Drummond Jno	700
Deane Tho	150
Duke Tho	750
Davey Francis	778
Doby Jno.	300
Duke Henry Jun	50
Duke Henry Esq.	2986
	11695

E

Elerby Elizabeth	600
Edmunds Elizabeth	175
Eggleston Joseph	550
Eglestone Benj.	1375
	2700

F

Fearecloth Tho	277
Farthing Wm.	50

Frayser Jno	250
Fox Wm.	50
Fouace Stephen	150
Fish Jno.	100
Freeman George	197
Furrbush Wm.	400
Flanders Francis	350
	1824

G

Goodrich Benj.	1650
Gwin Jno.	100
Garey Tho.	60
Guilsby Tho.	300
Graves Joseph	250
Goss Charles	171
Goodall Jno.	400
Geddes	476
Gill Jno.	100
Green Tho.	50
Gregory Nicho.	50
Green Wm.	100
Ginnings Phill.	400
Gibson Gibey	150
Goodman John	275
Goodwin Robert	150
Grice Aristotle	700
Greene Tho	500
	5882

H

Hudson Wm	50
Herd Leph.	100
Hadley Dyonitia	100
Hall Jno.	50
Harvey George	1425
Howard Jno.	25
Hughes Geo.	250
Harfield Mich	50
Hudson George	100
Hudson Leonard	170
Hood Jno.	250
Harris Wm.	140
Hamner Nicho.	500
Henley Leonard	360
Hooker Edward	1067
Higgins Jno.	75
Henley Jno.	100
Holiday Tho.	250
Hitchcock John	100
Holeman James	150

Hubert Matt	1834	**M**		
Handcock Robt.	300	Mookins Roger	160
Haley James	310	Macklin Wm	300
Hook Mick	260	Marston Wm	150
Hill Tho.	310	Morris Edward Jun	100
Hatfield Richard	100	Manningaren	150
Hilliard Jerimiah	225	Marston Tho	1000
Hilliard John	200	Martin Richard	150
Hopkins John	120	Maples Tho	300
Hunt Wm.	1300	Muttlow Jno	170
Hix John	115	Morris James	800
Harrison Wm.	150	Moris David	170
Hawkins John	200	Myers Wm Jun	100
Hix Joseph	100	Mountfort Tho	600
Harrison Benj. Jun	100	Morris John	195
		Marble Geo	135
	10936	Mallard Poynes	100
		Merryman James	300
J		Morecock Tho	700
Inch Jno.	30	Meekings Tho	175
Jone Fred	300	Marraw Dennis	30
Inglis Mingo	1300	Major John	100
Jenings Edmund Esq.	200		
Jaquelin Edward	400		5885
Jeffrys Tho	60		
Jackson Elizabeth	200	**N**	
Jackson Richard	150		
Jeffrys Matt.	100	Norrell Hugh	328
Johnson Antho	100	Nicholson Jno	144
Jones Wm.	50	Nicholls Henry	100
Johnson Jno	260	Nailer Wm	300
Jones Wm.	150	O'Mooney Mary	126
Jordan John	1000		
			998
	4265		
K		**P**	
Knowstarp	150	Prince George	50
		Page John	1700
L		Page Mary	900
Lawrence Richard	250	Pigot Benj.	90
Ludwell Phil Esq	6626	Pall Wm	450
Lattoon John	75	Parker Tho	1650
Lund Thomas	100	Peper Stephen	100
Lillingtone Benj.	100	Phillips Jno	300
Lidie Robt.	500	Pattison Alex	100
Loftin Comeles	200	Perkins Charles	320
Lightfoot Phil	1650	Philips Edward	100
Lightfoot Jno. Esq	250	Philips Wm	300
Love Jno.	100	Pearman Wm	270
Loftin Comeles Jun	200	Pearman Jno	200
Liney Wm.	55	Pendexter Tho	550
		Parish Tho	100
	10106	Pattisson Tho	200

Parke Daniell Esq	1800
Pattison Catherine	150
	9330

R

Rhodes Randall	50
Ryder Mary	350
Rhodes Francis	100
Rovell Jno	50
Revis Wm.	150
Russell Samuell	350
	1050

S

Stafford Mary	210
Sanders Jno.	50
Sewell Jno.	75
Sprattley Jno.	350
Smith Christo.	450
Short Jno.	90
Smallpage Robt.	190
Santo Robt.	100
Smith Jno.	114
Slade Wm.	80
Soane Henry	750
Sykes Barnard	1012
Selvey Jacob	50
Sharp Jno.	800
Shaley Jno	150
Simes Wm.	650
Sorrell Mary	500
Sherman Elizb.	500
	6121

T

Tinsley Edward	100
Tinsley Richard	100
Tomson James	100
Thackson John	289
Tyery Wm.	1590
Thurston John	500
Thomas Wm.	150
Tyler Henry	730
Tullett John	625
Thomas Hanah	100
Thomson Henry	150
Twine Tho.	100
Thomas Jno.	250
	4784

V

Vaughn Henry	1900
Udall Matthew	50
Verney Wm.	50
Vaiding Isaac	300
	2300

W

Weathers Tho.	130
Wood Richard	130
Whitaker Wm.	320
Ward Tho.	100
Weldon Sarah	100
Whaley Mary	200
Winter Timo.	250
Wilkins Samll.	170
Wright Samll.	100
Winter Wm.	100
Williams Matt.	75
Walker Alex.	500
Williamson John	120
Walker David	150
Walker Alex. Jun.	2025
Warberton Tho.	190
Weldey Geo.	317
Wragg Tho.	500
Wooton Jno.	150
Willson Jno.	140
Wilkins Tho.	600
Wood Edward	300
Wood Tho.	200
Walker David	100
Ward Robt.	800
Wright Mary	175
Woodward Lanslett	650
Woodward John	650
Woodward Geo.	350
Woodward Samll.	350
Ward Henry	150
Ward Edward	150
	10662

Y

Young Robt.	350
Young Thomas	350
	700
	114780

Benj. Shottwater of York
County 300
Tho. Sorrell 300
Mary Nosham at the
Blackwater 168
                    ———
                    768

Henry Soane Junr. Sher.

The Totall of the Acres
in James City County
                    114780
Discovered of this for which
the Shreiff is to be allowed

the Qt. Rts. according to
his Ex.cy odrs in Council
                         6000
                       ———
                      108780
108780 acres at 24 tob per
100 is .... 26107 tob
                         ———

Whereof pd in Aronoco at
6 per Ct 4000
                         12.0.0
In Sweet Scented at 3s " 4d
per Ct. 22107
                         92.2.3
                        104.2.3

New Kent County Rent Roll

A Rent Roll of the Lands held of her Maj^tie in the Parish of St. Peters
and St. Paulls. Anno 1704.

Alford John	240	Bradbury Geo	100
Allen Richard	550	Brothers Jno	200
Alex Abraham	100	Bayley Jno	80
Allen Robt.	100	Beck Wm Mr.	200
Austin	245	Butts Alice	150
Austin James	700	Burnell Mary Mrs.	2750
Amos Fran	100	Bassett Wm.	550
Ashcroft Tho	180	Ball David	200
Aldridge Jno	250	Baughan Jno Junr	300
Atkinson Jno	300	Bassett Tho	350
Anthony Mark	190	Blackburn Rowland	700
Anderson Jno	100	Baker Christo	100
Anderson Robt	900	Beer Peter	100
Arise Margt	200	Brooks Richd	85
Austin Rich	50	Burnell Edwd	200
Anderson Robt.	700	Brown Jno	100
Anderson David	300	Bullock Richd	450
Anderson Rich	200	Blackwell James Junr	200
Allen Reynold	205	Brooks Robt	45
Allvis George	325	Bulkley Benj	200
Aron Josiah	200	Blackwell	950
Amos Nocho	50	Baughan Jno	100
Allen Daniell	250	Baughan Joseph	100
Allen Samll	150	Bostock Jno	100
Anderson John	100	Bostock Wm	80
Ashley Charles	100	Bumpus Robt.	100
		Burwell Lewis	200
	6785	Bryan Charles	100
		Bullock Edwd	450
B		Blalock Jno	492
Bourn Wm	140	Baker Jno	130
Bray Sarah	790	Bearne Henry	50

Buhly Jno	225
Bow Henry	200
Bradley Tho	255
Barker Cha	100
Bugg Samll	60
Baskett Wm. Esq.	1250
Beck Wm.	433
Beare Joseph	150
Barrett Christo	60
Baughtwright Jno	250
Bad Samll	150
Banks Andrew	50
Baker Richd	80
Bowles John	500
Bunch John	100
Burnett Jno	150
Barnhowes Richd	1600
Barbar Tho	500
Burkett Tho	41
Bates Edwd	50
Breeding John	300
Brewer Mary	100
Bassett Wm. Esq.	4100
Bradingham Robt.	150
Baxter James	90
	——
	21786

C

Cotrell Richd	200
Clarkson David	200
Crump Stephen	60
Crump Wm.	330
Clopton Wm.	454
Chandler Robt.	160
Crump Richd.	60
Cambo Richd.	80
Crawford David Junr	400
Crawford David Mr.	300
Chambers Edwd	235
Clerk Edwd	282
Collett Tho	100
Clerk Christo	300
Cocker Wm.	1000
Case Hugh	100
Carley Richd	80
Chiles Henry	700
Cook Abraham	200
Crump Elizb	80
Colum Richd	130
Crump James	150
Crump Robt	150
Clough Capt.	80

Chandler Wm.	300
Chandler Francis	150
Cordey Tho.	150
Currell Andrew	30
Croome Joell	600
Crutchfield Peter	400
Chesley Wm.	500
Crutchfield Junr	400
Carlton Wm.	140
Chambers George	100
Cox Wm.	350
	——
	9251

D

Dolerd Wm	50
Dennett John	350
Durham James	100
Dumas Jerimiah	250
Deprest Robt	350
Dodd John	300
Dabony James	320
Davis Elizar	375
Duke Henry Esq.	325
Dibdall Jno	800
Darnell Rachell	100
Duke Henry Esq.	170
Davis John	80
Davenport Mest	125
Daniell John	150
	——
	3845

E

Eperson John	120
Elmore Tho	300
Elmore Tho Junr	100
Ellicon Garratt Robt	520
England Wm.	490
Elderkin John	300
Elmore Peter	100
English Mungo	500
Ellis Wm.	100
	——
	2530

F

Finch Edwd	300
Foster Joseph	800
Forgeson Wm	507
Fleming Charles	920
Francis Tho	150
Freeman Wm.	200

Fenton Widdo	270
Feare Edmd	200
Fisher Wm.	100
	3447

G

Goodger Jno	200
Green Edwd	200
Gibson Tho	370
Garrat James	375
Gonton Jno	250
Glass Tho	150
Graham Tho	250
Gleam Jno	300
Giles Jno	120
Gentry Nicho	250
Garland Edwd	2600
Glass Anne	150
Granchaw Tho	480
Greenfield Fran.	80
Gillmett Jno	160
Gawsen Phillip	50
Gillmett Richd	150
Glassbrook Robt	400
Gadberry Tho	200
Gill Nicho	222
Gosling Wm	460
Goodring Alexander	100
Gills John	100
Grindge Richd	225
	7442

H

Herlock John	320
Hilton Jno	300
Hughs Jno	180
Huberd Jno	827
Howle Jno	150
Howle Jno Junr	100
Hughs Robt	966
Harris Edmd	100
Harris Tho	100
Hawes Haugton	850
Harris John	146
Hill Jno	250
Hester Fra	300
Horsley Rowland	250
Horman Robt	300
Hughes Rees	400
Hill Samll	300
Holled Samll	100
Harrelston Paul	360

Hatfield Wm	318
Harris Wm	125
Harris Benj	100
Horkeey John	800
Hairy John	280
Haiselwood Jno	200
Haiselwood Tho	150
Hockiday Wm	300
Holdcroft Henry	95
Hogg Mary	140
Harmon Wm	350
Hogg Jno. Junr	260
Harris Wm	100
Hopkins Wm	200
Howes Job	300
Hight John	100
Hankins Charles	340
Harris Wm	150
Harris Robt	75
Handey Wm	150
Hogg Wm	200
Haselwood Richd	100
Harlow Tho	230
Hutton Geo	150
	11312

J

Jackson Tho	500
Izard Fran	1233
Jarratt Robt	1600
Johnson Mich	40
Jones John	100
Johnson Wm	265
Jones Jane	200
Johnson John	100
Johnson Edwd	150
Jennings Robt	100
Jones Fredirick	500
Johes John	100
Jeeves Tho	100
Jones Francis	200
Jones John	100
Jones Evan	500
	5838

K

King Elizb	300
Kembro Jno	540
Kembro Jno Junr	150
Keeling Geo	1500
	2490

L

Lightfoot John Esq.	3600
Littlepage Richd	2160
Losplah Peter	100
Lestrange Tho	200
Liddall Geo	100
Lawson Nicho	200
Levermore Phill	1000
Lewis John Esq	2600
Lawson John	50
Lewis John	375
Lovell Geo	920
Lovell Charles	250
Leak Wm	280
Logwod Tho	100
Lacey Wm	500
Lacey Tho	100
Lacey Emanuell	180
Luke Jno	150
Lochester Robt	80
Lewis Tho	115
Lee Edwd	120
Lochester Edwd	80
Law James	100
Laton Reubin	100
Linsey Joseph	1150
Linsey Wm	50
Lane Tho	100
	14760

M

Millington Wm Junr	450
Mitchell Stephen Junr	75
Millington Wm	200
Moss Samll	200
Mitchell Tho	300
Meanley Wm	100
Minis Tho	200
Mitchell Stephen	200
Moor Pelham	125
Martin Tho	100
Martin Martin	150
Morris Robt	245
Moss Tho	430
Morgan Edwd	50
Moon Stephen	70
Major Wm	456
Murroho Jno	100
Moor Jno	250
Masey Tho	300
Martin John	400
Masey Peter	100

Madox John	300
Martin Wm	230
Martin James	100
Moss James	720
Moon Tho	65
McKing Alexander	170
McKoy Jno	300
Merridith Geo	400
Melton Richd	290
Morreigh John	110
Merfield John	210
Mills Nicho	300
Mask Jno	411
Medlock John	350
Moor Edwd	65
McKgene Wm	13½
Merriweather Nicho	3327
Mage Peter	450
Mitchell Wm	512
Marr Geo	100
Moor Anne	75
Mutray Tho	382
Mirideth James	270
Mohan Warwick	850
Muttlow James	150
Morgan Matthew	210
Morris John	450
Markham Tho	100
Moxon Wm	100
Mackony Elizb	250
Meacon Gideon	270
	16149½

N

Nucholl James	300
Neaves James	150
Nonia Richd	100
Norris Wm	100
	650

O

Osling John	150
Otey John	290
Oudton Matt	190
	630

P

Page John Junr	400
Pendexter Geo	1490
Pattison David	300

Park Jno Junr	300	Smith Nathll	82
Park John	200	Sanders Wm	40
Pease John	100	Spear Robt	450
Philip Geo	100	Sanders James	60
Penix Edwd	200	Scott John	300
Plantine Peter	240	Scrugg Richd	100
Pendexter Tho	1000	Strange Alexander	450
Pyraul James	150	Smith Wm	110
Pullam Wm	575	Scrugg Jno	50
Purdy Nicho	200	Snead Tho	200
Page Mary Madm	3450	Sunter Stephen	478
Perkins John	120	Symons Josiah	100
Paite Jerim	220	Sanders John	130
Pasley Robt	300	Stephens Wm	100
Perkins Wm	305	Stanley Tho	150
Pait John	1500	Sandidge Jno	100
Petever Tho	100	Sprattlin Andrew	654
Pittlader Wm	147	Snead John	75
Pickley Tho	281	Smith James	80
Pittlader Tho	295	Sexton Wm	80
Petty Stephen	200	Sims Jno	1000
Porter John	100	Smith Roger	300
Petty John	2190	Sherritt Henry	100
Park Coll	7000	Salmon Thomas	50
Purly John	100	Sanders Tho	25
		Symons George	125
	21573	Stamp Ralph	625
		Stanop Capt	1024
R		Stanup Richd	325
Raglin Evan	300	Shears Paul	200
Raglin Evan Junr	100	Stepping Tho	350
Raglin Tho	100	Slater James	700
Ross Wm	150		
Richardson Henry	300		**9813**
Raymond James	80		
Reynold Tho	255	**T**	
Reyley Jno	100	Tony Alexandr	170
Reynolds Jonah	50	Tovis Edmd	100
Rhoads Charles	175	Turner Henry	250
Reynolds Samll	820	Turner Wm	250
Rice Tho	300	Turner Geo	400
Redwood John	1078	Thorp Tho	200
Rule Widdo	50	Thurmond Richd	131½
Richardson Richard	890	Tucker Tho	700
Russell John	550	Turner James	50
Richardson John	1450	Thompson James	100
Richard Eman	1250	Tully Wm	200
Round Free Wm	100	Turner Geo Junr	200
Randolph Widdo	100	Tate James	160
		Town Elizb	100
	8928	Thomasses Orphans	500
S		Tinsley Cournelius	220
Styles John	200	Tyler	100

Tinsley Tho	150
Tirrell Wm	400
Taylor Tho	25
Tinsley Jno	130
Tapp Jno	110
Tyrrey James	150
Tyrrey Alexandr	210
Thompson Capt.	2600
Tyrey Thom	190
Taylor Joseph	150
Taylor Lemuell	212
Taylor Thomas	350
Twitty Thomas	200

8708½

V

Upsherd Jon	60
Vaughan Wm	300
Via Amer..	50
Venables Abr.	100
Venables John	200
Vaughan John	250
Vaughan Vincent	410

1370

W

Wintby Jacob	250
Winfry Charles	100
Waddill Jno	40
Walker Wm	650
Walton Edwd	150
Wilson Jno	200
Waddill Wm	375
Warring Peter	88
Wingfield Tho	150
Weaver Sam	100
Wyatt Alice	1300
West Nath	6370
Webb Mary	200
Wilmore Jno	100
Webster Joseph	80
West Giles	200
Wharton Tho	270
Willis Fran	134
Waddy Samll	150
Willford Charles	100
Waid James	150
White Jno	320
Wood Henry	100
Woody Symon	50
Woody Jno	100

Winstone Antho	310
Winstone Isaac	850
Woody James	130
Winstone Sarah	275
Watson Theophilus	325
Woodson Jno	600
Walton Edwd	450
Wood Walter	100
Watkins Wm	50
Wilkes Joseph	250
Williams Clerk	300
Willis Stephen	500
Williams Tho	100
Worrin Robt	300
Woodull James	200
Walker Capt	400
Wilson James	60
Wheeler John	75
Williams Wm.	100
White John	190

17292

Y

Yeoman John	50
Yeoell Judith	150

200

Quit Rents that hath not been
paid this 7 year viz.

Richarson Matt	200
Wm Wheeler	150
Coll Parkes	300

650

Lands that the Persons lives
out of the County viz.

Coll Lemuell Batthurst	800
Robt Valkes	500
The Heirs of Bray	500

1800

A	6785
B	21786
C	9251
D	3845
E	2530
F	3447
G	7442
H	11312

J	5838	S	9813
K	2490	T	8708½
L	14760	V	1370
M	16149½	W	17292
N	650	Y	200
O	630		
P	21573		173870
R	8298	James Mosse Sherriff	

A full & Perfect Rent Roll of all the Land held of her Majtie in Charles City County this Present Year 1704 by Patents &c.

A

Aliat John 100

B

Bradley Joseph 200
Baxter John 250
Bishop Robt 200
Bedingfield Theo. 110
Botman Harman 100
Burton Henry 100
Burwell Lewis 8000
Brooks Robt 150
Blanks Richard Senr 250
Blanks Richd Junr 125
Blanks Tho 125
Bradford Richd 1397
Brown Marmaduke 100
Bray David 230

11337

C

Cole Robt 80
Codell Richd 100
Clark Edwd 962¼
Clark Daniell 250
Clark Joseph 230
Christian Tho 1273
Cock Edwd 350
Cock Richd 975

3258

D

Davis Thomas 200
Davis Richd 118

318

E

Edwards John 287½
Epes Littlebury 400

Epes John 500
Ele Samll 682
Evans John 800

2669½

F

Floyd Geo 243
Fowler Richd 150
Flowers Samll 200

593

G

Gunn James 250
Grosse Edwd 100

350

H

Hamlin Jno 143½
Hill Edwd 2100
Haynes Nicho 125
Harwood John 100
Howood James 200
Hattle Shard 112
Harwood Joseph 659
Harwood Samll 350
Harwood Robt 312½
Hunt Wm 3130
Hunt John 1500
Harmon Elizb 479
Hyde Wm 120
Hamlin Stephen 80
Hamlin Tho 264

16015

J

Irby Wm 103
Javox James 100

Jordin Edwd	100
Justis Justinian	200
	503

L

Lowlin Danll	600
Lawrence James	100
	700

M

Manders James	100
Minge James	1086
Mountford Jeffry	100
Marvell Tho	1238
Moodie Samll	82
Muschamp John	80
	2686

N

New Edwd	100
New Robt	300
	400

O

Owen Wm	100
Owen David	100
	200

P

Parker Tho	1667
Parish Wm	100
Parish Charles	100
Parker James	160
Parish Edwd	100
Parish John	100
	2227

R

Roach Jno Senr	630
Renthall Joseph	270
Russell Samll	253
Roper John	220
Royall Joseph	262
	1635

S

Smith Obidiah	100
Sampson Widdo	211
Stith Drewry	1240
Stith John	1395
Stockes John	476
Stockes Silvanus Senr	250
Stokes Silvanus Junr......	550
Speares Geo	225
	4447

T

Tanner Tho	2000
Tarendine John	150
Turner Edwd	195
Trotman Anne	120
	2465

V

Vernon Walter	240

W

Wyatt Widdo	800
Woodam Tho	100
Waren John	54
	954

A	100
B	11337
C	3258
D	318
E	2669½
F	593
G	350
H	16015
J	503
L	700
M	2686
N	400
O	200
P	2227
R	1635
S	4447
T	2465
V	240
W	954
	52059½

An account of what Land that
I cannot get the Quit Rents
the Persons living out of the
County

Josep Parish at Kiquotan... 100

Richd Smith James City Cty	350
Danll Hayley	200
Wm Lagg Henrico Cty	100
	750

Tho Parker Sherif

The Quit Rent Roll of King William County

Armsby John	200	Coates Wm	50
Alvey Robt	400	Douglas Wm	200
Andrew Wm	100	Davis Lewis	200
Abbott Robt	100	Davis Wm	200
Arnold Anthony	100	Downer John	300
Arnold Benj	1000	Downes Elias	300
Alcock John	190	Davenport Davis	200
Adam James	400	Dorrell Sampson Qr	5000
Anderson Wm Capt	150	Davenport Martin	100
Burwell Majr	4700	Davis Robert	200
Bunch Paul	150	Dickason Wm	100
Baker John	250	Dickason Thomas	100
Burges Edwd	150	Dillon Henry	150
Buttris Robt	400	Dabney James	200
Bibb Benj	100	Dabney George	290
Browne Joseph	270	Dabney Benj	200
Bell Edwds	580	Davis John	200
Burch Henry	200	Elly Richd	100
Burrel Suprian	350	Egny Elizb	100
Baker Tho	100	Elliot Thomas	480
Bobo Elizb	200	Edward James	350
Bird Wm Maj Qr	1200	Elliott James	1700
Burrus John	60	Fox John Capt.	600
Butler Thomas	150	Fox Henry	2000
Burrus Thomas	60	Finton Francis	100
Bassett Coll Qr	1550	Fuller Anthony	150
Bray James Qr	1400	Foord John Junr	300
Browne Abraham	250	Foord Wm	800
Brightwell Elizb	300	Fullalove Thomas	100
Bickley Joseph	150	Fleming Charles Qr	1700
Claibourne Wm Coll	3000	Graves John Qr	100
Claibourne Tho Capt	1000	Garratt Thomas	200
Claibourne John	50	Geeres Thomas	100
Coakes Robert	100	Green John	100
Cradock Samll	600	Gravatt Henry	150
Cockram Wm	200	Goodin Majr Qr	200
Cockram Joseph	600	Glover Wm	100
Celar John	100	Herriott George	200
Chadwick Wm	150	Hollins John	200
Cathern John	180	Higgason John	350
Carr Thomas	500	Holderbee Wm	100
Chiles Henry Qr	700	Holliday Wm	100
Craushaw Thomas	150	Hayfield Wm	100
Clark Margarett	100	Hampton John	50

Huckstep Edwd	150
Hurt Wm Junr	90
Hurt Wm Senr	250
Hurt John	500
Hendrick Hans	700
Handcock Thomas	200
Hayden John	150
Hobday Edwd	150
Hill Thomas	150
Hutchinson Wm	600
Hill Francis	300
Hill Gabriell	250
Hill Edwd Coll Qr	3000
Hayle Joseph	200
Johns Jane	240
Johnson Wm	300
Johnson Coll Qr	600
Johns Wm	100
Isabell Wm	150
James Jonathan	300
Inge Vincent	100
Jones Frederick Qr	2850
Jenings Coll Qr	4000
King Robert Qr	300
Kettlerise Symon	200
Lee John	20
Lypscomb Ambrose	600
Lasy Wm	100
Lypscomb Wm	300
Littlepage Richd Capt Qr	2600
Lypscomb John	200
Mallory Thomas	150
Mallory Roger	100
Miles Daniell	350
Mr Gehee Thomas	250
Marr John	200
Morris Wm	440
Maybank Wm	100
Mr Donnell John	150
Maddison Henry	650
Merriweather Nicho Qr	600
Mullene Matthew	150
Madison John Qr	300
Norment Joseph	800
Norment Samll	100
Noyce Wm	650
Napier Robert	100
Owens Hugh	300
Oustin John	350
Oakes John	350
Oliver John	140
Palmer Martin	1200
Peek John	100

Pynes Nathaniell	1400
Pee Thomas	400
Purlevant Arthur	100
Powers David	200
Pollard Wm Qr	500
Pemberton Geo	180
Page John Qr	1000
Pickrell Gabriell	100
Parks Coll Qr	4500
Quarles John	100
Reynolds Wm	100
Robert Maurice	200
Randall John	100
Ray James	100
Rhodes Nicholas	150
Sandlan Nicholas	700
Strutton Thomas	150
Streett Wm	350
Shilling George	300
Satterwhite Charles	150
Slaughter Geo	100
Slaughter Martin	130
Stark John	500
Sanders Jushua	100
See Mathew	200
Sellers Jacob	350
Spruse Jeremy	150
Smith Edmd	150
Spencer Thomas	600
Slaughter John	90
Smith Christo Qr	800
Slaughter Henry	100
Toms Wm	150
Towler Matthew	150
Terry Thomas	300
Terry Stephen	330
Tomason Thomas	150
Terry James	400
Traneer John	100
Vickrey Henry	450
West John Coll	1800
Winfree Henry	300
West Tho Capt	1000
Whitworth John	200
Whitlock John	200
Willeroy Abraham	550
Williams Phillip	100
Williams Griffith	240
Wood Thomas	300
Whitehead John	100
Woolsey Jacob	130
Williams John	150
Williams Samll	600

Wright Thomas	150	Wm Stanard M.S.	1000
Whitbee Robert	800	James Wood K.Q.	500
West Nathanll Capt	2000	Zachary Lewis K.Q.	450
Waller John Majr	800	Peter Kemp G.C.	600
Willis Wm	250	Wm Beck N.K.	1600
Wheelis Joseph	130	Tho. Hickman K.Q.	550
Wormley Madam Qr	3000	Benj Clement G.C.	600
Winston William	170	David Bray J.C.C.	1000
Whitehead Phillip	3000	Job House N.K.	2000
Yancey Charles	100	Harry Beverley M.S.	600
Yarborough John	150	Chillian White G.C.	300
Yarborough Richard	300		

100950

A True Account of the Lands in King & Queen County as it was taken by Robt. Bird Sherriff in the year 1704.

A

Alford John	200
Austin Danll	80
Asque John	320
Adams Johns	200
Arnold Edwd	150
Allin Thomas	100
Adkinson John	250
Austin Thomas	100
Adamson David	100
Anderson Richd	650
Allcock Dorothy	150

2300

B

Baker Wm	350
Beverley Robt. Qr.	3000
Bennett Alexander	200
Breeding Geo	200
Bennett Wm	150
Bowles Robt	100
Bennett Sawyer	150
Baylor John	3000
Bell Roger	150
Burford Wm	150
Bray John	230
Blake Wm	290
Boisseau James Quart	900
Blake Wm Junr	210
Brown Lancelet	385
Burch Jno	100
Burch Wm	100
Brown Tho. Blakes Land	300
Bridgeforth James	355

Bagby Robt	550
Banks Wm	1079
Bullock John	200
Bird Wm	572
Broach Jno	1200
Braxton Geo	2825
Blanchet John	125
Bowker Ralph	330
Bine Edmd	111
Barber James	750
Burgess Wm	100
Bond Jno	100
Breemer John	1100
Bland Henry	150
Breemer John Junr	200
Bowden Tho.	150
Barton Andrew	150
Barlow Henry	200
Baskett John	150
Batterton Tho.	100
Baker James	322
Bill Robt.	150
Bocus Reynold	150
Bourne George	200
Bird Robt.	1324

22535

C

Cane Jno	300
Chessum Alexandr	150
Cook Benjamin	200
Cook Thomas Junr	50
Cook Thomas Senr	100
Cook Jno	50
Cleyton John	400

Chapman Mary	200
Cleyton Jeremy	325
Crane Wm	120
Camp Thomas	250
Carleton Christo	200
Carleton Jno.	300
Carter Timo.	350
Coleman Tho.	300
Coleman Daniell	470
Cleyton Susannah Widdo	700
Collier Robt.	100
Crane Wm.	300
Crane Tho.	320
Chapman John	200
Caughlane James	100
Cotton Catherine	50
Collier Charles	450
Collier John	400
Collins Wm.	350
Cammell Alexandr.	200
Chin Hugh	100
Conner Timo.	1410
Collins James Yard Qr	300
Corbin Gowin	2000
Crisp Tobias	100
Carters Qr	300
Carlton Tho.	200
Carlton Anne	300
Clough George Qr	390
	12235

Clerk and Cordell both in Glocester	1000

D

Widdo Durrat	200
Day Alexander Maj. Beverley Qr	300
Doe Wm.	300
Dilliard Nicho.	150
Dilliard Edwd.	150
Dimmock Tho.	150
Dismukes Wm.	200
Duett Charles	900
Didlake James	200
Durham John	100
Dunkley John	380
Duson Tho.	448
Davis Nathll.	300
Deshazo Peter	450
Davis Jno	90
Davis Edwd	100

Dillard Thomas	170
Davis Richd	250
Dillard Geo	325
Duglas James	275
Dayley Owen	180
	5618

E

Eachols John	220
Ellis John	400
Eastham George	300
Ewbank Wm	350
Eastham Edwd Junr	800
Edwds John	100
Eastham Edwd	100
Eastes Abraham	200
Eyes Cornelius	100
Emory Ralph	100
Ellis Timothy	350
	3020

F

Forsigh Thomas	150
Farquson James	300
Flipp John	80
Farish Robt	1400
Fielding Henry	1000
Farmer John	50
Fothergill Richd	675
Fortcon Charles	400
Forgett Charles	150
Robt Fothergill	150
	4355

Farmer John not paid for..	200
Fox Margarett not pd for..	100

G

Gadberry Edwd	100
Griffin Edwd	100
George Richd	100
Griffin David	100
Graves Robt	150
Graves Jno	150
Gardner Ringing	200
Gray Joseph	200
Gilby John	300
Gray Samll	40
Gresham Jno.	200
Gresham Edwd	175
Good John	200
Gresham George	150

Garrett Danll	200	Holt Joseph lives in	
Gamble Tho. Majors Land	450	Maryland	321
Gresham Tho	225	Mayward Tho in Glocester..	600
Graves Jno	150		
Guttery Jno	230	**J**	
Greogory Frances Widdo ..	700	Jones Tho	150
Gough Alice Widdo	800	Jones Robt	200
Griggs Francis	250	Jeffrys Richd	337
Garrett John	330	Jones Robt Junr	130
Garrett Humphrey	200	Johnson James	200
Gibson Widdo	200	Jones Wm	900
Garrett Robt	200		
			1917
	6100		

H

		K	
Hand Thomas	150	King John	150
Hayle John Qr	685	Kallander Timo	100
Honey James	200	Kink Anne	275
Holloway Wm	100	King Edwd	200
Herndon James	100	Knowles Dorothy Qr	150
Hoomos George	725	King Robt	100
Hodges Thomas	250	Kenniff Danby	100
Hayle Joseph	250	King Daniell	200
Hayes John	100		
Haynes Wm	494		1335
Holcomb Wm Bradfords			
Land	700	**L**	
Henderson John Thackers		Loveing John	100
, Land	200	Lyon Peter	250
Hodgson Widdo	200	Leigh John	6200
Henderson Widdo	300	Lumpkin Robt	400
Henderson Wm	162	Lee Wm	230
Housburrough Morris, Harts		Loob Wm	100
Land	200	Loft Richd	320
Hesterley John	200	Lewis Tachary	350
Hill John	200	Lumpkin Jacob	950
Hordon Wm	70	Lewis David	120
Harris Wm	250	Lewis John Esq	10100
Hart Tho	200	Lewis Edwd	1400
Hockley Robt	100	Lemon Elizb	100
Howard Peter	300	Lynes Rebecea	405
Hardgrove Wm	100	Levingstone John	600
Herring Arthur	50	Levingstone Samll	100
Hickman Thomas	700	Lawrence Matthew	210
Hunt Wm	312	Letts Arthur	475
Hobs Wm	250	Langford John	150
Hicks Richd	250	Levingstone Jno Sowels	
Howden Wm	100	Land	750
Howerton Thomas	300		
			23310
	8098	Leftwich Thomas in Essex	75

M

May John	300
Musick George	100
Major Jno	250
Martin John	300
More Austines Qr	200
May Tho	300
Moore Samll	100
Maddison Jno	500
Morris Wm	130
Martin Elizb	400
Mackay Sarah	177
May John Piggs Land	200
Major Francis	700
Mansfield Thomas	60
Morris Henry	100
Major John	400
Melo Nicho	200
Marcartee Daniell	200
Morris Wm	300
Mead Wm	100
Matthews Edwd	160
Martin Cordelia Wido	200
	5377

N

Nelson Henry	440
Neal John	50
Nason Joshua	200
Norman Wm	300
Norris James	100
	1090

O

Owen Ralph	120
Ogilvie Wm	300
Orrill Lawrence	290
Orrill Wm	500
Orsbourn Michaell	90
Overstreet James Qr	180
ditto at home	50
	1530

P

Powell Robt	500
Prewitt Wm	200
Paine Bernard	130
Pomea Francis	100
Philip Charles	250
Pettitt Thomas	548

Pollard Robt	500
Pollard Wm	100
Phinkett Elizb	500
Pemberton Tho.	115
Pickles Tho	93
Potters Francis Wido Neals Land	100
Parks James	200
Purchase Geo Qr	580
Page Jno	100
Pritchett David	225
Pigg Henry	61
Page John Junr	300
Pigg Edwd	250
Phelps Tho	400
Pendleton Philip	300
Pendleto Henry	700
Pann John	200
Paytons quarts	500
Pigg John	100
Pamplin Robt	150
Pryor Christo	175
Paulin Elizb	175
	7552
Pate John in Glocester	1000

Q

Quarles James	300
Quarles Dyley Zacha: Lewis Land	300
	600

R

Richard Robt	300
Rings Quarter	1000
Robinson Daniel	100
Roger Giles	475
Rice Michaell	200
Richeson Tho	460
Richeson Elias	180
Read Elizb	550
Russell Alexandr Wyatts Land	400
Robinson Robt	980
Rowe John	100
Richards John	914
Richards Wm	400
Richards Oliver	250
Riddle Tho Reads Land	700
Roy Richd	1000
Ryley Elias	200

Rollings Peter 150

8359

John the son of Robt
Robinson hold, which
nobody pays for 750

S

Sebrill John 130
Stone Mary 100
Smiths in Bristoll Qr 2800
Stone Jno 295
Stubbelfield Geo Qr 400
Scandland Denis 1470
Swinson Richd 170
Smith Christo 200
Smith Jno Cooper 273
Smith Alexander 275
Seamour Wm 268
Sones Tho 150
Shepard Jane 100
Southerland Danll 200
Shoot Tho 100
Shepheard Joseph 100
Shea Patrick 200
Southerland Danll 200
Smith Nicho 700
Sanders Nathll 200
Smith John Sawyer 80
Shuckelford Roger 250
Skelton John 100
Snell John 150
Simpio Charles 100
Sawrey John 113
Stringer Margt 175
Spencer Tho 300
Sykes Stephen 50
Smith Francis 100
Smith Richd 150
Sparks John 200
Surly Tho 100
Stapleton Tho 200
Story John 3000
Spencer Katherine 600

14599

Shippath Sr Wm Which is
not paid for 700
Stark Tho of London which
is not paid for 920
Stubblefield Geo in Glocester 400
Smith Austin in Glocester.. 4000

T

Turner Richard 200
Todd Thomas Quarts 2300
Taylor James 4000
Toy Thomas 175
Taylor Danll 70
Thomas Rowland 610
Tunstall Tho 550
Todd Richd 1050
Towley John 200
Trice James 350
Tureman Ignatius 100
Turner Thomas 267
Thacker C. C. 1000

10872

U

Vaughan Cornelius 500
Vize Nathll 100
Uttley John 200

800

W

Wood James 800
Wilkinson John 100
Wright Tho 300
Watkins Wm 137
Wiltshier Joseph 60
Watkins Edwd 98
Watkins Philip 203
White Thomas 200
Walker John 6000
Wilson Benj Wyats Land.. 420
Wyat Richd 1843
Walton Thomas 200
Wyat John 530
Withy Thomas 50
Williams Thomas 200
Watts Tho 235
Ward Samll 160
Watkins Benj 60
Watkins Tho Junr 125
Williams Elizb 900
Waldin Samll 275
Ware Edwd 735
William John 125
Ware Vallentine 487
Willbourn Tho 250
Wildbore Wm 100
Ware Nicho 718
White Jerimiah 200

Whorein John	200	N	1090
Wise Richd quarts	209	O	1530
Walker John, Johnsons		P	7552
Land	1000	Q	600
		R	8359
	16920	S	14599
Wadlington Paul not paid		T	10872
for being	150	U	800
		W	16920
Y		Y	100
York Matthew	100		
			158522
A	2300		
B	22535	Lands returned not paid for	
C	12235	C	1000
D	5618	F	300
E	3020	H	920
F	4355	L	75
G	6100	P	1000
H	8098	R	750
J	1917	S	6020
K	1335	W	150
L	23310		
M	5377		10215

Glocester Rent Roll
A Rent Roll in Petso Parish

Capt David Alexander	1050	James Dudley	780
James Amis	250	Richd Dudley	400
John Acre	100	Thomas Dudley	200
Wm Armistead	430	Thomas Dixon	300
Ralph Baker	150	Jno Drument	80
Martha Brooken	600	Samll Fowler	150
Thomas Buckner	850	Wm Fleming	600
Samll Bernard	550	Wido Forginson	150
Wm Barnard	810	Wm Fockner	180
Richd Bailey	600	Jno Grymes	1400
Mary Booker	100	Susannah Grinley	200
Thomas Cook	350	Darcas Green	400
Wm Crymes	400	Jno Grout	300
Jno Cobson	100	Jno Harper	100
Robt. Carter	1102	Wm Howard	300
Wm Collone	400	Richd Hubard	100
Hannah Camell	100	Wm Hasford	500
Benj Clements	400	Jno Hanes	150
Jno Cleake	100	Alextnder How	120
Wm Cook	135	Richd Hill	70
Jno Coleman	200	Robt Hall	100
Jno Day	400	Richd Hull	250
Jerim Darnell	150	Sanll Hawes	200
Jno Darnell	60	Stephen Johnson	150

Wm Jones for Northington	530	Edward Symons	500
Glebe Land	127	Nicho Smith	280
Jno Kingson	400	John Stubs	300
Capt Edwd Lewis	1000	Thomas Sivepson	280
Richd Lee Esq	1140	John Smith	1300
Nicho Lewis orphen	350	Augustin Smith	200
Wm Milner	900	Augustin Smith Junr	500
Richd Minor	250	Wm Starbridge	159
Edwd Musgrove	100	Wm Thornton Senr	525
Hayes an orphan	60	Wm Thornton Junr	800
Elizb Mastin	360	Wm Thurston	200
Jno Mackwilliams	50	Wm Upshaw	490
Robt Nettles	300	Francis Wisdom	150
Wm Norman	150	Thomas West	112
Isaac Oliver	100	Thomas Whiting	450
Dorothy Oliver	130	George Williams	100
Jno Pritchett	850	Conquest Wyatt	2200
Jno Pate	1100	Seth Wickins	50
Richd Price	600	Walter Waters	200
Madm Porteus	500	Jane Wothem	60
Madm Page	550	Robt Yard	450
Pobt Porteus	892	Robt Hall	250
Guy Parish	100	Wm Whittmore Desarted	150
Wm Roane	500	Wm Parsons Orphen	100
James Reynolls	200	Edwd Stephens	70
George Robinson	300	John Kelley Orphen	150
John Royston	570		
Thomas Read	2000		41132
Wm Richards in Pamunkey	150	Tho Neale	
Jno Shackelford	280		

Glocester Rent Roll
A Rent Roll of Kingston Parish

Rose Curtis	400	Tho Cray	200
Robt Peyton	680	Hen. Knight	240
Richd Perrott	35	John Williams	50
Henry Preston	1500	Richd Beard	380
Sarah Green	200	Timothy Hundley	300
Robt Cully	200	Thomas Bedford	50
Thomas Hayes	140	Jno Floyd	250
Andrew Bell	128	John Bohannah	113½
Humphry Toy	1100	Capt Armistead	3675
Anne Aldred	350	Christopher Dixon	300
Dunkin Bahannah	113½	Robt Bristow Esqr	900
Richd Hunley	50	Edwd Gowing	100
Capt Gayle	164	Tho Ryland	272
Math. Gayle Junr	250	John Nevill	100
James Hundley	100	Lawrence Parrott	340
John Hundley	130	Wm Brooks	720
Philip Hundley	660	Joseph Bohannah	148

Wm Hampton	348	Benj. Read	550
Widdo Green	150	Walter Keble	550
Capt Dudley	650	Joseph Brooks	500
Capt. Knowles	575	Capt. Gwin	1100
Capt. Tho. Todd	775	Lindseys Land	390
Wm Beard	100	Thomas Garwood	77
Wm. Tomkins	100	John Callie	1000
Henry Bolton	50	Tho. Miggs	100
Wm Eliott	1060	Richd Glascock	500
Humphrey Tompkins	100	Jno Lylley	584
Daniel Hunter	200	Geo. Billups	1200
Thomas Peyton	684	Robt. Singleton	650
Richd Dudley	350	James Foster	225
James Ransom Junr	310	John Andrews	50
Tho. Peters	30	Thomas Rice	34
Robt. Elliott	1247	John Martin	200
Mich. Parriett	100	Capt. Smith	550
Jno. Meachen Junr	600	Capt. Sterling	1100
Caleb Linsey	140	John Diggs	1200
Alexandr Ofield	23	Wm. Howlett	300
Mark Thomas	300	Jno. Miller	100
Jno. Garnet	250	Andrew Ripley	40
Wm. Plumer	510	Francis Jarvis	460
Wm. Brumley	750	Wm. Armistead	300
Wm. Credle	50	John Banister	650
Charles Jones	225	Tho. Plumer	400
Robt. Sadler	50	Isaac Plumer	200
Edwd Sadler	20	James Taylor	50
Geo Roberts	170	Edwd Borum	360
Richd Longest	600	Widdo Davis	300
Tho. Fliping	300	Sam. Singleton	300
Charles Watters	100	Wm. Morgan Senr	50
Wm. Grundy	200	Wm. Morgan Junr	200
Thomas Kemp	200	John Bacon	825
Tho. Allaman	842	Henry Singleton	600
Coll Kemp	200	John Edwards	534
Ralph Shipley	430	Patrick Berry	250
George Turner	50	Anne Forest	500
Coll. James Ransom	1400		
Thomas Putman	300		46537
Richd Marchant	180	Ambrose Dudley	
Widdo Sinoh	300	1705	
Christopher Rispue	200		

Glocester Rent Roll
A Rent Roll in Ware Parish

Thomas Poole	600	Simon Stubelfield	200
Anne Croxson	300	Jno. Price	600
Thomas Purnell	163	Saml. Vadrey	400
Nocholas Pamplin	210	Samll Dawson	350

Nathan: Burwell	600	Giles Cook	140
John Dawson	780	Wm. Jones	120
Tho. Bacop	200	Tho. Collis	100
Robt. Francis	400	Philip Smith	700
Walter Greswell	50	Tho. Cheesman	650
Tho. Read	400	Geo. More	40
James Shackelfield	35	James Morris	250
Robt. Freeman	135	Abraham Iveson Senr.	1000
Jno. Marinex	100	Robert Bristow Esqr.	2050
Isaac Valine	100	Anthony Gregory	700
Tho. Haywood	70	Richd. Bailey	800
Hugh Marinex	50	Wm. Foulcher	100
Leonard Ambrose	200	Widdo. Jeffes	216
Philip Grady	200	Richd. Dudley Junr.	300
Capt. Wm. Debnam	1250	John Buckner	900
James Burton	100	Thomas Todd	884
Jno. Spinks	300	John and Peter Waterfield	143
Wm. Hurst	200	Henry Whiting	800
Sarah More	67	Madm. Whiting	950
John Ray	100	Jno. Goodson	150
Robt. Pryor	300	Wm. Morris	350
Christo. Greenaway	270	Mary Lassells	200
Capt. Throgmorton	500	Peter Ransone	220
James Clark	250	Charles Waters	200
Philip Cooper	200	Dorothy Kertch	220
Jno. Kindrick	100	Dorothy Boswell	1600
Samll. Simons	120	Richd. Cretendon	280
Wm. Radford	200	Elizb. Anniers	250
John Robins	900	Elizb. Snelling	250
Alice Bates	200	Joseph Boswell	230
Jno. Easter	350	John Bullard	100
James Davison	100	Anthony Elliot	100
Robt. Morrin	200	Wm. Armistead	100
Anne Bray	100	Peter Kemp	650
Grace Easter	200	Majr. Peter Beverley	800
Sampson Dorrell	300	Ditto per Tillids Lands	150
Capt. Francis Willis	3000	Dudley Jolley	100
Thomas Powell	460	Robt. Couch	100
Wm. Holland	300		
Capt. Cook	1500		31603

Glocester Rent Roll
A Rent Roll of Abbington Parish

Mr. Guy Smith	30	Henry Stevens	60
James Cary	50	Chillion White	100
Wm. Sawyer	150	Jerimah Holt	350
Edwd. Cary	100	of Ditto for the Widdo Babb	150
Robt. Barlow	62	Robt. Yarbborrow	100
Tho. Cleaver Sworne	200	Robt. Starkey	100
Edwd. Stevens	80	Henry Seaton	170

Hugh Howard	200	Peter Richeson	250
Capt. Booker	1000	Benja Clements	500
Jno. Stoakes	300	Thomas Graves	70
Jno. Dobson	400	Robt. Page	75
Wm. Dobson	950	Joseph More	150
Edmd. Dobson	350	Richard Dixon	200
Hugh Allen	1250	Elizb. Turner	150
George Jackson	117	Owen Grathmee	250
Jno. Teagle	30	Richd. Woodfolk	125
Widdo Jones	45	Jno. Waters	50
Mary Thomas	100	Wm. Hilliard	80
Thomas Seawell	200	Richd. Heywood	100
Benj. Lane	50	Mary Hemingway	150
Valentine Lane	80	Wm. Kemp	75
Jeffry Garves	33	Robt. Francis	104
Thomas Coleman	250	Joshua Broadbent	200
Johanna Austin	40	Joseph Coleman	200
Majr. Burwell	3300	Grustam Clent	100
Jno. Satterwight	50	Philip Grady	150
Jerimiah Holt Junr.	150	Jno. Hall	125
Charles Stevens	75	Tho. Walker	300
Richd. Roberts for wife	300	Jno. Mixon	400
Jno. Sadler	125	Tho. Sanders	450
James Steavens	100	Wm. Smith for Kittson	50
Susannah Stubbs	300	John Banister	2750
Richd. Foster	150	Madm. Mary Page	3000
Henry Mitchell	50	Jno. Lewis Esq.	2000
Nathanll. Russell	550		
Elizb. Richardson	500		28426
Wm. Camp	175		
James Row	300	Richd. Cordell	
John Butler	100	Ware	31603
John Smith Esqr.	2000	Petso	41123
Ditto for Robt. Byron	400	Kingston	46537
Capt. Blackbourne	550		
			147698

A Perfect Role of the Land in Middlesex County Anno Dom. 1704

Richard Atwood	100	Wm. Daniell	150
Richard Allin	150	Robt. Daniell	225
Tho. Blewford	100	Henry Freeman	200
Mrs. Blaiss	300	John Goodrich	50
John Bristow	140	Geo. Goodloe	50
Robt. Blackley	100	Geo Guest	50
Coll Corbin	2260	Richd Gabriell	30
Coll Carter	1150	Wm. Finley	50
John Cheedle	50	Wm. Gardner	100
Wm. Carter	170	Robt. George	180
Widdo Chaney	800	David George	150
Nath. Cranke	50	Widdo. Hazellwodd	200
Tho. Dyatt	200	John Hoare	100
John Davie	75	Richd. Reynolds	50

Jno. Southerne	100	Richd. Daniell	210
Richd. Shurly	200	Geo. Blake	100
Tho. Hapleton	200	Edwd Williams	100
Wm. Southworth	50	Pat Mammon	100
Wm. Jones	300	Alexander Murray	250
Evan Jones	50	Poplar Smith	550
Esqr. Wormley Estate	5200	Olixer Seager	380
Wm Churchhill	1950	Edwd Gobbee	90
Jacob Briston	100	Henry Barnes	200
Jno. Pace	200	John Davis	100
John Logie	300	Paul Thilman	300
John Price	519	Hugh Watts	80
Henry Perrott	1100	Edwd Clark	300
Richd Kemp	1100	Charles Williams	100
Tho Kidd	250	Edwin Thacker Estate	2500
Francis Weeks	225	Thomas Dudly	200
Widdo Weeks	225	Thomas Mackhan	200
Henry Webb	100	Richd. Paffitt	200
Tho Wood	70	Tho. Hiff	100
Robt. Williamson	200	Peter Bromell	100
Tho Lee	100	Tho Blakey	100
Edmd. Mickleburrough	200	John Robinson	1350
Valentine Mayo	100	Roger Jones	100
Wm. Mountague	500	John Nicholls	200
Garrett Minor	225	George Berwick	100
Marvill Mosseley	225	Widdo Hurford	50
Joseph Mitcham	75	Widdo Hackney	300
Minie Minor	225	Wm. Kilbee	600
Humphrey Jones	150	Ezikiah Rhodes	300
Jno. North	200	John Handiford	100
Henry Tugill	200	John Miller	200
Henry Thacker	1875	Wm. Scarborow	200
Thomas Tozeley	500	Wm. Herne	75
Charles Moderas	100	Robt. Dudley	300
Wm. Mullins	150	Widdo Mason	100
John Smith	700	Peter Chilton	100
James Smith	400	Francis Dobson	150
Harry Beverley	1000	James Dudley	200
George Wortham	400	Capt. Berkley	750
Capt. Grimes	900	Wm. Sutton	150
Sarah Mickleborough	1000	Sr. Wm. Skipwith	350
Christo. Robinson	4000	Coll Kemp	900
John Vibson	100	Wm. Barbee	150
James Daniell	150	Wm. Wallis	300
James Curtis	300	Adam Curtin	200
Tho. Cranke	54	Capt. Wm Armistead	2325
Phil. Calvert	200		
John Hipkins	100		49008

A True & Perfect Rent Roll of all the Lands held in Essex County this present year 1704

Abbott Wm.	150	Bradburn Richd.	100
Andrews Geo	200	Brown Francis	150
Adcock Edwd	230	Brown Danll. Junr.	150
Adcock Henry	250	Bryom Henry	100
Acres James	100	Burnett Tho. Junr.	1000
Arving Wm.	100	Baughan James Senr.	600
Allin Erasmus	100	Baughan James	150
Allin Wm.	100	Baughan Henry	100
Ayres Wm.	200	Brown Danll. Senr.	450
Acres Wm.	200	Brown Tho.	50
		Blackiston Argail	200
	1630	Burnett John	365
Baulwar James	800	Burnett Tho. Junr.	130
Bendall John	135	Bailer Jno.	800
Butler John	125	Brakins Qrtr.	250
Bowers Arthur	600	Bell Thomas	100
Baulwar James	200		
Beesley Wm.	100		19980
Barron Andrew	50	Condute Nathll.	20
Bartlett Tho.	100	Cary Hugh	50
Brown Buskinghan	400	Connoly Edwd.	200
Beeswell Robt.	100	Cogwell Fredirick	250
Beeswell Robt. Junr.	150	Copland Nicho.	300
Brown Wm.	420	Cattlett Jno.	1800
Brown Charles	1000	Covengton Richd.	1000
Buckner Richd.	1200	Cook John	112
Buckner Tho.	1000	Chew Larkin	300
Brice Henry	400	Crow Tho.	300
Bourn Jno.	100	Covington Wm.	400
Beverly Harry	1000	Cheney John	200
Battail John	1100	Cole Wm.	200
Baulwar John	50	Cheney Wm.	700
Booth Widdo	800	Corbin Tho. Qr	440
Butler Jno.	100	Cockin Tho.	120
Butcher Jno.	150	Coates Samll	300
Bendrey Widdo	700	Cooper Richd.	100
Bird Widdo	100	Cooper Tho.	100
Beckham Symon	100	Copland Jno.	175
Brutnall Richd	100	Crow Jno.	440
Brook Robt.	400	Chew Larkin	550
Ball Jno.	150	Cooper Wm.	50
Brooks James	100	Compton Wm.	50
Billington Mary	200	Cox Wm.	500
Brooks Peter	275	Callaway Jos.	87
Bowman Peter	400	Coleman Robt.	450
Brooks Robt.	150	Cobnall Symon	100
Brasur Jno.	300	Chamberlain Leond.	350
Brush Richd.	250		
Baker Henry	350		9764

Daniell James	100	Hinshaw Samll.	200
Devillard Jacob	80	Hutson Tho.	100
David Tho.	150	Harrison James	400
Dudding Andrew	230	Harrison Andrew	300
Davis Evans	150	Hilliard Thomas	100
Dobbins Danll.	550	Harper Wm.	240
Dressall Timo.	175	Harmon Henry	75
Daughty John	200	Hoult Richd.	100
Dyer Wm.	100	Humphrie Joe	100
Daingerfield Jno.	270	Hail Jno.	900
Daingerfield Wm.	270	Harper John	748
Dunn Wm.	220	Harper Tho.	350
Dyer Jeffrey	100	Hould David	100
Day Richd.	100	Hudson Wm.	100
Dicks Thomas	500	Hinds Thomas	100
		Howerton Thomas	175
	12959	Hodges Arth	100
		Hows Qrtr	300
Evans Rice	200	Harwood Peter	125
Edmondson James	500	Harway Tho.	1000
Elliott Alice	75	Hudson Tho.	50
Evitt Tho.	100	Hudson Wm.	300
Emondson Tho.	700	Hill Leond.	300
Flowers Isaac	250	Harwar Samll.	300
Faulkner Nicho.	100	Jamison David	250
Farrell Charles	50	Jones Wm.	165
Franklin Nicho.	130	Jenkins David	50
Foster Robt.	200	Jewell Tho.	100
Foster Jno.	200	Johnson Widdo.	300
Fisher Jonathan	250	Jones Walter	100
Fisher Benja.	150	Johnson Richd.	50
Frank Tho.	175	Johnson Wm.	650
Fullerton James	400	Jones John	300
Fossett Wm.	100	Jones Richd.	350
Ferguson Jno.	150	Jenkins John	93
Faulkner Edwd.	530	Jones Wm.	300
		Journey Wm.	243
	17219	Johnson Thomas	500
		Jones Rice	500
Green George	300	Key Robt.	209
Gray Abner	350	Kerby Henry	60
Goulding Wm.	200	Landrum John	300
Gannock Wm.	2100	Landrum James	100
Gaines Barnerd	450	Long Richd.	300
Griffin Tho.	200	Lomax John	2000
Gibson Jonathan	700	Loyd George	800
Grigson Tho.	300	Lawson Claudy	100
Gouldman Francis	300	Little Abraham	60
Goulding John	200	Lacy John	100
Goulding Edwd.	380	Law John	300
Good Richd.	200	Lattaine Lewis	250
Garnett John	150	Leveritt Robt.	100
Glover John	100	Micou Paul	150
Hawkins John	1066		

Martin John	400		Quarter Xtpher Robinson..	2200
Morgain John	100		Quartr Tho. Corbin	4000
Miller John	150		Qrtr Robt. Thomas	200
Medor Tho.	300		Quartr John Hay	1000
Moseley Benja.	1100		Quartr. Wm. Smith	3000
Mottley John	100		Quartr Gawen Corbin	2000
Morris John	200		Quartr Peter Ransom	300
Moss Robt.	180		Quartr David Gwin	950
Merritt Tho.	124		Quartr Wm. Upshaw	1000
Merritt John	100		Quartr Leversons	600
Munday Tho.	500		Quartr Tho Todd	550
Magcon David	400		Ridgdall John	300
Mice Hno.	200		Ramsey Tho.	550
Mosseley Robt.	100		Rowze Ralph	610
Mayfield Robt.	100		Rucker Peter	500
Matthews Richd.	250		Rowze Edwd.	300
Moseley Edwd.	550		Royston John	1000
Merriweather Francis	3200		Roberts Edmd.	300
Mefflin Zach	400		Rebs Henry	400
Michaell Jno.	200		Reeves Joseph	200
Merriweather Tho.	2100		Reeves James	200
Mefflin Lath	400		Roberts John	50
Medor John	100		Richardson Robt.	200
Morse John	400		Reynolds James Senr.	500
Matthews Benja.	200		Reynolds James	500
Mountegue Wm.	850		Ransom Peter	1200
Newbury Nathll.	200		Strange Jno.	100
Nixson Henry	500		Stepp Abra.	390
North Wm	900		Samll. Antho.	300
Newton Nicho.	100		Sail Cornelius	73
Nightingall John	100		Salmon John	60
Osman James	300		Spiers Jno.	160
Presser John	450		Smith Wm.	150
Poe Samll.	800		Stokes Richd.	500
Pley Widdo.	800		Smith Charles	3000
Parker Jno.	250		Sullenger Peter	400
Pitts Jon.	200		Sales Widdo	1150
Piskell Jno.	300		Shipley Jno.	200
Pain Jno.	135		Spearman Job	300
Price Wm.	100		Smith Francis	500
Peteras Tho.	200		Stallard Samll..	100
Powell Honor	72		Ship Jos	350
Powell Wm.	72		Short Tho.	150
Powell Place	72		Scott Wm.	1100
Powell Tho.	72		Stogell Jno.	100
Payne Widdow	1000		Stephens Jno.	100
Perkin Henry	300		Slaughter Phebe	352
Prichett Roger	167		Smith Jno.	75
Paggett Edmd.	700		Smith Jonas	100
Price John	1100		Sanders John	300
Pickett John	800		Stanton Jno.	95
Perry Samll.	225		Shepherd Jeremiah	300
Price Wm.	100		Smith Tho.	50

Shackelford Francis	300	Webb Robert	375
Sthrashley Tho	200	Webb Isaac	200
Staners Tho	500	Woodnatt Henry	300
Snead Tho	950	Waginer John	400
Shackelford Henry	50	Ward Geo.	350
Thorp Widdo	400	Wheeler Tho	250
Tinsley Tho.	111	Young Wm.	1000
Thacker Samll.	110	Young Giles	100
Tomlin Widdo	400	Muscoe Salvator	100
Taliaferro Francis	1300	Moody John	150
Thornton Fran.	700	Maguffe John	100
Tomlin Wm.	1600	Brookins Quartr.	250
Thomas John	100	Smith Jno. Quartr	1000
Taliaferro Charles	300	Newton Henry	100
Thomas Wm.	200	Newton Henry	175
Taliaferro John	2000	Nowell Dall	400
Turner George	200	Nowell Widdo	300
Tomlin Wm.	950	Garrett Tho	1000
Trible Peter	100	Gould Price	200
Taylor Richd.	650	Green Samll.	97
Tilley Matthew	200	Gouldman Fran.	300
Vanters Bartho	400	Gawdin Wm.	100
Virget Job	50	Grimmall Wm.	100
Vincent Vaus	450	Gaitwood John	400
Wakeland Wm.	100	Games John	475
Wood Tho.	50	Samll. Thompson	1000
Winslow Tho.	150		
Winslow Henry	100		140580

Williams John	450
Williams Wm.	100
Wilson David	50
Wilton Richd.	150
Wheeden Edwd.	50
Ward Widdo.	200
Whitehorn Widdo.	260
Wms. Emanuell	100
Watkins Thomas	400
Waters John	150
Webb James	200
Webb John	200
Wead Wm.	200
Wood Tho	300
Williamson Tho	100
Williamson Wm.	100
Williamson John	100

Lands held in the above said County the Rents not paid and held by the severall Gentlemen as followth vizt.

John Smith Esqr. of Glocester County	800
Wm. Buckner of Glocester by information	1500
Jno. Lightfoot Esqr. New Kent County	900
Jno. Bridgate in Engld.	700
Richd. Wyatt & Jno. Pettus of King & Queen Cty.	800
Wm. Berry of Richmond County	400

Richard Covington

Accomack Rent Roll

A

Alexander Richards	150	Ann Simkins	1000
Arthur Upshot	2020	Arthur Donas	100
Antho. West	700	Arnoll Harrison	630
		Alex. Harrison	400

Alex. Bagwell	413
Anne Chase	200
Arthur Frame	500
Alexdr West	550
Abraham Lambedson	100
Alex Benstone	270
Anne Blake Widdo	120
Anne Bruxe	180
Ar. Arcade Welburn	1854
	9187

B

Burnell Niblett	100
Majr. Bennit Scarbrough	521
	621

C

Corneline Hermon	321
Christo Stokly	200
Charles Scarbrough	1000
Charles Leatherbeny	1100
Charles Bally	959½
Charles Pywell	150
Churchhil Darby	125
Charles Evill	550
Charles Champison	270
Christo Hodey	500
Cornelius Lofton	166
Charles Stockley	170
Charles Taylor	580
Catherine Gland	217
	6312½

D

Dorman Derby	225
Daniell Derby Senr.	300
Dorothy Littlehouse	250
David Watson	200
Delight Shield	300
Daniel Derby Junr	125
Daniel Harwood	100
Dennis Mores	200
Daniel Gore	3976
	5676

E

Coll Edmd Scarbrough	2000
Edwd Hitchins	170
Edwd Turner	750

Edwd Killam	720
Edmd Allin	200
Edwd Bagwell for Coll Wm. Custis	200
Edmd. Jones	800
Elizb. Tinley	200
Edwd Taylor	300
Edmd Tatham	200
Edmd Bally	800
Edmd Ayres	1000
Edwd. Miles	413
Elizb. Mellchop	210
Edwd. Bell	101
Edwd. More	500
Edwd. Gunter	600
Edwd Brotherton	600
Elias Blake	430
Edwd Robins	782
Edwd Bally	300
Elias Taylor	1500
Elizb. Wharton	200
Mrs. Elizb Scarbrough	4205
	17181

F

Mr. Francis Mackenny	5109
Francis Robts.	200
Francis Wainhouse	700
Francis Crofton	200
Francis Young	100
Finley MackWm	100
Francis Ayres	300
Francis Jester	200
Francis Benstone	400
Francis Wharton	600
	7909

G

Geo. Anthony	100
Geo. Hastup	300
Coll Geo Nicho Halk	2700
Capt. Geo Parker	2609
Gervis Baggally	700
Garrat Hictlims	170
Geo Parker Sco. Side	1200
Griffin Savage	650
Geo Middleton Senr	588
Geo Trevit	400
Geo. Pounce	400
Geo Middleton Junr	150
Geo Johnson	200

Capt. Geo Hope 900

11067

H

Henry Armtrading	175
Henry Chance	445
Henry Selman	180
Henry Ubankes	400
Henry Lurton	363
Henry Stokes	208
Henry Custis	774
Henry Bagwell	412
Henry Read	350
Henry Ayres	250
Hill Drummond	483
Henry Toules	300
Henry Hickman	135
Henry Gibbins	250
Henry Truett	240

4965

J

John Tounson	200
Joseph Stokley	664
Jno. Read	200
Jno. Blake	310
Joseph Ames	375
Joseph Clark	200
Jno. Fisher	200
James Gray	900
Jno. Huffington	240
Jno. Legatt	300
James Lary	100
James Longoe	200
Jno. Merrey	350
Jno Milloy	500
Jno. Pratt	50
Jno. Revell	1450
Jno Road	110
Jno. Rowles	650
Jno. Savage Senr	350
Jno Charles	480
Jno Willis Senr	430
Jno Willis Junr	350
James Fairfax	900
Joseph Milby	830
John West Junr	500
Jno Jenkins	400
Jonathan James	150
John Rodgers	100
Jno Collins	100

Jno Sincocke	125
Jno Metcalfe, Isaac Metcalfe and Samll. Metcalfe	600
Joseph Touser	200
Jno Stanton	200
Jno Bally	1000

13715

Jno Melson	180
Jno Bernes Senr	657
Jno Littletone	200
John Nock	300
Jno Killy	100
Jacob Morris	200
Jno Morris	640
Jona. Aylworth	200
James Davis	1000
Jno Parkes	200
Jno Evans	200
Jno Hull	100
Jno Blocksom	700
Jno Abbott	1170
Jno Arew	234
Jno Grey	116
Jno Baker	400
Jno Wharton	150
James Taylor	100
Jno Glading	207
Jno Loftland	167
James Smith	756
Majr Jno Robins	2700
Jno Collins for Asban......	1666
James Walker	525
Jno Whelton	90
Jno Marshall	1666
Jona Owen	230
Jacob Wagaman	150
Capt John Broadhurst	1100
Jno Dyer	200
Mr. John Watts	2450
Jno Booth	300
John Bradford	364
Ingold Cobb	150
Jno Griffin	150
Jno Mitchell	400
John Parker	970
James Alexander	1250
Jno Burocke	200
James Sterferar	50
Jno Perry	217
Jno Drummond	1550
Jno Carter on Foxs Island	203

Jno Warington	100
Jno Bagwell	465
Jno Wise Senr	800
Jno Wise Junr	400
Jno Dix	500
Isaac Dix	500
Jno Hickman	454
Jno Onians	200
Coll Jno Custis Esqr.......	5950
John Coslin	50
	46692

M

Michaell Recetts	300
Mrs. Mattilda West	3600
Marke Evell	250
Mary Wright	200
	4350

N

Nicholas Mellchops	285
Nathaniel Williams	64
Nathaniell Rattcliff	300
	649

O

Owen Collonell	500
Overton Mackwilliams	200
Obedience Pettman	115
	815

P

Peter Major	113
Philip Parker	150
Peter Rogers	167
Perry Leatherbury	1750
Peter Turlington	79
Peter Ease	250
Philip Fisher	433
Peter Chawell	250
	3192

R

Robt. Bell	650
Richd Bally Senr.	2100
Richd Bally Junr	180
Richd Garrison	468

Roules Major	157
Rouland Savage Senr	950
Robt. Taylor	95
Richd. Rodgers	450
Richd Killam	1900
Robt. Wattson	425
Richd Jones	500
Robt. Hutchinson	934
Reynold Badger	150
Robt. West	400
Richd Cuttler	450
Robt. Cole	125
Richd Drummond	600
Robt. Stocomb	300
Robt Norton	1050
Richd Grindall	350
Roger Hickman	135
Robt Lewis	200
Roger Abbott	450
Richard Hill	350
Ralph Justice	1050
·Richd Hinman	1800
Robt Davis	384
Ragnall Aryes	300
Roger Miles	200
Richd Bundike	773
Richd Kittson	1300
Robt. Bally	100
Richd Starlin	150
Richd Flowers	200
Richd Price	100
Robt. Pitts	2300
Robt Adkins	200
Rebeckha Benstone	270
Richd Hillayres	300
	22816

S

Samuell Benstone	300
Sarah Beach	300
Sillvanus Cole	250
Symon Sosque	325
South Littleton Widdo	2870
Stephen Woltham	244
Steph. Warrington	400
Symon Mitchell	300
Stephen Drummond	300
Selby Harrison	50
Sollomon Evell	125
Samll Young	50
Sarah Reyley	150
Sebastian Dellistations Senr	500

Sebastian Dellistations Junr	400
Skinner Wollope	2485
Samll. Sandford	3250
Sebastian Silverthorn	150
Symon Smith	200
Sarah Coe	900
Samll Taylor	1232
Sarah Evins	150
Sebastian Croper	600
Samuell Jester	200
	15731

T

Tho Burton	600
Tho Bud	500
Tho Boules	300
Tho Clark	100
Tho Middleton	350
Tho Stringer	600
Tho Haule	500
Tho Taylor	100
Tho Fockes	300
Tho Bagwell	465
Madm Tabitha Hill	3600
Tho Rose	7
Tho Webb	50
Tho Savage	450
Tho Jones	100
Tho Scott	100
Tho Reyley	225
Tho Ternall	150
Tho Simpson	520
Tho Coper	711
Tho Miles	202
Thomas Bonwell	300
Tho Bell Senr.	100
The Bell Junr	100
Tho Touson Kiquotan	800
Tho Stockley	363
Tho Jester	100
Tho Smith	300
Thomas Crippin	648
Tho Wilkinson	50
Tho Jenkinson	374
Tho Moore	166
Tho Allen	700
Tho Smith Savannah	200
Tho Perry	232
Tho Tonnson	400
Tho Smith Gingateague	693
Lieut Coll Robinson	600
	15956

W

Wm. Robins	200
Wm Patterson	200
Wm Bevens	400
Wm Matthews	400
Wm Shepherd	200
Wm Whett	400
Winfred Woodland	333
Wm Andrews	300
Wm Custis	1500
Wm Darby	83
Wm Fletcher	200
Wm Killam	450
Wm Lingoe	300
Wm Major	130
Wm Meeres	150
Wm Mack Sear	800
Wm Savage	150
Wm Waite	110
Wm Sill	200
Wm Waite Junr	600
Wm Bradford	3500
Wm Rogers	200
Wm Wise	400
Wm Finey	800
Wm Consalvins	100
Wm Phillips	200
Wm Parker	362
Wm Cole	375
Wm Merill	150
Wm Johnson	150
Wm Lewis	150
Walter Hayes	130
Wm Chance	450
Wm Milby	250
Wm Nicholson	600
Wm Burton	500
Wm Willett	842
Wm Hudson	270
Wm Lewis	300
Wm Young	144
Wm Liechfield	154
Wm Bunting	150
Wm Nock Junr	400
Wm Lucas	300
Mary Mellechop	498
Wm Daniell	200
Wm Silverthorn	160
Wm Garman	475
Wm White	600
Wm Broadwater	500
Wm Taylor	100
Wm Williamson	600
Wm Brittingham	538

Wm. Benstone Jun.	270
Wm Dickson for Mr. Littleton	1050
Wm Waite Senr	225
Wm Taylor	1400
	24599
	196899½

Added to this Rent Roll the following Lands of which the Quit Rents may possibly be recovered tho the Owners live out of the Country Viz.

Jonas Jackson	500
Robt. Andrews	500
Joseph Morris	200
Robt. Meros	200
Hillory Stringer	950
Tho Fisher	133
Jno Fisher	133
Timo Coe	4100
David Hagard	130
	6846

An Account of what Land in Accomack County the owners whereof are not dwellers.

Tho Preson of Northampton	200
Geo Corbin Ditto	150
Joshua Fichett Ditto......	200
Alexdr Merey Maryld	200
Tho Dent	500
Mr. Wm Kendalls orphans of Northampton County.	2850
Mr Hancock Lee dividing Creeks	4050
Richd Watters in Maryland	1057
Francis Lailor Northamp..	100
Obedience Johnson Qtrs...	300
Henry Smith at the Southerd	1000
Grattiance Michell North..	200
Matt. Tyson Southerd.....	300
Teagle Woltham Maryld..	200
Peter Waltham New Engld	200
Jno Waltham Maryld......	200
	11707

Jno Wise Sheriff

The Rent Roll of Northampton County for the Year of our Lord God 1704

A

Andrews Robt.	300
Andrews Andrew	100
Addison John	350
Abdell Tho	125
Abdell Jno	200
Abdell Wm	125
Alligood John	300
Angell James	100
Alligood Henry	100

B

Bullock Geo	100
Boner Geo	150
Brown Tho	1862
Benthall Joseph Senr	793
Benthall Joseph Junr	150
Branson Francis	100
Bateson	200
Billot Jno	400
Bell Geo	400
Billott Wm	100

Brewer Jno	50
Blackson Jno	100
Brooks Jeane	100
Beadwine Jno	200
Berthall Danll	258
Baker John	400
Brickhouse Geo	2100

C

Cob Samll	130
Coape Wm	200
Custis Jno Coll	3400
Collier Bartho.	150
Carpenter Charles	240
Cox Jno	500
Church Samll	143
Cleg Jno. Senr	204
Clog Henry	204
Carvy Richd	100
Cowdry Josiah	167
Cormeck Mich	100
Clerk Jno	100

Corban Geo 250
Clerk Geo 833
Caple Nath 100
Callinett Jno 100
Crew John 300
Costin Francis 275
Custis Majr John 3250
Custis Hancock 50
Chick Tho. 100

Downing Jno. 70
Dewy Geo 300
Dewy Jacob 100
Delby Margery 450
Dowty Rowland 150
Dunton John 170
Dunton Tho 400
Dowman John 100
Dullock John 100
Denton Tho 400
Dunton Tho Junr 120
Dunton Wm 420
Dunton Benj 220
Duparks Tho 90
Davis Jno 850
Dunton Joseph 120
Dixon Michaell 460

E
Eshon Jno 600
Evans John 200
Edmunds David 500
Evans Tho 300
Esdoll Geo 100
Eyres Tho 1133
Eyres Nich 325
Eyres Capt Jno 774
Eyres Anne Wido. 733
Esdoll Edwd. 100

F
Fisher John 637½
Francisco Dan 150
Fisher Tho 637½
Foster Robt. 150
Fabin Paul 60
Frost Tho 100
Frank Jno 500
Floyd Charles 378
Freshwater Geo 200
Frizell Geo 140
Freshwater Wm 200

Fitchett Joshua 100
Floyd Berry & Matthew .. 555

G
Gogni David 150
Gill Robt. 200
Gascoyne Robt. 125
Gascoyne Wm 525
Greene Jno Senr 2200
Giddens Tho 227
Grice Peter 200
Godwin Devorix 600
Goffogan Tho 100
Guelding Charles 200
Griffith Jerimiah 345
Griffith Benja 200

H
Hill Francis 100
Henderson John 250
Haggaman Isaac 750
Harmonson Jno 1600
Harmonson Henry 1250
Hanby Charles 25
Hanby Richd 75
Hanby Danll 50
Hanby John 150
Harmonson Capt Wm 308
Harmonson Geo 1586
Harmonson Tho 400
Hawkins Jno Senr 66
Hawkins Jno Junr 66
Hawkins Gideon 66
Hunto Groton 485
Hunt John 440
Hunt Tho 290
Hall Francis Widdo 340

J
Johnson John Senr 250
Johnson John Junr 100
Johnson Jacob 350
Isaacs John Jnr 100
Joynes Major 150
James Joan Widdo 250
Johnson Obedience Capt ... 400
Johnson Tho Junr 75
Johnson Thomas Senr ... 400
Jackson Jonah & John 625
Joynes Edmd 200
Joynes Edwd 200
Johnson Jeptha Senr 50

Jacob Phillip Senr 350
Johnson Jepha Junr 200
Johnson Obedience & Jepha
Sen 250
Johnson Edmd 400
Jacob Richd 200
Jacob Abraham 50

K

Kendall Wm 2410
Knight John 100

L

Lawrence John 120
Lailler Luke 100
Lucas Tho 100
Lewis Robt 100
Littleton Susannah Wido.. 4050
Luke John 400

M

Marshall Geo 250
Farshall Jno 250
Maddox Tho 1500
Michaell Yeardly 400
Matthews John 275
Major John 390
Map John 50
Moore Matthew 175
Mackmellion Tho 300
More Gilbert 225
Morraine John 119½
More Jno 545
More Eliner 175

N

Nicholson Wm 600
Nottingham Wm 150
Nottingham Joseph 150
Nottingham Richd 350
Nottingham Benja 300
Nelson John 100

O

Only Clement 200
Odear John 100

P

Parramore Tho 400
Preson Tho 610
Powell Frances Widdo ... 1225
Palmer Samll 1562

Pyke Henry 150
Powell John 636⅓
Pittett Tho 300
Pittet Justian 200
Pittett John 275
Powell Samll 200
Paine Daniell 150
Piggott Ralph 1368

R

Read Thomas 150
Rascow Arthur 100
Ronan Wm 150
Roberts Jno 200
Richards Lettis 150
Robins Jno Majr 1180
Robins Littleton 1000
Rabishaw Wm 55
Roberts Obedience 260
Robinson Benjamin 250

S

Shepherd Jno 200
Smith Joseph 250
Smith Samll 150
Smith Jno 200
Savage Tho 450
Smith Tho 400
Smith Abrah 300
Seady Antho 120
Sott Widdo 750
Smith Richd minor 300
Scot Geo 100
Smith Richd 99
Scot Jno 100
Scott Henry 800
Scot David 300
Smith Peter 450
Sanders Richd 100
Smaro John 800
Shepherd Tho 140
Sanders Eustick 100
Sanderson John 636
Savidge John 410
Stringer Hillary 1250
Savidge Capt Tho 1600
Savidge Elkington 750
Scot Wm Senr 153
Straton Benja 745
Smith Geo 133
Stockley Jno Senr 370
Shepheard Widdo 830
Seamore John 200

T

Tilney John	350
Tryfort Barth	147
Teague Simeon	100
Turner Richd	50
Teague Tho	200
Tankard Wm	450
Tanner Paul	148

W

Webb Henry	100
Wills Thorn	300
White John	400
Wilson Tho	250
Westerhouse Adryan Senr.	200
Walker John	300
Ward Tho	120
Walter John	400
Waterfield Wm	200
Warren John	525
Warren Argoll	350
Widgeon Robt	100
Wilkins Jno	150
Webb Edwd	200
Wilcock Jno	200
Warren James	50
Waterson Wm	855

Warren Robt.	190
Water Lieut-Coll Wm	700
Webb Charles	133¼
Willett Wms	2650
Waterson Richd	150
Wilkins Argoll	150
Walter Elizb Widdo	100
Warren Joseph	50

99671

Lands not paid for vizt

Gleab formerly Capt Fox-crofts	1500
John Majr at Occahannock	200
Hogbin not being in Virginia	100
Tho Smith	300
Tho Marshall orphan	75
Jno Rews not in Virginia ..	100

2275

The total on the other side is	99671 acres
Added to it ye Glebe land	1500

101171 acres

The preceding Sheets are true copys of the Rentrolls for the year 1704 given in and accounted for by the several Sherifs in April 1705 and sworne to before his Excellcy according to which they made up their accounts of the Quitrents with

Will Robertson Clerk.

INDEX

INDEX

251

Webster, Roger,
    servant, *Burgess* in 1632, 74.
Whitlock, Thomas,
    will of, 105-106.
Williamsburg,
    35; 54.
Williams, William,
    buys 200 acres, 50.
Wills,
    throw light on distribution of servants
    and slaves, 59; 73; headrights mentioned
    in, 76.
Wine,
    prospect for in Virginia, 15.
Woolens,
    need of potash for, 8; French duty on,
    13.
Woolritch, William,
    landowning freedman, 74.
Wormsley, Ralph,
    109; letter to from *Fitzhugh*, 130.
Wray, Thomas,
    granted 50 acres, 81.

Y ATES, William,
    has 55 slaves, 158.
Yeomanry, largest class in Virginia, 59, 62;
    freedmen in, 72-82; 85; desperately
    poor, 90-91; driven to revolt by poverty,

92-93; no advancement for after 1660,
97-100; enjoy plentiful food, 101-103;
often suffer for proper clothing, 103-
105; *Burgesses* represented interests of,
109; aid in ejecting Harvey, 110; many
favor *Parliament in Civil War*, 110-111;
in control from 1652 to 1660, 112; chief
sufferers from *Navigation Acts*, 113;
support Bacon in rebellion, 113; struggle
for political rights, 114; few recruits to
at end of 17th century, 122; condition
of at end of 17th century, 123; effect of
slavery on in ancient Rome, 137-139;
migration of from Virginia, 139-146;
produce higher grades of tobacco, 146-
147; misery of in 1713, 150; many sink
into poverty, 151-154; many become
slave holders, 152-159; slaves make less
industrious, 155; 160.
Yeardley, Sir George,
    29; instructed to enforce free exchange
    of goods, 65.
York,
    land transfers in, 46; plantations of
    small, 53; farms and tithables of, 58;
    servants and slaves in, 59; landowners
    of who had been headrights, 76; 79;
    107; 130.
Young, Richard,
    granted 100 acres, 81.